rigins of Human
_ommunication

The Jean Nicod Lectures
Francois Recanati, editor

Origins of Human Communication

Michael Tomasello

A Bradford Book
The MIT Press
Cambridge, Massachusetts
London, England

First MIT Press paperback edition, 2010
© 2008 Massachusetts Institute of Technology

MIT Press books may be purchased at special quantity discounts for business or sales promotional use. For information, please e-mail special_sales@mitpress.mit.edu or write to Special Sales Department, The MIT Press, 55 Hayward Street, Cambridge, MA 02142.

This book was set in Palatino by SNP Best-set Typesetter Ltd., Hong Kong, and was printed and bound in the United States.

Library of Congress Cataloging-in-Publication Data

Tomasello, Michael.
Origins of human communication / Michael Tomasello.
    p.   cm.—(Jean Nicod lectures)
Includes bibliographical references and index.
ISBN 978-0-262-20177-3 (hc. : alk. paper)—978-0-262-51520-7 (pb. : alk paper)
1. Language and languages—Origin. 2. Animal communication. I. Title.

P116.T66   2008   2007049249
401—dc22

10 9 8 7

Point to a piece of paper. And now point to its shape—now to its color—now to its number. . . . How did you do it?

—Wittgenstein, *Philosophical Investigations*

Contents

Series Foreword

The Jean Nicod Lectures are delivered annually in Paris by a leading philosopher of mind or philosophically oriented cognitive scientist. The 1993 inaugural lectures marked the centenary of the birth of the French philosopher and logician Jean Nicod (1893–1931). The lectures are sponsored by the Centre National de la Recherche Scientifique (CNRS), in cooperation with the Ecole des Hautes Etudes en Sciences Sociales (EHESS) and the Ecole Normale Superieure (ENS). The series hosts the texts of the lectures or the monographs they inspire.

Jean Nicod Committee
Jacques Bouveresse, President
Jérôme Dokic and Elisabeth Pacherie, Secretary
François Recanati, Editor of the Series

Daniel Adler   Jean-Pierre Changeux
Stanislas Dehaene   Emmanuel Dupoux
Jean-Gabriel Ganascia   Pierre Jacob
Philippe de Rouilhan   Dan Sperber

Preface and Acknowledgments

This volume is based on the Jean Nicod Lectures delivered in Paris in the Spring of 2006. Given the people at the Jean Nicod institute, I chose to focus on communication. I have done a fair amount of empirical and theoretical work on: (i) great ape gestural communication; (ii) human infants' gestural communication; and (iii) human children's early language development. I have also worked a good bit on more general cognitive and social-cognitive processes involved in human communication and language: (i) social and cultural cognition; (ii) social and cultural learning; and (iii) cooperation and shared intentionality. My attempt in this volume is to bring all of this together into one coherent account of the evolution and development of human communication. The single animating idea of this attempt is that there must be some fairly specific connections between the fundamentally cooperative structure of human communication, as initially discovered by Grice, and the especially cooperative structure of human, as opposed to other primate, social interaction and culture in general.

The ideas in this volume have come mainly from my cooperative research and discussions with my many colleagues in the Department of Developmental and Comparative Psychology at the Max Planck Institute for Evolutionary Anthropology. Much of what is presented here originated in these interactions, and I only wish I could recall all of the particular sources more clearly.

But what is clear is the large debt I owe to several specific people. Most important in the context of this volume is Malinda Carpenter. Malinda and I have discussions on almost a daily basis about topics that relate to the current volume more or less directly. My thinking has been shaped by these discussions in such fundamental ways that, unfortunately, it is impossible to give specific credit for specific things (or to indicate all those points with which Malinda disagrees). Also of particular importance were the many discussions I have had over the years with Josep Call about great ape gestural communication, and with Elena Lieven about child language acquisition.

I presented an early version of the ideas in this volume to the members of our social cognition research group (the infamous September Sessions), and received extremely helpful feedback from Hannes Rakoczy, Tanya Behne, Henrike Moll, Ulf Liszkowski, Felix Warneken, Emily Wyman, Suse Grassmann, Kristin Liebal, Maria Gräfenhain, Gerlind Hauser, and others—including the suggestion to leave out a number of diagrams even crazier than those that are currently here. I also received a number of useful suggestions from the attendees at the Jean Nicod Lectures themselves, especially Dan Sperber.

Several people read more or less the entire volume and helped me to improve it immensely: Malinda Carpenter, Elena Lieven, Bill Croft, Adele Goldberg, and Gina Conti-Ramsden—along with an anonymous reviewer for MIT Press. Others who read selected portions and gave valuable feedback as well are: Hannes Rakoczy, Henrike Moll, Joe Henrich, Danielle Matthews, Nausicaa Pouscoulous, Felix Warneken, Colin Bannard, Emily Wyman, and Kristin Liebal. The thoughtful criticisms of these readers have made this a much more empirically accurate, theoretically coherent, and user-friendly volume. I also thank Esteban Rivas for supplying me with helpful information for table 6.1.

Finally, as always, is Henriette Zeidler, who not only helped with several specific aspects of the book, but also ran things at the department with her usual skill and good cheer while I was home writing. I am also grateful to Annett Witzmann for help with the references, and to Tom Stone at MIT Press for his oversight of the entire publication process.

1   A Focus on Infrastructure

What we call meaning must be connected with the primitive language of gestures.

—Wittgenstein, *The Big Typescript*

Walk up to any animal in a zoo and try to communicate something simple. Tell a lion, or a tiger, or a bear to turn its body like "this," showing it what to do by demonstrating with your hand or body and offering a delicious treat in return. Or simply point to where you would like it to stand or to where some hidden food is located. Or inform it that a fearsome predator is lurking behind a bush by both pointing to the location and pantomiming the predator's actions. They don't get it. And it is not just that they are not interested or motivated or intelligent in their own way, but the fact is that you simply cannot *tell* animals anything, even nonverbally, and expect them to understand.

    Human beings, of course, find such gestures as pointing and pantomiming totally natural and transparent:

just look where I am pointing and you will *see* what I mean. Indeed, even prelinguistic infants use and understand the pointing gesture, and in many social situations in which vocal language is not possible or practical—for example, across a crowded room or in a noisy factory—humans naturally communicate by pointing and pantomiming. Tourists manage to survive and interact effectively in many situations in foreign cultures, in which no one shares their conventional language, precisely by relying on such naturally meaningful forms of gestural communication.

My central claim in these lectures is that to understand how humans communicate with one another using a language and how this competence might have arisen in evolution, we must first understand how humans communicate with one another using natural gestures. Indeed, my evolutionary hypothesis will be that the first uniquely human forms of communication were pointing and pantomiming. The social-cognitive and social-motivational infrastructure that enabled these new forms of communication then acted as a kind of psychological platform on which the various systems of conventional linguistic communication (all 6,000 of them) could be built. Pointing and pantomiming were thus the critical transition points in the evolution of human communication, already embodying most of the uniquely human forms of social cognition and motivation required for the later creation of conventional languages.

The problem is that, compared with conventional human languages (including conventionalized sign languages), natural gestures would seem to be very weak communicative devices, as they carry much less information "in" the communicative signal itself. Consider pointing, which I will argue later was the primordial form of uniquely human communication. Suppose that you and I are walking to the library, and out of the blue I point for you in the direction of some bicycles leaning against the library wall. Your reaction will very likely be "Huh?," as you have no idea which aspect of the situation I am indicating or why I am doing so, since, by itself, pointing means nothing. But if some days earlier you broke up with your boyfriend in a particularly nasty way, and we both know this mutually, and one of the bicycles is his, which we also both know mutually, then the exact same pointing gesture in the exact same physical situation might mean something very complex like "Your boyfriend's already at the library (so perhaps we should skip it)." On the other hand, if one of the bicycles is the one that we both know mutually was stolen from you recently, then the exact same pointing gesture will mean something completely different. Or perhaps we have been wondering together if the library is open at this late hour, and I am indicating the presence of many bicycles outside as a sign that it is.

It is easy to say that what carries the meaning in these different examples is "context," but that is not very helpful since all of the physical features of the immediate communicative context were (by stipulation) identical in the various scenarios. The only difference was our shared experience beforehand, and that was not the actual content of the communication but only its background. And so our question is: how can something as simple as a protruding finger communicate in such complex ways, and do so in such different ways on different occasions?

Any imaginable answer to this question will have to rely heavily upon cognitive skills of what is sometimes called mindreading, or intention-reading. Thus, to interpret a pointing gesture one must be able to determine: what is his intention in directing my attention in this way? But to make this determination with any confidence requires, in the prototypical instance, some kind of joint attention or shared experience between us (Wittgenstein's [1953] forms of life; Bruner's [1983] joint attentional formats; Clark's [1996] common conceptual ground). For example, if I am your friend from out of town and there is no way I could be familiar with your ex-boyfriend's bicycle, then you will not assume that I am indicating it for you. This is true even if, by some miracle, I do indeed know that this is his bicycle, but you do not know that I know this. In general, for smooth communication it is not enough that you and I each know separately and privately that this is his bicycle (and even that the other knows this); rather, this fact must be mutually known common ground between us. And in the case in which it is common ground between us that this is his bicycle, but not that the two of you have just broken up (even if we each know this privately), then you will probably think that I am indicating your boyfriend's bicycle as a way of encouraging our entrance into the library, not discouraging it. The ability to create common conceptual ground—joint attention, shared experience, common cultural knowledge—is an absolutely critical dimension of all human communication, including linguistic communication with all of its *he's*, *she's*, and *it's*.

The other remarkable aspect of this mundane example of human pointing, from an evolutionary perspective, is its prosocial motivation. I am informing you of your ex-boyfriend's likely presence or the location of your stolen bicycle simply because I think you would want to know these things. Communicating information helpfully in this way is extremely rare in the animal kingdom, even in our closest primate relatives (in chapter 2 we will deal with examples such as warning cries and food calls). Thus, when a whimpering chimpanzee child is searching for her mother, it is almost certain that all of the other chimpanzees in the immediate area know this. But if some nearby female knows where the mother is, she will not tell the searching child, even though she is perfectly capable of extending her arm in a kind of pointing gesture. She will not tell the child because her communicative motives simply do not include informing others of things helpfully. In contrast, human communicative motives are so fundamentally cooperative that not only do we inform others of things helpfully, but one of the major ways we request things from others is simply to make our desire known in the expectation that they will volunteer help. Thus, I may request a drink of water by simply stating that I want one (informing you of my desire), knowing that, in most instances, your tendency to be helpful (and our mutual knowledge of this) turns this act of informing into what is effectively a full-blown request.

Human communication is thus a fundamentally cooperative enterprise, operating most naturally and smoothly within the context of (1) mutually assumed common conceptual ground, and (2) mutually assumed cooperative communicative motives. The fundamentally cooperative nature of human communication is, of course, the basic insight of Grice (1957, 1975), and it is assumed—to varying degrees and in various ways—by others who follow in this tradition such as Clark (1992, 1996), Sperber and Wilson (1986), and Levinson (1995, 2006). But if we are to understand the ultimate origins of human communication, both phylogenetically and ontogentically, we must look outside of communication itself and into human cooperation more generally. It turns out that human cooperation is unique in the animal kingdom in many ways, both structurally and motivationally.

Specifically, human cooperation is structured by what some modern philosophers of action call shared intentionality or "we" intentionality (Searle 1995; Bratman 1992; Gilbert 1989). In general, shared intentionality is what is necessary for engaging in uniquely human forms of collaborative activity in which a plural subject "we" is involved: joint goals, joint intentions, mutual knowledge, shared beliefs—all in the context of various cooperative motives. The jointness involved is especially salient in institutional interactions involving such culturally constructed entities as money, marriage, and government, which exist only within an institutional reality, collectively constituted, in which we all believe and act together as if they do exist. But shared intentionality is involved in simpler and more concrete collaborative activities as well, for example, when we form the shared goal to construct a tool together or to take a walk together, or when we simply admire a mountain vista together or engage in a religious practice together. The proposal is thus that human cooperative communication—whether using "natural" gestures or "arbitrary" conventions—is one instance, albeit a special instance, of uniquely human cooperative activity relying on shared intentionality (Tomasello, Carpenter, Call, Behne, and Moll 2005). The skills and motivations of shared intentionality thus constitute what we may call the cooperative infrastructure of human communication.

If human communication is cooperatively structured in ways that the communication of other primates is not, the question naturally arises how it could have evolved. The issue is that in modern evolutionary theory the emergence of cooperation, or at least altruism, is always problematic. But if the infrastructure of human cooperative communication is basically the same as that of all other collaborative activities, then one possibility is that it

evolved as part of a larger human adaptation for cooperation and cultural life in general. Thus, for reasons we do
not know, at some point in human evolution individuals
who could engage with one another collaboratively with
joint intentions, joint attention, and cooperative motives
were at an adaptive advantage. Cooperative communication then arose as a way of coordinating these collaborative activities more efficiently, first inheriting and then
helping to build further a common psychological infrastructure of shared intentionality. This all began almost
certainly in mutualistic activities in which an individual
who helped her partner was simultaneously helping
herself. But then there was a generalization to more altruistic situations in which individuals simply informed or
shared things with others freely, possibly as a way to
cultivate reciprocity and a reputation for cooperation
within the cultural group. Only later still did humans
begin to communicate in this new cooperative way
outside of cooperative contexts for higher-up, noncooperative purposes—leading to the possibility of deception
by lying.

The initial steps in this process almost certainly took
place in the gestural modality. This becomes especially
clear when we compare the vocal and gestural communication of our nearest primate relatives, the great apes.
Great ape vocalizations are almost totally genetically
fixed, based on almost no learning, tightly tied to specific
emotions, and broadcast indiscriminately to everyone in
the immediate vicinity. In contrast, many great ape ges-

tures are learned and used quite flexibly in different social circumstances for different social ends—with new gestures sometimes learned for interacting with humans—and communicators direct these gestures at specific individuals taking into account their current attentional state. Learning, flexibility, and attention to the partner are obviously fundamental characteristics of the human way of communicating, and things simply could not move in the human direction until they were present. It is also important, as many gestural origins theorists have noted previously, that the human use of pointing and pantomiming—as the successors to ape gestures after things became cooperative—are "natural" in a way that "arbitrary" linguistic conventions are not. Specifically, pointing is based on humans' natural tendency to follow the gaze direction of others to external targets, and pantomiming is based on humans' natural tendency to interpret the actions of others intentionally. This naturalness makes these gestures good candidates as an intermediate step between ape communication and arbitrary linguistic conventions.

And what about language? The current hypothesis is that it is only within the context of collaborative activities in which participants share intentions and attention, coordinated by natural forms of gestural communication, that arbitrary linguistic conventions could have come into existence evolutionarily. Conventional languages (first signed and then vocal) thus arose by piggybacking on these already understood gestures, substituting for the

naturalness of pointing and pantomiming a shared (and mutually known to be shared) social learning history. This process was, of course, made possible by humans' unique skills of cultural learning and imitation, which enable them to learn from others and their intentional states in uniquely powerful ways (Tomasello 1999). As part of this same evolutionary trajectory, human beings also began to create and pass along culturally various grammatical conventions organized into complex linguistic constructions that codified complex *types* of messages for use in recurrent communicative situations.

We thus need basic evolutionary processes, working in several different ways, to explain the origin of the underlying psychological infrastructure of human cooperative communication. But then in addition, to explain the origins of humans' 6,000 different conventional languages, we also need cultural-historical processes in which particular linguistic forms are conventionalized in particular speech communities, and then sequences of these are grammaticalized into grammatical constructions, and then all of these conventions and constructions are passed along to new generations via cultural learning. We thus may see here especially clearly the ongoing dialectic between evolutionary and cultural-historical processes as first described by Vygotsky (1978) and, in a more modern evolutionary framework, by Richerson and Boyd (2005)—and with which I myself have been obsessed for some time (Tomasello, Kruger, and Ratner 1993; Tomasello 1999; Tomasello et al. 2005). This perspective on human communication and language thus basically turns the Chomskian proposal on its head, as the most fundamental aspects of human communication are seen as biological adaptations for cooperation and social interaction in general, whereas the more purely linguistic, including grammatical, dimensions of language are culturally constructed and passed along by individual linguistic communities.

In all, the road to modern human communication was almost certainly a long and circuitous one, with many twists and turns along the way. To provide a theoretical account based mainly on empirical data, then, we must consider many different aspects of ape and human life—which makes this account a long and circuitous one as well. But despite the many complexities along the way, our final destination is easily stated and crystal clear: identification of the species-unique features of human communication and their ontogenetic and phylogenetic roots. Toward this end, in what follows I evaluate three specific hypotheses:

1. Human cooperative communication emerged first in evolution (and emerges first in ontogeny) in the natural, spontaneous gestures of pointing and pantomiming.

2. Human cooperative communication rests crucially on a psychological infrastructure of shared intentionality, which originated evolutionarily in support of collaborative activities, and which comprises most importantly:

(a) social-cognitive skills for creating with others joint intentions and joint attention (and other forms of common conceptual ground), and

(b) prosocial motivations (and even norms) for helping and sharing with others.

3. Conventional communication, as embodied in one or another human language, is possible only when participants already possess:

(a) natural gestures and their shared intentionality infrastructure, and

(b) skills of cultural learning and imitation for creating and passing along jointly understood communicative conventions and constructions.

2   Primate Intentional Communication

Any logic good enough for a primitive means of communication needs no apology from us. Language did not emerge from some kind of ratiocination.

—Wittgenstein, *On Certainty*

The human way of communicating—by intentionally informing others of things for cooperative motives—comes so naturally to us that we can hardly conceive of any other. But in the biological world, communication need not be either intentional or cooperative. For biologists, communication comprises any and all physical and behavioral characteristics that influence the behavior of others—from distinctive colorations to dominance displays—regardless of whether the signaler has any intentional control over the signal (or even knows it is affecting others). And for biologists, the proximate motives of the communicator, cooperative or otherwise, simply do not matter (Dawkins and Krebs 1978; Maynard-Smith and Harper 2003).

But from a psychological point of view, these things matter. We must begin, therefore, by distinguishing between what we may call communicative displays and communicative signals. Communicative displays are prototypically physical characteristics that in some way affect the behavior of others, such as large horns which deter competitors or bright colors which attract mates. Functionally, we may also group with displays reflexive behaviors that are invariably evoked by particular stimuli or emotional states and over which the individual has no voluntary control. Such inflexible physical and behavioral displays, created and controlled by evolutionary processes, characterize the vast majority of communication in the biological world. In sharp contrast are communicative signals that are chosen and produced by individual organisms flexibly and strategically for particular social goals, adjusted in various ways for particular circumstances. These signals are *intentional* in the sense that the individual controls their use flexibly toward the goal of influencing others. Intentional signals are extremely rare in the biological world, perhaps confined to primates or even great apes.

In this way of looking at things, the key role is that of the communicator. Recipients are simply individuals going about their business attempting to assess the situation and figure out what to do. They are seeking relevant information, from whatever source, and so the communicative display of another individual is just another source of information—regardless of whether the "communicator" even knows it exists (e.g., he may not even know he has a red tail). In contrast, when communicators are attempting to influence the behavior or psychological states of recipients intentionally, we now have the starting point for communication from a psychological point of view. When such intentionality exists, and in addition recipients recognize it to at least some degree, then we may refer to the overall process as intentional communication. To qualify as *cooperative* communication, among other things the communicator's proximate goal must be somehow to help or share with the recipient—even though, of course, evolutionarily there must be some benefit to the communicator for being so helpful as well.

Beginning with this basically psychological perspective on communication, the best place to look for the evolutionary roots of human cooperative communication is, of course, nonhuman primates—and especially (or so I will argue) to their gestural, as opposed to their vocal, communication.

2.1 Vocal Displays

When a vervet monkey hears a "snake alarm call," it knows that a snake is nearby; when it hears an "eagle alarm call" it knows that an eagle is nearby. Vervet monkey recipients thus extract referentially specific information from alarm calls, and this has been demonstrated repeatedly by playback experiments in which the call is

played over a loudspeaker when no predator is nearby—
and recipients still engage in the appropriate predator-
specific avoidance behavior (Cheney and Seyfarth 1990a).
Impressively, individuals of a number of monkey species
may even learn during ontogeny to use the alarm calls of
other species, including those of some birds, to obtain
information about nearby predators (Zuberbühler 2000).
Although great apes do not produce any referentially
specific calls (i.e., beyond calling at different rates or in
slightly modified form for different amounts or qualities
of food; Hauser and Wrangham 1987; Crockford and
Boesch 2003), they also extract information from vocal
calls, and may even learn during ontogeny to respond to
novel calls (Seyfarth and Cheney 2003).

In stark contrast to this picture of flexible comprehension, monkeys and apes do not learn to produce their
vocal calls at all, and they have very little voluntary
control over them. Here are some important facts (see
Tomasello and Zuberbühler 2002 for a review):

• within any monkey or ape species all individuals have
the same basic vocal repertoire, with essentially no individual differences in repertoire;

• monkeys raised in social isolation and monkeys cross-
fostered by another monkey species (with very different
vocal calls) still produce their same basic species-typical
vocalizations (and not those of the other species);

• the connection between a vocal call and its eliciting
emotion or situation is mostly very tightly fixed; non-

human primates do not vocalize flexibly by adjusting to the communicative situation; and

• human attempts to teach new vocalizations to monkeys and apes always fail, and attempts to teach them to produce their own vocalizations on command either fail or take many thousands of trials to work only a little.

The one dimension of flexibility that has been systematically documented is that individuals may not give certain calls when they are alone or without kin, as opposed to in the presence of others or with kin, but other animal species also refrain from alarm calling in these situations as well (including prairie dogs and domestic chickens; see Owings and Morton 1998), and so one may easily imagine that this is part of the genetically fixed adaptive specialization.

The reason for this lack of flexibility in vocal production is that nonhuman primate vocalizations are mostly very tightly tied to emotions. Goodall says:

The production of a sound in the *absence* of the appropriate emotional state seems to be an almost impossible task for a chimpanzee. (1986, p. 125)

Evolutionarily, this is because vocal calls are often associated with especially urgent functions such as escaping predators, surviving in fights, keeping contact with the group, and so forth. In such cases urgent action is needed, and there is little time for thoughtful deliberation. In all cases, each particular call has been selected evolutionarily because it benefits the caller in some way.

Thus, in recent analyses it has been stressed that vervet monkey alarm callers benefit directly from the call because, for example, the predator is directly deterred by the noxious noise, or because the call alerts the predator that it has been detected (Owren and Rendell 2001; see also Bergstrom and Lachman 2001). The other vervets inform themselves by eavesdropping, but they are not the target of the caller's calls. Tellingly, when macaque mothers in experiments see a "predator" approaching their offspring, they do not give an alarm call so long as they themselves are not at risk (Cheney and Seyfarth 1990b). In all, this pattern of flexible comprehension but totally inflexible production in primate vocalizations is captured quite nicely by Seyfarth and Cheney:

Listeners acquire information from signalers who do not, in the human sense, intend to provide it. (2003, p. 168)

Another important characteristic of primate vocalizations, deriving simply from the physics of the acoustic channel, is that they are broadcast indiscriminately to everyone nearby. This is an obvious advantage in highly emotional, evolutionarily urgent situations, but what this means psychologically is that the caller need not pay any attention to the recipient(s), and indeed cannot easily direct vocal calls to selected individuals to the exclusion of others. Evidence that the caller typically ignores the audience comes from the fact that vervet monkeys quite often persist in giving their alarm calls even when all the individuals of the group are already in some safe position looking at the predator (Cheney and Seyfarth 1990a; see also Gouzoules, Gouzoules, and Ashley 1995), and chimpanzees give "pant-hoots" upon finding large amounts of food even if the whole group is already there and eating (Clark and Wrangham 1994; though see Mitani and Nishida 1993). On the whole, primate vocalizations would seem to be mainly individualistic expressions of emotions, not recipient-directed acts. According to Zuberbühler:

Nonhuman primates vocalize in response to important events, irrespective of how potential recipients may view the situation. (2005, p. 126)

Recognizing all of this, some theorists (e.g., Seyfarth and Cheney 2003) have argued that primate vocal communication was an important step on the way to human language mainly in terms of skills of vocal comprehension. The problem is that such "comprehension" skills are not specialized only for communication; they are merely general skills of cognitive assessment. Thus, when a monkey learns that a certain alarm call of a certain bird species, or even of its own species, predicts the presence of a leopard, it is not clear that this is best thought of as the comprehension of a communicative act. The monkey has simply learned that one thing predicts another, or even causes another, in the same basic way as many other phenomena in their daily lives. If we are looking for evolutionary steps along the way to human communicative activities, therefore, we must look at how the *production* of communicative signals works, since these are specifically communicative. And from the perspective of production, general mammalian, including primate, vocal displays, with their genetically fixed and highly inflexible structure, would seem to be a very long way from human-style communication.

2.2   Gestural Signals

Nonhuman primates also communicate with one another on a regular basis gesturally, where gesture designates a communicative behavior (not a physical characteristic) in the visual channel: mostly bodily postures, facial expressions, and manual gestures. Although many of these are as genetically fixed and inflexible as primate vocalizations—and thus should be called displays—an important subset are individually learned and flexibly used, especially in the great apes, and so may be properly called intentional signals. These intentional gestural signals often concern less emotionally charged and evolutionarily urgent social activities such as play, nursing, begging, and grooming.

By far the most research on primate gestural communication has been conducted on great apes. Evidence that an important subset of great ape gestures are individually learned, intentionally and flexibly produced communicative signals is as follows (see Tomasello et al. 1985, 1994, 1997, 1989; Call and Tomasello 2007):

• there are many and very large individual differences in the gestural repertoires of different individuals of the same species, even within the same group, including some idiosyncratic gestures produced by single individuals;

• individuals regularly use the same gesture for different communicative ends, and also different gestures for the same communicative end;

• individuals typically produce a gesture only when the recipient is appropriately attentive, and afterward they often monitor the recipient's reaction and wait for a response;

• individuals sometimes use sequences or combinations of multiple gestures when the other does not react appropriately; and

• individuals with significant human contact invent or learn different kinds of novel gestures quite easily.

And so, although primate vocal communication obviously shares with human linguistic communication the vocal-auditory channel, great ape gestural communication shares with human linguistic communication foundational aspects of its manner of functioning, namely, the intentional and flexible use of learned communicative signals.

2.2.1   Two Types of Gesture

There are two basic types of great ape gesture, based on how they function communicatively: intention-movements and attention-getters. Unlearned intention-movement displays are ubiquitous in the animal kingdom, and indeed they were first noted informally by Darwin (1872), and then named and systematically described by Tinbergen (1951) in his classic studies of seagulls. Intention-movements occur when an individual performs only the first step of a normal behavioral sequence, often in abbreviated form, and this first step is already enough to elicit a response from a recipient (i.e., the same response that would normally be given to the entire behavioral sequence). For example, wolves growl and bare their teeth, ritualized from preparations for actual biting, which leads a recipient to withdraw, and some birds perform various preparations for mating that signal their impending sexual advances. The normal case is that such displays are "ritualized" phylogenetically; for example, wolves who conspicuously prepare for biting by baring their teeth and growling have an adaptive advantage, as do wolves who respond to this preparatory behavior by withdrawing before the actual biting comes. Over evolutionary time, this results in the genetic fixation of intention-movement displays performed invariably in specific emotional and/or social circumstances.

But what we are interested in here are intention-movement *signals* that have been ritualized (learned) ontogenetically and so are used with more flexibility. Ontogenetically ritualized intention-movement gestures in chimpanzees—the ape species studied most intensively—are such things as *arm-raise* to initiate play and *touch-back* (by infants to moms) to request being carried (see table 2.1 for a list of examples). Like intention-movement displays, these intention-movement signals are basically abbreviations of full-fledged social actions, and they are almost always dyadic in the sense that the communicator is attempting to influence the behavior of the recipient directly in the interaction (not communicate about some third entity). For those intention-movement gestures that are learned, the learning process, using *arm-raise* to illustrate, seems to go something like this:

(i) initially one youngster approaches another with rough-and-tumble play in mind, raises his arm in preparation to play-hit the other, and then actually hits, jumps on, and begins playing;

(ii) over repeated instances, the recipient learns to anticipate this sequence on the basis of the initial arm-raise alone, and so begins to play upon perceiving this initial step; and

(iii) the communicator eventually learns to anticipate this anticipation, and so raises his arm, monitors the recipient, and waits for her to react—expecting this arm-raise to initiate the play.

We now have an ontogenetically ritualized gesture, *arm-raise*, that the communicator produces intentionally—

Table 2.1
Some intentional gestural signals used by chimpanzees in their spontaneous social interactions in social groups (C = communicator; R = recipient). See Call and Tomasello 2007.

	Gestural Action	Goal/Function
Intention-Movements		
Arm-raise	C raises arm toward R, beginning hitting.	Initiate play
Touch-back	C touches back of R lightly, beginning climbing on.	Request ride-on-back
Hand-beg	C places hand under R's mouth, beginning taking food.	Request food
Head bob	C "bobs and weaves" in bowing position at R, beginning play.	Initiate play
Arm-on	C approaches R and places arm on R's back, beginning dragging.	Initiate tandem walk
Attention-Getters		
Ground-slap	C slaps the ground (or an object) and looks to R.	Often play
Poke-at	C pokes a body part of R.	Various
Throw-stuff	C throws something at R.	Often play
Hand-clap	C slaps own wrist or hand, as approaches R.	Often play
Back-offer	C insistently puts its own back in the face of R.	Typically grooming

with a plan and with monitoring of the recipient's response (trying something else if the desired response is not forthcoming)—in order to initiate play. The *touch-back* gesture is learned in a similar way, as the infant initially grabs the mother's back and pulls it down physically so as to climb on. Mom comes to anticipate on the basis of the first touch, and so lowers her back when just this initial part of the sequence is produced. The infant learns to anticipate this response, and so comes to use the gesture intentionally, touching mom's back lightly and waiting for her to lower it in response as expected.

The main competing explanation for how apes acquire intention-movement gestures is imitation. But there is basically no evidence for this and much against it. Evidence that chimpanzees and other apes learn their most flexible intention-movement gestures mainly by ontogenetic ritualization, and not by imitation, includes at least the following (see Tomasello et al. 1994, 1997; Call and Tomasello 2007):

· when different captive groups are compared, there are no systematic group differences, but many individual differences within both groups;

· individuals in natural social groups acquire gestures they have had little or no opportunity to observe (e.g., infant nursing gestures), and there are some idiosyncratic gestures used only by single individuals (who of course had no one else to observe);

• youngsters raised in captive peer groups, with no adult gestures to observe, acquire many of the same gestures as youngsters in natural groups—because they engage in many of the same activities (play, nursing, etc.) within which these gestures are ritualized;

• in the experiment of Tomasello et al. (1997), when one individual was taken from a captive group, trained to use a novel gesture for a reward, and put back in the group, no other individuals learned the new gesture (the experiment was performed twice with different demonstrators and gestures).

Intention-movements are thus created as two interactants anticipate and so shape one another's behavior dyadically over repeated instances of the same interaction. Importantly, this means that the "meaning" or communicative significance of intention-movements is inherent in them, in the sense that they are one part of a preexisting, meaningful social interaction—which is what is being anticipated back and forth in the first place. Because of this, individuals do not need to learn, by imitation or any other means, to connect the signal with its "meaning"—the "meaning" comes built in. Also, because of the way ritualization works, these gestures are only "one-way" (not bidirectional) communicative devices in the sense that the communicator and recipient each learn it in terms of their own role only—without knowing the role of the other (so that the communicator would not recognize the gesture as "the same" as his own if someone directed it at him). Finally, some researchers have claimed that some intention-movements are actually functioning iconically, for example, when one gorilla moves its arms in a particular direction in a sexual or play context and a recipient responds by moving in that direction (Tanner and Byrne 1996). But these are most likely garden-variety ritualized behaviors that appear to humans to be iconic because they derive from attempts to actually move the body of the other in the desired direction; they are not functioning iconically for the apes themselves.

The other kind of ape gesture is attention-getters, and these kinds of gestures most assuredly are *not* widespread in the animal kingdom; they may even be unique to primates or even great apes. Attention-getters are such things as *ground-slap, poke-at*, and *throw-stuff*, which serve to attract the attention of the recipient to the slapping, poking, or throwing communicator—again mostly in dyadic fashion without external referents (see table 2.1 for a list of examples). Initially in our research, because these gestures are used quite often by youngsters in play contexts, we classified them as play gestures. But then we saw them being used in other contexts, and we realized that they operate somewhat differently from intention-movements. What happens in the prototypical case is that the youngster is in a play mood—which is apparent from her mood-induced "play face and posture" display— and the attention-getter serves to draw attention to the display. Another example is when male chimpanzees who are in the mood for sex engage in *leaf-clipping* behavior, which makes a sharp, loud noise that attracts the attention of females to their erect penis (Sugiyama 1981). Importantly, in both of these cases the "meaning" or function of the communicative act as a whole resides not in the attention-getting gesture, but rather in the involuntary display, which the individual knows the recipient must see in order to react appropriately. Evidence for this interpretation is that on some occasions apes will actually hide a display from others, for example, covering up a facial fear-grimace display with their hands (Tanner and Byrne 1993; de Waal 1986).

One small variation on this theme is a very interesting subset of attention-getters that operate without displays, and may even move in the direction of triadic (referential) communication. These involve such things as the communicator "offering" to another individual either a body part, typically for grooming, or an object, which is then quickly retracted, as a solicitation for play. There are even some rare observations of apes "offering" unwanted food to others (Liebal, Pika, and Tomasello 2006). Although rare, individuals directing the attention of conspecifics in this way is theoretically very important, because it is the closest thing we have to apes directing others' attention intentionally to external things triadically, referentially, in the manner of virtually all of human communication.

Because they operate differently from intention-movements, attention-getters are learned in a somewhat different way as well. They are not bound up with any particular social activity, and so they cannot be ritualized from recurrent social behaviors directly (and there is no evidence that they are imitated). Instead, they are learned by individuals engaging in behaviors like slapping the ground or throwing things or pushing others for noncommunicative reasons, which naturally attracts the attention of others—and this result is then noticed and exploited in the future by the behaving individual. Once learned, an attention-getter may be used quite widely for many different social goals such as play, grooming, nursing, and so forth. And it is precisely this indirectness that is the true novelty here. The communicator has some action he wants from the recipient—what we may call his *social intention*—and to attain this he attempts to draw the recipient's attention to something—what we may call his *"referential" intention*[1]—in the expectation that if she looks where he wishes, she will do as he wishes. This two-tiered intentional structure is a genuine evolutionary novelty—almost certainly confined to great apes and perhaps other primates—and may be considered the closest thing we have to a "missing link" between nonhuman primate communication and the sophisticated attention-directing and attention-sharing characteristic of human referential communication.

---

1. "Referential" is in scare quotes because, I would argue, what apes are doing is a precursor to human reference while differing in some respects—which can only be fully characterized after human reference is described in the next chapter.

Finally, it is important that apes regularly string together sequences of gestures, involving both intention-movements and attention-getters. Systematic investigation of these, however, has revealed no "grammar" in the sense of specific combinations creating new communicative functions or "meanings" (Liebal, Call, and Tomasello 2004). What seems to happen—and this provides further support for the intentional nature of great ape gestural communication—is that the communicator tries one gesture, monitors the response of the recipient, and, if needed, repeats or tries a different gesture. This shows persistence to a goal with adjusted means as necessary—the prototype of intentional action—but it does not show any kind of combinatorial or grammatical capacity (see chapter 6).

2.2.2   *Attention to the Attention of the Other*

A crucially important difference between communication in the vocal and gestural modalities is how the participants monitor one another's attention in the process. In vocal communication, there is basically no monitoring. In most cases, the communicator is simply expressing his individual emotion, and so his call is broadcast relatively indiscriminately throughout the surrounding environment. In contrast, most gestural communication takes place in the visual channel, spatially directed toward a single individual, which requires the communicator to check that the recipient is visually attending, or else the gesture will not work. For her part, the recipient needs to determine if the gesture is directed to her or her neighbor, to know whether she should or should not respond.

In our twenty years of research on ape gestures, we have documented many times that ape gestures are produced with sensitivity to the attentional state of the recipient—in the sense that purely visually based gestures are given almost exclusively when the recipient is already visually oriented to the communicator (see Call and Tomasello 2007 for a review). There are some well-known experimental studies by Povinelli and Eddy (1996) showing that when chimpanzee communicators are faced with the choice of two potential human recipients—one of whom is unable to see her because, for example, he has a bucket on his head—they produce visually based begging gestures toward both humans equally, suggesting little sophistication in judging the attentional states of others. But choosing whom to direct gestures to is a very unnatural communicative situation, and when the experimental paradigm is changed so that the chimpanzee does not have to choose—on one trial he faces a human who can see him and on another trial he faces one who cannot (and these are then compared across trials)— their performance looks much better (although they still do not, as do human infants, attend much to the role of the eyes specifically; Kaminski, Call, and Tomasello 2004). And other studies in noncommunication paradigms have demonstrated in many different ways that apes—for example, in competition with one another, or when concealing things from a human competitor—understand what others do and do not see (see Tomasello and Call 2006 for a review).

With all of this attention to the attention of the other, a natural question is whether chimpanzees and other apes produce some sequences of gestures with the specific ordering: attention-getter (to obtain the recipient's attention) followed by intention-movement (visually based and therefore requiring the recipient's visual attention). The answer is that they do not. That is to say, they do produce such sequences on occasion, but they produce all kinds of other sequences as well (including the reverse), and so this is not an especially privileged sequence (Liebal, Call, and Tomasello 2004). On the face of it this would seem not to fit with the finding of sensitivity to the attention of the other. But the reason apes do not privilege attention-getter > intention-movement sequences is because they have an alternative strategy. When they need to produce a visually based intention-movement gesture, they quite often walk around in front of the other to produce it. We observed this first naturalistically, but then later experimentally. When a human faced an ape with some food behind her, the ape gestured to her face straightaway; but when the human turned her back, even if the food was directly in front of the ape, the ape walked around and gestured to the human's face (Liebal, Pika, Call, and Tomasello 2004). The species who did this most readily were humans' two closest relatives, chimpanzees and bonobos. Why apes use this "walk around" strategy rather than using an attention-getter-to-intention-movement sequence is unknown at this time.

All of this attention to the attention of the other during communication is unprecedented in nonprimate, and maybe even non-ape, communication.

2.2.3 *Summary*

From a functional, communicative point of view, then, on practically every dimension imaginable, great apes display more sophisticated communicative skills in the gestural rather than in the vocal modality (see also Pollick and de Waal 2007). First, many ape gestures are individually learned and flexibly used, including in combination, whereas this is not true of ape vocalizations. Second, many ape gestures are used with attention to the attentional state of the recipient, which is mostly not even relevant in ape vocal communication. The overall communicative act in ape gestures is thus: check the attention of other > walk around as necessary > gesture > monitor the reaction of other > repeat or use another gesture. This would seem to be a paradigm case of intentional action, in this case toward others and with some understanding of the way the other's reaction depends on her abilities to perceive and intend things. It is also important evolutionarily that gestural communication is more sophisticated in apes (humans' closest relatives) than in monkeys and other mammals (Maestripieri 1998), whereas something close to the opposite is true of vocal communication. These considerations all give us good reason to think that great ape gestures are the more likely candidate, in comparison with great ape vocalizations, for the evolutionary precursor of human-style communication.

2.3   Communication with Humans

For better or for worse, many monkeys and apes grow up in one or another kind of human context, either a zoo, a research facility, or a human home. There are no systematic reports of any monkey acquiring any new communicative skills naturally as a result of their exposure to humans. And apes, as noted above, do not acquire anything new in the vocal domain when they grow up in the midst of humans. But apes who grow up with humans do acquire some new gestures specifically for use with humans. Most interesting in the current context is the fact that many apes—some with no explicit training—learn to do something that might be called "pointing," as a powerful extension of their natural attention-getting gestures.

2.3.1   *Pointing and Other Imperatives*

Chimpanzees and other apes growing up in human captivity learn to indicate for their human caretakers things they want but cannot obtain on their own. The most basic such behavior, documented extensively by Leavens and colleagues (e.g., Leavens and Hopkins

1998; Leavens, Hopkins, and Bard 2005), is chimpanzees "pointing" to out-of-reach food so that a human will retrieve it for them. Approximately 60 to 70 percent of all captive chimpanzees engage in this behavior when presented with the appropriate situation, spontaneously with no explicit training from humans. Typically, they are doing this through a cage, and so they orient their body toward the out-of-reach food, and thrust their fingers and hands through the caging toward the food as well. They are not reaching for the food, because when a human is not present they do not engage in this behavior. How these chimpanzees acquire their pointing skills is not known.

This "pointing" is used relatively flexibly. For example, if several different types of food are available, apes will point to the most desirable one, and they will continue pointing to that one persistently even if given a less desirable food (Leavens, Hopkins, and Bard 2005). Also, when human-raised apes observe a human hiding food in an open area outside their cage, many hours later they will still point, for a naive human, to the location where the food is hidden (Menzel 1999). And when apes observe that a human needs a tool to retrieve food for them, and that tool is then hidden while the human is away, when the human returns they will point to the location of the hidden tool (Call and Tomasello 1994). This is still best seen as a request that the human retrieve the tool (so that he can retrieve the food) because apes do not gesture in this situation if the tool is for the human's own use

(Haimerl et al., in prep.); but its indirectness is neverthe-less remarkable.

Also important is the fact that apes raised in rich human contexts, similar to the way human children are raised, have been observed to request things imperatively in other ways as well. For example, some human-raised apes point to a locked door when they want access behind it, so that the human will open it for them—or in some cases they lead the human to the door or a high shelf by pulling his hand, stopping and waiting in front of it expectantly (Gomez 1990). Another common observa-tion, based on my own personal experience interacting with young chimpanzees, is that they will bring a recal-citrant object (e.g., a locked box) to humans for help, and they will grab a human's hand and put it in or on his pocket, and wait for a good result. Apes in zoos often develop attention-getters for the human visitors, such as clapping their hands, so that they will attend to them and throw food. And apes may be taught something like human sign language signs or touching visual symbols for communicating with humans as well (Gardner and Gardner 1969; Savage-Rumbaugh et al. 1986, 1993). It is thus clear that human-raised apes have a fairly flexible understanding that humans control many aspects of their world, and that these humans can be induced to do things that help them reach their goals in this human environ-ment with some kind of attention-directing behavior. The fact that apes often look to the eyes of the human when making such requests is perhaps also important, as it suggests that they know that the causality/intentionality somehow emanates from behind the eyes and not just from the external limbs carrying out the desired actions (Gomez 1990, 2004).

The most reasonable interpretation of ape pointing, then, would seem to be that it is a natural extension of their attention-getting gestures. Just as they attract attention to the self by slapping the ground or even attract attention to their shoulder for grooming, in the right circumstances with humans they attract attention to desired food by indicating it "referentially"—because they have some social intention they think this will help them to achieve. In all of these cases, ape communicators presumably can predict from past experience in similar situations what the human recipient will do if she indeed sees what they want her to see. One obvious question, however, is why apes point for humans, but not for one another. The obvious answer is that other apes are not motivated to help them in the same way as humans. If an ape pointed to food as a request to another ape, it is not very likely that he would end up getting it—whereas captive apes have much experience of humans giving them food freely. The evolutionary implication of this obvious fact is that if the social environment of apes suddenly became more cooperative, they could point imperatively to request help from each other with no additional cognitive machinery necessary.

But at the same time it is critically important to note that no apes in any kind of environment produce, either

for other apes or for humans, acts of pointing that serve
functions other than the imperative function. That is, they
do not point declaratively to simply share interest and
attention in something with another individual (Gomez
2004), and they do not point informatively to inform
another of something she might want or need to know—
as human infants do from very early in ontogeny (see
chapter 4). Tomasello and Carpenter (2005) even presented three young human-raised chimpanzees with situations that reliably elicit expressive-declarative pointing
in human infants (e.g., surprising, interesting events),
but observed no declaratives from them in response.
And even the signed productions of "linguistic" apes are
almost all imperatives—approximately 96–98 percent in
the only two systematic studies (Rivas 2005; Greenfield
and Savage-Rumbaugh, 1990), with the other 2–4 percent
having no clear functional interpretation (they are not
clearly declarative or informative, but more recognitory
or classificatory, as the ape simply recognizes something
and produces the associated sign in recognition). This
functional restriction probably accounts in large part for
apes' surprising troubles in comprehending human
pointing gestures designed to inform them of things
helpfully, as we shall now see.

2.3.2 *Comprehending Pointing*

Great apes follow the gaze direction of others, even to
hidden locations behind barriers (Tomasello, Hare, and

Agnetta 1999; Bräuer, Call, and Tomasello 2005). If a human points and looks toward some food that an ape currently does not see, and by following the pointing/looking the ape comes to see the food, she will go get it. In this sense, one could say that the ape understood the intention behind the human's attention-directing gesture in this simple situation.

But a seemingly minor change in this procedure leads to a drastically different result—which might lead us to reassess the simpler situation. Tomasello, Call, and Gluckman (1997) introduced apes to a game in which one human, the hider, hid food in one of three buckets and a second human, the helper, helped them find to it—what has been called the object choice task. Apes knew from previous experience that there was only one piece of food hidden, and they would get only one choice. In the key experimental condition, the hider hid the food from the ape while the helper peeked, and then the helper simply pointed informatively for the ape to the bucket in which the food was hidden. Astoundingly, apes then chose buckets randomly, even though they were highly motivated to find the food on almost every trial. Quite often an ape followed the helpers' pointing and looking to the correct bucket but then did not choose it. This means that following the directionality of the point was not the problem; they just did not seem to understand its meaning, its relevance to their search for the food. It is as if the apes said to themselves "OK. There's a bucket. So what? Now where's the food?" Human infants perform well in this seemingly trivial task by 14 months of age, mostly before language (Behne, Carpenter, and Tomasello 2005).

Task failures may be explained in an unlimited number of ways. But a follow-up study constrains the possibilities considerably. Hare and Tomasello (2004) conducted a competitive version of the basic object choice task. Chimpanzees participated in two experimental conditions. One condition, the cooperative condition, was identical to the basic task, and so, not surprisingly, the results were identical as well: despite following the point to the correct bucket the apes chose randomly. In the other, competitive condition, however, a human began in the warmup session by competing with the chimpanzee for food, and then in the experimental session attempted to continue competing. Specifically, without looking to the ape in any way, the human reached toward the correct bucket, but due to the physical constraints in the situation (her arm would not go very far because the hole in the Plexiglas was not large enough), was unable to reach it. When the buckets were now pushed to the ape (by another experimenter), she now knew where the food was! Even though the superficial behavior in the two experimental conditions was highly similar—arm extended toward correct bucket—the apes' understanding of the humans' behavior was seemingly very different. They were thus able to infer: she wants to get into that bucket for herself; therefore, there must be something good in there. But they still were *not* able to infer: she wants me to know that the food is in the bucket.

What are we to make of apes' behavior in this task? They follow the pointing gesture to the correct bucket naturally, but then they do not seem to know what it means. Based only on the standard object choice task, we might suppose that they cannot go beyond what they see to infer the location of hidden food. But many other studies show that they can make inferences in other situations (Call 2004), and in the follow-up study of Hare and Tomasello (2004) they made this inference easily (i.e., "his reaching suggests that there must be something good in there"). One reasonable hypothesis, then, is that apes simply do not understand that the human is communicating altruistically in order to help them toward their goals. That is, they themselves communicate intentionally only to request things imperatively, and so they only understand others' gestures when they are imperative requests as well—otherwise they are simply mystified as to what the gesticulating is all about.

2.3.3 Summary

Overall, the most important facts about apes communicating with humans are three: (i) again, it is the gestural modality that wins the day; (ii) again, it is ape attention-getters (i.e., "pointing") with their split between the social intention and the referential intention that are most

Box 2.1
On Dogs and Other Mammals

Interestingly, domestic dogs perform very well in the basic object choice task with a human pointing informatively to the location of hidden food. Wolves perform poorly, and dog puppies perform very well even before they have had much experience with humans (Hare et al. 2002). It would thus seem that when humans were domesticating dogs, over the past 10,000 to 12,000 years, they somehow selected for individuals with characteristics enabling them to understand, in some sense, what the human is doing in this situation. We do not know how the dogs do this—research is ongoing—but one hypothesis is that they do not actually understand that the human is informing them of the location of the hidden food cooperatively, but rather, they understand the pointing as imperative: the human is ordering them to that location. This makes sense because dogs have been selected/domesticated in large part to follow human orders. Another plausible interpretation is in terms of helping: because of their unique evolutionary histories, domestic dogs understand in a way that apes do not that the human is actually attempting to help them. These two interpretations are given added plausibility by the fact that basically all of the animals who do well in this task are either domesticated animals or animals who have been raised or trained extensively by humans—including trained dolphins, domestic goats, and some human-raised apes (see Call and Tomasello 2005 for a review). In any case, in the current context, we may at least note that dogs' and other domesticated animals' excellent performance provides an existence proof that at least some animals respond appropriately to human

Box 2.1

(continued)

> pointing in the object choice task. The basis on which they do this is still unknown.
>
> In terms of production, there are observations of dogs and other domesticated animals communicating with humans in seemingly complex ways. There are not so many systematic studies of this (see Hare, Call, and Tomasello 1998), but even accepting these observations to some degree, it is important to note that these animals do not communicate with conspecifics in these same complex ways—only with humans. And so, these communicative skills may be thought of as, in a sense, "unnatural," as they are instances of interspecific communication resulting at least partly from the process of domestication.

human-like; and (iii) even with relatively sophisticated means of communication taught to them by humans, apes still communicate almost exclusively imperatively, to get others to do things, and indeed it appears that they do not even comprehend cooperative informatives.

2.4   Intentionality in Ape Communication

For people who study only humans, and who have never looked in detail at animal communication, it is difficult to appreciate how astounding are apes' flexible skills of gestural communication. The vast majority of animal communication is basically genetically fixed. Even among monkeys and apes, vocal communication is mostly genetically fixed. And the gestural communication of monkeys, though it has not been studied in much detail (see Maestripieri 1998), has a distinctly stereotypic appearance. The flexibility of great ape gestural communication is thus truly an evolutionary novelty.

Behavioral flexibility is generally a sign that learning is involved, and indeed we presented evidence that many ape gestures are learned. But this could, in theory, be either relatively simple associative learning—when a certain situation presents itself a certain gesture is likely to be effective—or else relatively complex cognitive processes involving an understanding of the intentionality of the communicative partner. We believe that complex cognitive processes are involved, and that this view is supported by studies documenting great ape understanding of intentionality in other domains of activity.

2.4.1 Understanding Intentional Action

Just as animals may solve physical problems without understanding all of the underlying causality involved, animals may communicate without understanding all of the intentionality involved—and indeed that is what they mostly do. They know that when they do X, recipients do Y, without any understanding of how this works. But for more flexible communication in which, for example, different signals are chosen on different occasions depending on such things as the attentional state of the recipient, as in ape gestural communication, the communicator needs some kind of cognitive model of how the recipient perceives the signal and acts as a result.

Recent research has demonstrated that great apes understand much about how others work as intentional, perceiving agents. Specifically, great apes understand something of the goals and perceptions of others and how these work together in individual intentional action in ways very similar to young human children (though see Povinelli and Vonk 2006 for a different view). First, great apes (most of the research is with chimpanzees) understand that others have goals. Evidence is as follows:

• When a human passes food to a chimpanzee and then fails to do so, the ape reacts in a frustrated manner if the human is doing this for no good reason (i.e., is unwilling) whereas she waits patiently if the human is making good-faith attempts to give the object but failing or having accidents (i.e., is unable) (Call et al. 2004; see Behne et al. 2005 for similar findings with human infants).

• When a human or conspecific needs help reaching an out-of-reach object or location, chimpanzees help them in a way very similar to human infants—which requires an understanding of the other's goal (Warneken and Tomasello 2006; Warneken et al. 2007).

• When a human shows a human-raised chimpanzee an action on an object that is marked in various ways as a failed attempt to change that object's state, the ape, in her turn, actually executes the intended action (and not the action actually demonstrated, e.g., hands slipping off the object) (Tomasello and Carpenter 2005; based on Meltzoff's 1995 study with human infants).

• When a human shows a human-raised chimpanzee a series of two actions on an object, one of which is marked in various ways as accidental, the ape, in her turn, usually executes only the intended action (Tomasello and Carpenter 2005; based on Carpenter, Akhtar, and Tomasello's 1998 study with human infants; see also Call and Tomasello 1998 for further evidence).

• When a human-raised chimpanzee observes a human produce actions that are either freely chosen or forced by circumstances, the ape understands the difference—as demonstrated by her selective imitation of freely chosen acts but not those forced by circumstances (if the circumstances do not apply to her)—thus demonstrating an understanding not just of the intentionality of action, but also its rationality (Buttelmann et al. 2007, based on the study of Gergely, Bekkering, and Király 2002 with human infants).

The conclusion is thus that apes and young human children both understand in the same basic way (in simple situations) that individuals pursue a goal in a persistent manner until they have reached it—and they understand the goal not as the result produced in the external environment, but rather as the actor's internal representation of the state of the world she wishes to bring about. They also understand that the actor chooses an action to pursue a goal "rationally" in the sense that they consider the actor's reasons for doing what he is doing.

Second, great apes (most of the research is again with chimpanzees) also understand that others have perceptions. Evidence is as follows (see Tomasello and Call 2006 for a review):

• When a human peers behind a barrier, apes move over to get a better viewing angle to look behind it as well (Tomasello, Hare, and Agnetta 1999; Bräuer et al. 2006; see Moll and Tomasello 2004 for a similar study with human infants).

• When a human's gaze is directed toward a barrier and there is also an object further in that same direction, apes look only to the barrier and not to the object—unless the barrier has a window in it, in which case they look to the object (Okamoto-Barth, Call, and Tomasello 2007; see Caron et al. 2002 for similar findings with human infants).

• When apes beg a human for food, they take into account whether the human can see their gesture (Kaminski, Call, and Tomasello 2004; Liebal, Pika, Call, and Tomasello 2004).

• When chimpanzees compete with one another for food they take into account whether their competitor can see the contested food (Hare et al. 2000; Hare, Call, Tomasello 2001), and even on occasion attempt to conceal their approach from a competitor (Hare, Call, Tomasello 2006; Melis, Call, and Tomasello 2006).

The conclusion is thus that apes and young human children both understand in the same basic way (in simple situations) that individuals perceive things in the world and react to them—and they understand that the content of the other's perception is something different from their own.

The last-cited competition experiments are especially important because they demonstrate that chimpanzees do not just understand goals and perception separately, but rather understand how they are interrelated in the basic logic of intentional action: agents *want* certain environmental states to obtain (have goals); agents *see* the world and so can assess the situation with respect to the desired goal state; and agents *do* things when they perceive that the environment is not in the desired goal state. This kind of understanding of intentional action supports a basic form of practical reasoning that enables individuals to understand and predict what others are doing and will do, even in novel circumstances. Thus, in the Hare et al. competition experiments, participants understand that if their competitor can see his goal (the food) he will pursue it, whereas if he cannot see it he will not pursue it; and conversely, if the competitor sees something that is not its goal (e.g., a rock), he will not pursue that. And they can understand basic things about opportunities and obstacles to goals for others in novel situations—for example, when the other has a free path to food or his path is blocked—and how this affects their behavioral choices. This kind of practical reasoning about others—in terms of the psychological predicates *want, see,* and *do*—is foundational to all kinds of primate and human social interaction, including intentional communication viewed as social action in which individuals attempt to get others to do what they want them to.

The overall conclusion is thus that apes understand others in terms of their goals and perceptions and how these work to determine behavioral decisions, that is, they understand others as intentional, perhaps even rational, agents. Based on this understanding, they can engage in the kinds of practical reasoning that underlie flexible, strategic social interaction and communication— for example, determining what the other wants, the reason he wants it, and what he is likely to do next. Importantly, because ape gestures arise directly out of meaningful social interactions as expressed in overt behavior—whereas vocalizations are more individualis- tic expressions of emotions with few overt behavioral manifestations—practical reasoning skills about inten- tional action would seem to be applicable in an especially natural way in the case of gestural communication.

2.4.2   How Ape Gestures Work

It is possible that great apes use none of this under- standing of individual intentionality in their gestural communication, that they simply rely on associative learning or some such. But this seems highly unlikely. If they know what others see and want and do in the above-cited experiments, they presumably know these things also when they are gesturing and being gestured to. Nevertheless, we must still be careful not to give things a human interpretation where it is not warranted. This "third way" theoretical stance (cognitivist, but not anthropocentric; Call and Tomasello 2005) leads to the following analysis of great ape intention-movement and attention-getting gestures in terms of the primitive psychological predicates of *want, see,* and *do,* as justified by the experiments cited above.

Apes' intention-movement gestures emanate from the communicator's social intention that the recipient *do* something such as play, lower her back, or groom. The communicator's expectation is that if the recipient *sees* his gesture, she will *do* what he wants, because that is what she has done in past (the basis of the ritualization process). For her part, upon seeing the intention-movement the recipient knows that the communicator *wants* her to *do* some particular thing (based on her intention-reading abilities and her past experience in similar interactions). In contrast, apes' attention-getting gestures emanate from the communicator's social intention that the recipient *see* something, which he expects, based on his intentional understanding (in combination with past experience), will most likely lead her to *do* what he wants. This creates a two-tiered intentional structure comprising the communicator's social intention, as his fundamental goal, and his "referential" intention, as a means to that goal. For her part, upon seeing the attention-getter the recipient knows that the communicator *wants* her to *see* something, and, possibly, that he is doing this as a means to get her to *do* something. Thus, the recipient typically looks in response to the attention-getting gesture, and then responds naturally to what she sees, and possibly to what the communicator wants, if she is for her own reasons so inclined.

Thus, at this point, our analysis of the two types of ape gesture, from the communicator's point of view, may be represented schematically as in figure 2.1. The critical point is this. Because intention-movements are simply

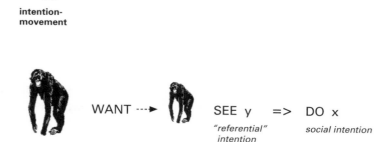

WANT ‑‑‑►   DO x
             social intention

intention-
movement

WANT ‑‑‑►   SEE y   =>   DO x
             "referential"   *social intention*
             intention

attention-
getter

Figure 2.1

ritualizations (abbreviations) of initial steps in intentional actions, their "meaning" is built in; it is simply what the communicator intends the other to do in the interaction, which was already present in some preexisting act in the social interaction before the signal was ritualized. In contrast, attention-getters introduce a modicum of indirectness into the process. Their two-tiered intentional structure creates a "distance" between the overt communicative means (act of "reference") and the covert communicative end (social intention). The recipient then potentially infers from what she is looking at what the communicator wants (although it is also possible that she simply reacts to it naturally without such an inference).

Amazing though this process is from the point of view of animal communication in general, it still differs from human communication in some fundamental ways. These will be spelled out more fully in the next chapter, but for now we may focus on one key difference, from the point of view of the recipient. When one human points for another, the recipient implicitly asks herself why—why does he think that looking in that direction will be useful or interesting for me? This is based on the assumption that he is indeed pointing for her benefit (at least immediately). Thus, young children know that an adult's pointing to a bucket in the context of a searching activity is probably relevant in some way to their joint goal of finding the toy. In contrast, great apes cannot and do not assume that the other is pointing for their benefit, and so they do not ask themselves "why does he think this is relevant for me?" They want to know what he wants for himself (since when they point it is always for themselves), not how he thinks their looking in this direction will be relevant for them—and so they simply do not see another's pointing gesture as relevant to their own goal. (For what it is worth, the same is true of recipients of ape vocalizations: they hear an excited or fearful scream and they ask what prompted it, but they do not ask how the screamer thinks it is relevant for them.) The general point is that when communication becomes governed by more cooperative motives—not just individual intentionality, but shared intentionality—a whole new inferential process ensues, as we shall see in some detail in the chapter that follows.

2.5 Conclusion

The vast majority of studies of nonhuman primate communication focus on their vocal displays, and virtually all treatises with titles such as "Primate communication and human language" focus on the vocal channel, often without even mentioning gestures (two recent exceptions are Corballis 2002 and Burling 2005). In my opinion, this is a huge mistake. Primate vocal displays are basically no different from those of other mammals; there is no growth in sophistication or complexity from other mammals to primates or, within primates, from monkeys to apes. For all mammals, including nonhuman

primates, vocal displays are mostly unlearned, genetically fixed, emotionally urgent, involuntary, inflexible
responses to evolutionarily important events that benefit
the vocalizer in some more or less direct way. They are
broadcast mostly indiscriminately, with little attention to
potential recipients. When apes grow up in the presence
of humans they learn no new vocalizations, and cannot
even be trained to vocalize in new ways. How could such
mechanical reflexes be a direct precursor to any of the
complexities of human communication and language,
beyond simple cries of "Ouch!"?

In stark contrast, a significant number of nonhuman
primate gestures, especially those of great apes, are individually learned and flexibly produced communicative
acts, involving an understanding of important aspects of
individual intentionality. Apes' intention-movement gestures express the intention that I want you to do something, and they are chosen in light of the attentional state
of the recipient. Apes' attention-getting gestures express
the two-tiered intention that I want you to see something
so that you will do something, with some attention-
getters even being used triadically (e.g., to "offer" a body
part or object to another, or to "point" for humans). Ape
attention-getters are an extremely rare form of communication evolutionarily—I have even referred to them here
as a kind of "missing link" to human communication and
all of its attention directing and sharing—because they
introduce a split between the referential intention that the
recipient look at something and the social intention that

she do something as a result. In all, I personally do not see how anyone can doubt that ape gestures—in all of their flexibility and sensitivity to the attention of the other—and not ape vocalizations—in all of their inflexibility and ignoring of others—are the original font from which the richness and complexities of human communication and language have flowed.

3   Human Cooperative Communication

I wouldn't know what I should point to in the picture as a correlate of the word kiss . . . or . . . the word taller. . . . [But] there is an act of "directing attention to the size of people" or to their actions. . . . This shows how it was possible for the general concept of meaning to come about.

—Wittgenstein, *The Big Typescript*

It would be easy to think that nothing great apes do is of much importance to human communication because humans communicate using language, and language works in an utterly unique way—as a kind of abstract symbolic code that conveys meaning directly. But if our question is about origins, this way of thinking has two fundamental problems.

The first is that although conventional languages are in some sense different codes, linguistic communication relies to a much greater degree than is readily apparent on uncoded communication and other forms of mental attunement. To give just two very simple examples: (1) everyday linguistic communication is peppered with

expressions such as *it, she, they, here, the guy we met,* whose
referents cannot be determined directly from any code
but must be inferred from common conceptual ground;
and (2) everyday conversation is full of communicative
exchanges such as, Ernie: "Wanna go to the movie?,"
Bert: "I've got a test in the morning"—in which Ernie can
only understand Bert's response given much shared
background knowledge and inferences from facts outside
of any code (e.g., knowing that having a test in the
morning means studying the night before, which pre-
cludes going to a movie). The linguistic "code" rests on
a nonlinguistic infrastructure of intentional understanding and common conceptual ground, which is in fact
logically primary (Wittgenstein 1953).

The second problem concerns origins directly. The
basic point is that human communication could not have
originated with a code, since this would assume what it
attempts to explain (as do all social contract theories).
Thus, establishing an explicit code requires some preexisting form of communication that is at least as rich as
that code. For example, if two employees want to establish a code whereby they knock twice on the wall to warn
that the boss approaches, how can they establish this
except through some other form of communication? A
symbolic communicative code assumes some preexisting
form of communication that is being codified—in much
the same way that money assumes a preexisting practice
of barter and trade that is being, in a sense, codified.
Explicit codes are thus by their very nature derivative.

But what about more naturally arising "codes" like languages? They are not explicitly formulated ahead of time, and so perhaps they are not subject to this same bootstrapping problem. Alas, no. One of the central insights of Wittgenstein's (1953) trenchant analysis of linguistic communication is that new potential users of a language—for example, children—can break into the code only if they have some other means of communicating with, or at least communing with, mature users. Otherwise, they are in the position of Quine's (1960) visitor to a foreign culture who hears a native utter "Gavagai" as an animal runs past, with no clue as to which aspect of the situation the native intends to indicate with this unknown linguistic expression. The native might "show" the stranger what he means, but this showing will, in the end, come down to some form of uncoded communication or, again, some other, uncoded way in which the two of them attune to one another mentally.

If we want to understand human communication, therefore, we cannot begin with language. Rather, we must begin with unconventionalized, uncoded communication, and other forms of mental attunement, as foundational. Excellent candidates for this role are humans' natural gestures such as pointing and pantomiming. These gestures are simple and natural, but still they are used to communicate in very powerful, species-unique ways. Our first question must therefore be how these gestures work—before we take on language and its myriad complexities. Our answer will focus on the mostly hidden, highly complex, species-unique, psychological infrastructure of shared intentionality within which humans use their natural gestures—which generates a whole new world of things to communicate about. Specifying the components of this infrastructure systematically—in terms of both the cognitive skills and the social motivations involved—amounts to constructing a model of human communication, what we will call the cooperation model.

3.1   Pointing and Pantomiming

Much of the research on human gestures has focused on the conventionalized sign languages of the deaf (e.g., Armstrong, Stokoe, and Wilcox 1995; Liddell 2003). But since such languages have basically all the complexities of modern vocal languages, they presumably do not represent the earliest evolutionary stages of uniquely human gestural communication. Other research has focused on the gestures that accompany vocal language, which have a number of unique qualities owing to their merely supporting role in the communicatory process (McNeil 1992; Goldin-Meadow 2003a). But if gestures came first in human evolution, then humans' earliest gestures would have been used without any conventionalized languages, either vocal or signed, on their own. Our interest here then, at least initially, is not in human gestures used as substitutes for or supplements to vocal language, but rather gestures used as complete communicative acts in themselves—because it is here that we may see most clearly all the different components of human cooperative communication working together, as they do for prelinguistic infants and as they presumably did for early humans before language. We want to know both how humans' unique forms of gesture might have emerged from the gestures of apes evolutionarily, and how these gestures might then subsequently have paved the way toward fully conventionalized natural languages.

If we look at human gestures from a functional, psychological point of view—at how human gestures are used to communicate—it is widely agreed that there are at bottom two basic types, based on how they are used to make reference (see Kendon 2004, p. 107). Humans gesture to:

• direct the attention of a recipient spatially to something in the immediate perceptual environment (deictically)

• direct the imagination of a recipient to something that, typically, is not in the immediate perceptual environment by behaviorally simulating an action, relation, or object (iconically)

By drawing the recipient's attention or imagination to something, these referential acts are intended to induce her to infer the communicator's social intention—what the communicator wants the recipient to do, know, or feel.

These two basic types of human gesture are, in a very general way, parallel to the two types of great ape gesture. Human pointing gestures are similar to ape attention-getters in that they are both aimed at directing the attention of a recipient to something in the immediate perceptual environment. Human iconic gestures are similar to great ape intention-movements in that they are both actions but not real actions: intention-movements are abbreviated from the real thing, and iconic gestures depict the real thing symbolically in its absence. But there are important differences as well. Thus, whereas ape attention-getters rest on the natural tendency of recipients to attend to the source of noises or touches, human pointing rests on the natural tendency of recipients to follow the gaze direction, and so the pointing direction, of others to external targets. And whereas ape intention-movements rest on the natural tendency of recipients to anticipate the next step in an action sequence—thematically, so to speak—human iconic gestures rest on the natural tendency of recipients to understand intentional actions—in this case, outside their normal context as used to communicate about a situation "like this one" symbolically and categorically.

3.1.1   Pointing

Arguably the most fundamental type of human gesture used as a complete communicative act is what we may call attention-directing or deictic gestures, the prototype of which is human pointing. Although there are significant variations of form (e.g., in some cultures the norm is lip-pointing or chin-pointing rather than index finger pointing), the basic interpersonal function of directing someone's attention to something gesturally is present in all known human societies (Kita 2003). Attention-directing gestures work by directing the attention of the recipient spatially to some location in the immediate perceptual environment (including holding up objects to show them to others). Extra cognitive work must then be done for the social intention—why this referential act has been performed, what the communicator wants from the recipient—to be inferred. Exactly how human beings learn to point, if indeed they do, is not known, but we discuss some alternatives in chapter 4 on ontogeny.

Over the past few years I have from time to time looked for examples of people pointing in natural contexts, mostly without language. These occur in situations in which, for one reason or another, language is not practical or appropriate. Some are quite simple, while others are like mini soap operas, with whole stories behind them. Each can be glossed in terms of the referential intention ("attend to") plus the social intention. Some examples are:

Example 1: A man in a bar wants another drink; he waits until the bartender looks at him and then points to his empty shotglass. *Gloss*: Attend to the emptiness of the glass; please fill it up with liquor.

Example 2: We are climbing up a steep riverbank, me already on top, and the person following, in order to have her hands free for climbing, hands up to me a book and points to the protruding end of a pen. *Gloss*: Attend to the precariousness of the pen; please be careful and don't let it drop out.

Example 3: People standing in line. The line has moved forward and a man hasn't noticed this because he is turned around talking to the person behind him. Someone from still further back points for him to the newly opened gap. *Gloss*: Attend to the empty space; please move up into it.

Example 4: A well-known professional athlete is standing in line at the airport. From some distance away, one man points to him for his companion. *Gloss*: Attend to Charles Barkley; it's cool we see him, don't you think?

Example 5: I am standing in the rear of the airplane, just to stretch for a bit, and this is near the bathroom. A woman approaches, and when she sees me points to the bathroom door with a quizzical look on her face. *Gloss*: Attend to the bathroom; are you waiting for it?

The main thing to notice in these utterly quotidian observations is simply the variety and complexity of ways in which pointing may be integrated into the various forms of life in which we operate on a daily basis. All of these observations involve the split between the referential and the social intention, as the communicator attempts to direct the recipient's attention to something for some reason, and the recipient attempts to follow this attention directing and to infer this reason—sometimes with a great inferential "distance" to be covered. For example, on the basis of my friend pointing to a pen in a notebook, I am supposed to infer that she wants me to make sure it stays safe; on the basis of someone pointing to a place on the floor, the recipient is supposed to know that she is being requested to move her body there; on the basis of the woman pointing to the airplane bathroom, I am supposed to tell her if I am waiting. Each of these depends on all kinds of background knowledge to make sense (and, as I shall argue below, this knowledge must be shared common ground). Thus, for me to comprehend the social intention of the woman inquiring about the bathroom—which, of course, I did immediately—requires a large amount of common conceptual ground between us about airplanes, airplane bathrooms, human biology and waste management, waiting in line, politeness conventions, and so forth. Even the very simple first example requires a common understanding that customers are at the bar because they want to drink, that an empty glass does not afford drinking, that the bartender has drink if the customer can pay, that a shotglass usually holds liquor and not beer or wine, and so forth.

One might suppose that only someone who is linguistic already could use a pointing gesture to communicate in such complex ways—that somehow the ability to communicate so richly with a simple pointing gesture is parasitic on linguistic skills. But, as we shall see in the next chapter, human infants, before they have much or any language, can already use pointing to direct others to all kinds of referents in order to communicate all kinds of complex social intentions.

3.1.2   Iconic Gestures (Pantomiming)

The second type of human gesture used as a complete communicative act is iconic gestures or pantomimes (depictive, imagistic, characterizing, representational, and symbolic gestures are other terms that have been used). In one form or another, iconic gestures are presumably culturally universal as well. In using an iconic gesture the communicator enacts some action with her hands and/or body (or perhaps depicts a referent statically), and this is intended to induce the recipient to imagine some corresponding perceptually absent referent (or some perceptually absent aspect of a present referential situation), for example, an action the communicator wants the recipient to perform or an object he wants her to fetch. In other words, the gesturer symbolizes the referential situation for the recipient. Again in this case, extra cognitive work must be done after the referent is identified for the social intention to be inferred.

Because iconic gestures are typically simulations of actions that are not currently happening (or objects or relationships not currently perceptually present), they depend, in a way that pointing does not, on skills involving some kind of imitation, simulation, or symbolizing—which goes a long way toward explaining why apes do not use them. The seemingly most common uses of iconic gestures are (i) to indicate that *this* is the action I want you to perform, or that I intend to perform myself, or that I want to tell you about; and (ii) to request or otherwise indicate an object that "does *this*" or an object that "one does *this* with." Of course these are instantiated in an almost infinite variety of contexts. Here are some observed examples, again glossing in such a way that the referential and social intentions are clearly differentiated:

Example 6: I am in a cheese shop in Italy, and I ask for "parmegiano." The proprietor asks me something I do not understand, but guessing—and not having the appropriate word—I twiddle my fingers as if sprinkling grated cheese onto my pasta. *Gloss*: Imagine what I am doing this to; and give me some of it.

Example 7: I am at the front of the lecture hall, getting ready to give a lecture. A friend in the audience fiddles with her shirt button, frowning at me, and sure enough when I look down mine is unbuttoned. *Gloss*: Imagine buttoning a button like this; do it on yourself.

Example 8: The airport security guard motions his hand in a circular motion to tell me to turn around so he can scan my back. *Gloss*: Imagine your body doing this motion; do it.

Example 9: At a vegetable stand, the proprietor—from a few meters away with back partially turned—is following a customer's request to fill a bag with potatoes. She pauses with a questioning look to query nonverbally "Should I stop here?" The customer motions his hand in a shoveling motion like the one she was just doing. *Gloss*: Imagine doing this action (which you were just doing); do it (i.e., "Keep going").

Example 10: At a loud construction site, one worker pantomimes to another ten meters away as if he were using a chainsaw. *Gloss*: Imagine me doing this; bring me the thing I need to do it.

Example 11: On television, a soccer match. A shot on goal narrowly misses the net. The TV camera focuses on the coach. He arranges his thumb and index finger about two inches apart and holds them up to his assistant. *Gloss*: Imagine a tiny distance like this; "It only missed by *this* much."

The basic behavior here is to enact an action, or in the last example a spatial relationship, not currently perceptually present, in order to induce the recipient to imagine a corresponding real action or relationship (and hence, in some cases, a related object), which—given some common conceptual ground—should allow her to infer the social intention. Thus, my sprinkling gesture at the cheese shop indicates what I will do with the object I desire, and the proprietor's comprehension is premised on shared knowledge of how grated cheese works. It is important to note that the comprehension of iconic gestures depends fundamentally on an understanding of the intention to communicate behind the gesture: without a recognition of my intention to communicate the proprietor will see my sprinkling motion as some kind of strangely mis-placed instrumental action, rather than an action designed to inform him of something (see Leslie's 1987 argument for the need to "quarantine" pretend acts from real acts).

Because iconic gestures are almost always aimed at absent entities (including actions that perceptually present entities might or should perform), they work somewhat differently from pointing—in this case in terms of what is "in" the gesture symbolically and what must be inferred. For example, a customer at a bar with no empty glass in front of him might iconically gesture to the bartender for a drink by pantomiming pouring a drink or bringing a glass to his lips—that is, by simulating either the initiating or final consum-matory act of drinking. In contrast, in pointing to the perceptually present empty glass (as in example 1), what is indicated is its emptiness, and what is requested is its fullness, which will then lead the bartender to perform the desired action. To my knowledge, there is no sys-tematic research concerning which aspects of a situation are indicated by different kinds of gestures on different occasions when language is impractical, including when a person might choose a pointing versus an iconic gesture. It seems plausible that people point to perceptually present things as their first option, when that is feasible and likely to suffice communicatively, and that only when, for whatever reason, pointing is impractical (e.g., when the intended referential situation is not currently present perceptually) do people use iconic gestures.

Once again one might suppose that only someone who already has language could use iconic gestures to communicate in such complex ways. But again in this case, as in pointing, human infants before they begin acquiring language in earnest begin to use iconic and/or conventionalized gestures in complex ways—although not nearly to the same extent as they do with pointing (see chapter 4). Also, deaf children who have not been exposed to any conventional vocal or signed language invent iconic gestures to communicate in extremely rich and complex ways early in development (Goldin-Meadow 2003b; see also chapter 6). Iconic gestures thus do not rely on language.

It is important to reiterate that although iconic gestures are most often used to simulate actions, the referential intention involved can also target an object: "the object that does *this*" or "the object that one does *this* with" (analogous to a relative clause in language), as in example 10 in which the worker asks for the chainsaw by pantomiming the way one uses it. It is thus not the case that pointing is only for objects and iconic gestures are only for actions. We will therefore not posit in chapters 4 and

5 that pointing is a precursor for nouns and iconic gestures are precursors for verbs in the development and evolution of language; rather, we will associate pointing with demonstratives and other deictics (indicated in space), whereas we will associate iconic gestures with contentful linguistic conventions, including both nouns and verbs.

3.1.3 Summary

These acts of pointing and pantomiming did not originate from any preestablished code between interactants, linguistic or otherwise, and so our question is: how can they communicate so richly? How can we account for the great diversity and complexity of communicative functions involved, including even reference to different perspectives on entities and to absent entities? How does the recipient cover the great inferential distances from the indicated referent to the communicator's social intention? The answer to these questions is a whole set of complex processes that will take some time to spell out—integrated, ultimately, into what we will call the cooperation model of human communication—and indeed the complete answer requires in addition an explication of the ontogenetic and phylogenetic processes involved (in the two chapters that follow). But for now, we may sketch out the basic elements of this model, so that we may see clearly the endpoint of the path human beings had to traverse to get from ape gestures to human pointing and pantomiming.

3.2   The Cooperation Model

The ultimate explanation for how it is that human beings are able to communicate with one another in such complex ways with such simple gestures is that they have unique ways of engaging with one another socially in general. More specifically, human beings *cooperate* with one another in species-unique ways involving processes of shared intentionality.

According to a number of philosophers of action, shared intentionality refers to behavioral phenomena that are both intentional and irreducibly social, in the sense that the agent of the intentions and actions is the plural subject "we." For example, Gilbert (1989) looks at extremely simple collaborative activities such as taking a walk together—as opposed to walking down a sidewalk in parallel to an unknown person—and concludes that the agent of the social activity is "we." The difference can be clearly seen if one person simply veers off in another direction unannounced. If we just happen to be walking in parallel, this deviation means nothing; but if we are walking *together*, my veering off is some kind of breach and you may rebuke me for it (since we have made a joint commitment to take a walk together and so certain social norms now apply). Scaled up, we may even get to phenomena in which "we" intend things together in such a way that they take on new powers—such as when pieces of paper become money, and ordinary people are transformed into presidents within institutional realities

(Searle 1995). The proposal is that because humans are able to engage with one another in acts of shared intentionality—everything from a joint walk together to joint participation in transforming people into institutional officials—their social interactions take on new qualities.

The basic psychological underpinning of the ability to participate with others in acts of shared intentionality, including communicating with them in human-like ways, is the ability to engage with others in a human-like cooperative manner, characterized by Searle as follows:

> [Shared] intentionality presupposes a background sense of the other as a candidate for cooperative agency . . . [which] is a necessary condition of all collective behavior and hence all conversation. (1990, pp. 414–415)

For current purposes, we may decompose this understanding of others as cooperative agents into: (i) the cognitive skills for creating joint intentions and attention (and other forms of common conceptual ground) with others; and (ii) the social motivations for helping and sharing with others (and forming mutual expectations about these cooperative motives).

3.2.1 Cognitive Skills: Creating Common Ground

All the instances of pointing and pantomiming just recounted involve one person simply directing another's attention or imagination to some referent. The recipient then looks to the indicated referent, or imagines it, and from this discerns what the communicator is attempting to communicate—anything from "Are you waiting for the bathroom?" to "I'd like my cheese grated." How do we do it? Where does this communicative complexity come from, if it is not "in" the protruding or sprinkling fingers?

The answer is of course "context," but this only takes us so far. Thus, great apes often operate in complex social contexts without seeming to communicate so richly. It is possible that adult humans can conceive of more complex contexts than apes and that this is the answer. But, as will be documented in the next chapter, even prelinguistic infants communicate gesturally in much more complex ways than apes, though it is not clear their conceptual skills are so much greater. Instead, in the current view, a large part of the explanation for humans' uniquely complex ways of communicating gesturally is that "context" for humans means something very special. For humans the communicative context is not simply everything in the immediate environment, from the temperature of the room to the sounds of birds in the background, but rather the communicative context is what is "relevant" to the social interaction, that is, what each participant sees as relevant and knows that the other sees as relevant as well—and knows that the other knows this as well, and so on, potentially ad infinitum. This kind of shared, intersubjective context is what we may call, following Clark (1996), common ground or, sometimes (when we wish to emphasize the shared perceptual context), the joint attentional frame. Common ground includes everything we both know (and know that we both know, etc.), from facts about the world, to the way that rational people act in certain situations, to what people typically find salient and interesting (Levinson 1995).

Common ground is necessary for the recipient to determine both what the communicator is directing attention to (his referential intention) and why he is doing it (his social intention). Thus, in the relatively simple first example of pointing given above (a customer points for the bartender to his empty shotglass to request another drink), without some kind of common ground the bartender cannot know if the customer is pointing to the glass as a whole, or its color, or a small crack in it. Indeed, in the actual example, the customer is pointing not to the glass itself but to its emptiness (imagine the difference if the pointed-to glass were already full—the customer's meaning would have to be something very different). And even keeping the exact same referent, the social intention may be different depending on common ground. Thus, in the normal situation the customer is pointing to his empty shotglass to request it being filled with liquor—which the bartender understands because they both know together that, as noted above, customers are at the bar because they want to drink, an empty glass does not afford drinking, the bartender has drink if the customer can pay, and so forth. But, if the customer and bartender are actually buddies who regularly attend Alcoholics Anonymous together, the customer could be pointing to the emptiness of his shotglass in this case to indicate to his buddy that he has still managed, after an hour at the bar, to resist having a drink.

The critical point about common ground is that it takes people beyond their own egocentric perspective on things. For example, modifying an example from Sperber and Wilson (1986), suppose that in a park I point to direct your attention to a location some meters away. There are three people there: an ice-cream vendor, a jogger you have never seen before, and William, who is your lover. If you are being egocentric, you assume in the first instance that I am drawing your attention to William, as he is very relevant for you, whereas the other two are not relevant for you. In the normal case, though, your search for relevance is not egocentric but takes place within the context of our shared common ground from the beginning, for example, taking into account from the beginning whether we both know together that we both know about William. Thus, suppose that I do not know about William and you know this for certain (he is your *secret* lover), and suppose further that you and I both know that we both share a passion for ice cream (we have explicitly discussed this). If I now direct your attention in the general direction of these same three people, no matter how relevant William is for you egocentrically, and even if you were lying to me about the ice cream (so that it is not in reality relevant for you at all), you will still assume that I am indicating for you the ice-cream vendor, since we both "know" from our previous discussion that we both love ice cream and you think I do not know about you and William. In direct competition, shared common ground trumps individual personal relevance every time.[1]

Of course, you may hypothesize that I really do know about William somehow and proceed on that assumption. But then you are, essentially, guessing about the kind of common ground that would make the process the canonical one. In the normal case, you want to know from the outset why I think that looking in that direction will be relevant for you, with a prerequisite being that we know together about the potential referent and its relevance for you. And so what comes to your mind most readily as an interpretation of my pointing gesture, at the top of the stack as it were (even though you may have your own personal interests as well), will be those things that are in our common ground. Another variation is cases in which we do not have direct personal common ground, but we both, as members of a particular culture or social group, have assumptions about what the other should know (and know I know, etc.). Thus, I might point to a sight for you out the airplane window even though

1. If we want to get really perverse, we can, following Clark and Marshall (1981), imagine a situation in which I have found out, unbeknownst to you, that William is your secret lover. Then we both know that he is extremely relevant for you, but since you do not know that I know this, you will not assume I am referring to him. This recursion may continue ad infinitum, with successful reference not possible with any finite number of iterations. It is required that we both know together, it is in our common ground, that William is especially relevant for you.

we have never before met, as I assume that you can
identify the referent based on (presumably) shared
assumptions about what people typically find salient,
beautiful, and so forth. But note that in both of these
cases—guessing and general cultural common ground—
the recipient attempts to comprehend the communicative
act by, in effect, imagining or assuming some form of
common ground that she must share with the communicator if the whole thing is to make sense. The normal
case—the one with which young children begin and the
one that adults process without hesitation—is thus the
case in which we both recognize our common ground
within which the communicative act is immediately
comprehensible.

This leads us to propose a kind of typology of common
ground based on three distinctions (see Clark 1996 for
a slightly different typology). The first is whether the
common ground is based in our immediate perceptual
environment, what I will call joint attention (what Clark
1996 calls perceptual co-presence), or rather is based in
shared experiences from the past. Second, we may also
distinguish between common ground created by top-
down processes—for example, we are pursuing a shared
goal together and so know together that we are focusing
on certain things relevant to our goal—and common
ground created by bottom-up processes—for example,
we both hear a loud noise and know together that we did.
Later I will argue that common ground created by top-
down processes in an immediately copresent perceptual

environment—specifically in the joint attention of collaborative activities—is in some sense primary in that it
provides for especially salient and solid common ground.
Third and finally, common ground may be based on such
generalized things as common cultural knowledge, never
explicitly acknowledged between us—often signified by
cultural markers of various sorts—or it may be based on
things overtly acknowledged, for example, when we look
to one another knowingly as a mutually known friend
approaches. Explicitly acknowledged common ground
may also have special salience and importance in some
communicative situations, or for novices such as human
children.

Importantly, for all types of human communication
including language, the relationship between the overt
communicative act and common ground—of whatever
type—is complementary. That is, as more can be assumed
to be shared between communicator and recipient, less
needs to be overtly expressed. Indeed, if enough is shared
in common ground, the overt expression of either motive
or referent may be totally eliminated without diminish-
ing the message at all. For example, in the dentist's office
the dentist may sometimes point to the instrument she
wants without overtly expressing her desire per se to the
assistant, since her desire to have the instrument is mutually assumed in this mutually known context (cf. Wittgenstein's builders). Conversely, the dentist may simply
hold out her hand, indicating that she wants an instrument, and the assistant, based on shared knowledge of

the procedure, puts the correct one (of many on the table) in her hand without the intended referent ever having been indicated specifically. An observed real example in which the referent is not indicated but assumed, based on shared common ground, is as follows:

Example 12: In an airplane, I take my seat on the aisle. There is a woman sitting next to the window in my row. A man comes into the row behind us, talking extremely loudly and obnoxiously. I look to the woman and roll my eyes, expressing an attitude best glossed as "Ugh, this is going to be a long trip." I did not need to indicate the referent of my exasperation for her; it was clear to us both.

Note that if the man had taken his seat in an utterly quiet manner, and I now wanted to refer my seatmate to him, I would need to somehow indicate him to her overtly since there would be no basis for joint attention. Interestingly, if the common ground or joint attention is strong enough, for example, if it is routinized or even institutionalized, it is also easy to actually point about absent referents. For example, if many mornings I must remind my child to bring her backpack, and today she has forgotten it, at the critical moment I may simply point to her back, or to mine, and she will know exactly what I mean. Without this shared routine, the same pointing gesture could not indicate the absent backpack. And even though iconic gestures and language express much more referential content "in" the signal than does pointing, they still depend on common ground in the same basic way as pointing. Thus, when the airport security guard whirls his hand in a circular motion (example 8), no matter how descriptive the act, it presupposes a mutually known context of airport security procedures for appropriate interpretation. Without this common ground—imagine a child at an airport for the first time—it is not clear what goes around or is supposed to go around in such a circular motion. And of course everyday language is full of referential expressions such as pronouns that depend absolutely on a shared context for interpretation.

In all, then, it is only because humans are able to construct with others various forms of conceptual common ground and joint attention that very simple pointing and iconic gestures can be used to communicate in complex ways—ways that go far beyond what great apes are able to communicate with their intention-movement and attention-getting gestures. Indeed, in many cases, when the common ground is particularly well defined, simple gestures may communicate as powerfully as language. Most basically, as can be clearly seen in the examples in which the referent of pointing changes with the common ground—for example, pointing to the shotglass to indicate either the object itself, its color, its emptiness, or its state of repair—a certain kind of perspective shifting is involved. It is thus possible that this kind of reference shifting in gesturing—accomplished by making contact in different ways with communicator-recipient common ground—paves the way for perspectival linguistic conventions both phylogenetically and ontogenetically.

Moreover, although reference to entities displaced in space and time has traditionally been seen as the exclusive province of language—and there is no doubt that language does this by far most productively—within an appropriate shared context, people may point or gesture iconically to direct attention to the nonpresence of expected entities (e.g., a missing backpack) or even to indicate absent entities directly (e.g., the desired chainsaw in example 10), which may also pave the way for displaced reference in language.

What this means is that many of the especially powerful properties that people often attribute to language—including referring others to perspectives on things and to absent referents—are actually present more fundamentally in human cooperative communication with very simple gestures. This is possible because of—and only because of—various types of common conceptual ground and joint attention between communicators.

3.2.2   Social Motivations: Helping and Sharing

The other side of the picture is humans' especially cooperative social motivations. In his seminal analysis, Grice (1975) emphasized that, most fundamentally, communicators and recipients interact cooperatively to get the message across (i.e., to get the recipient to know the communicator's social intention), which is their joint goal. This means that the communicator makes efforts to communicate in ways that are comprehensible to the recipient, who in turn makes efforts at comprehension by making obvious inferences, asking for clarification when needed, and so forth (see Clark 1996 for a description of reference as a joint activity). It is not clear that other animal species collaborate in this way in communication; for example, there is no evidence that other animals ever ask one another for clarification.

The underlying reason for the cooperative spirit by which humans work to get the message across is their species-unique cooperative motivations for communicating in the first place. These are evolved motivations, and so we must have some phylogenetic story for their emergence and structuring of human communication, including how both communicator and recipient benefit from interactions so motivated—which we do in chapter 5. For now, we may begin by noting that communicators often overtly express these motives emotionally in the communicative act—to give recipients information, in addition to the act of reference, for inferring their specific social intention. For example, I might point to a pen for you with a demanding or pleading facial expression to request that you fetch it for me; or with a surprised or excited demeanor to simply share my happiness that my lost pen is here; or with a quizzical expression to ask if that is your lost pen; or with a neutral expression to simply inform you of the pen's presence. Although specific social intentions are innumerable, there are just three basic human communicative motives—justified by the fact that they emerge earliest in ontogeny (chapter 4) and that they have plausible evolutionary roots in human social interaction more generally (chapter 5).

The first and most obvious human communicative motive is requesting—getting others to do what one wants them to—which, in a general way, is characteristic of the intentional communicative signals of all apes. The difference is that instead of ordering the other what to do, humans often do something more gentle like requesting help (from someone who likes helping). That is, unlike ape imperatives, human imperatives can range from orders to polite requests to suggestions to hints, depending most fundamentally on the degree to which a cooperative attitude may be assumed of the recipient. Thus, if you are on my land I can order you to leave, or I can simply inform you that I would like you to leave (or even that it is *my* land) if I think you will readily comply. We might call the first type individual imperatives or requests—since I tell you what to do directly—and the second type cooperative imperatives or requests—since I simply inform you of my desire and assume that you will decide to help me fulfill it (i.e., if I simply inform you of my desire that you leave, you must care about my desire if the request is to work).[2] In all likelihood, chimpanzees pointing for humans to desired

---

2. Following Searle (1969, 1999) and others, it is most natural to classify questions as simply requests for information from others (and again I could either torture or threaten the information out of you, or I could simply state that I would like it or ask a conventionalized question). Also note that requesting an object is actually requesting that someone fetch it for you.

food is not a cooperative imperative, as the ape is trying to get the human to do something directly, not informing her of his desire—and he has no expectation that, if he did, the human (much less another chimpanzee) would care. But human recipients often do care. For reasons of their own, they like fulfilling the requests of others if they are not too onerous; and knowing this, human communicators in many situations need only make their desires known.

The second fundamental human communicative motive, seemingly unique to the species, results from the fact that individuals often want to offer help to others without even being requested to—specifically, by informing others of things, even when they themselves have no personal interest in the information. And informing is indeed offering help, since typically I inform you of things that I think *you* (not I) will find helpful or interesting, given my knowledge of your goals and interests (even if on a higher, individual level I have other selfish motives for doing so). Thus, it is assumed that I am being helpful, or at least attempting to be helpful, when I point out the paper you just dropped or tell you that the boss is in a bad mood today. Socializing a well-known formula of Searle's (1999), we may say that requests reflect a You-to-Me direction of fit, as I want you to conform to my desire, whereas informatives reflect a Me-to-You direction of fit, as I want to conform to your desires and interests. Obviously, helping others by informing them of things they will find useful or interesting—and also complying with requests by helping the requesting person—involves altruistic motives of a type that will require a special evolutionary explanation (see chapter 5)—again, even if I may sometimes inform you of things (or comply with your requests) for higher, individual motives that are anything but altruistic.

In addition to these two most basic motives, we must posit a third basic communicative motive as well—although the reasons for positing it as basic will become clear only after we have considered things from both ontogenetic and phylogenetic perspectives. People often simply want to share feelings and attitudes about things with others—what I will call an expressive or sharing motive. For example, on a beautiful day it is quite common to say to your officemate upon arrival at the office, "What a beautiful day today!"—which derives not from any imperative or informative motive involving help, but rather from a purely social one. This kind of communicative act is simply a sharing of attitudes and feelings so as to expand our common ground with others. This sharing motive underlies much of the everyday talk of people as they gossip about all kinds of things, expressing opinions and attitudes which they hope the other will to some degree share. It turns out that this motive emerges ontogenetically quite early in infants' prelinguistic pointing, as they, for example, point for a parent to a colorful clown and squeal with glee. Although infants might sometimes point simply to inform the parent of the presence of the clown, they often point and squeal with glee even when the parent has already seen the clown or even is currently looking at it—because they want the adult to share their enthusiasm nonetheless. We will discuss this motive more fully in chapter 4 on ontogeny where I present experimental evidence for its fundamentally social nature, and also in chapter 5 on phylogeny where I stress its importance in individuals identifying with a specific community of like-minded people (to the exclusion of other communities of people with whom one does not gossip and share in this same way).

We may thus posit three general types of evolved communicative motives. They are determined by the kind of effect the communicator is attempting to have on the recipient, expressed here in terms of the shared intentionality motivations of helping and sharing with others:

Requesting: I want you to do something *to help me* (requesting help or information);

Informing: I want you to know something because *I think it will help or interest you* (offering help including information);

Sharing: I want you to feel something so that *we can share attitudes/feelings together* (sharing emotions or attitudes).

These three most basic of human communicative motives underlie a virtual infinity of particular social intentions in particular contexts, and they will play a pivotal role in both our ontogenetic and phylogenetic accounts of the emergence of human cooperative communication.[3]

3.2.3 Mutual Assumptions of Helpfulness and Cooperative Reasoning

The facts that communicators operate with these cooperative motives and that recipients are inclined to respond appropriately (all other things being equal) are part of the common ground between human communicators. Indeed, this is what motivates them to cooperate in getting the message across in the first place—they both assume mutually that it will be to their individual and mutual benefit to do so. Because the communicator knows this, he makes sure that the recipient knows that he is attempting to communicate, as if to say: "You're going to want to know this" (i.e., that I have a request of you, that I have something I want to inform you about, that I have an attitude I want to share). This additional layer of intentionality—"I want you to know that I want something

---

3. There is some correspondence here with the basic speech act functions posited by theorists such as Searle (1999), though the mapping is not totally straightforward. We should also note a number of specialized motives for specialized situations that are ontogenetically early and very likely culturally universal: greeting/leave-taking ("Hello" and "Goodbye"), expressing gratitude ("Thanks"), and expressing regret ("Sorry"). These are special because they are not referential in the normal way and so work a bit differently—and they apply to highly restricted and socially important circumstances that are crucial to human social evolution (see ch. 5).

from you"—is absolutely critical to the process and is most commonly referred to as the (Gricean) communicative intention.

Grice (1957) observed that human communicative acts involve an intention about the communication specifically. That is, when I point to a tree for you, I not only want you to attend to the tree, I also want you to attend to my desire that you attend to the tree (often signaled by eye contact, etc., and also implicit quite often in the expression of motive, as a sign that this act is done "for you"). This additional intentional layer is necessary to motivate you to make the kinds of relevance inferences required to identify both my referent and my social intention (Sperber and Wilson 1986). Thus, when you see me pointing to a tree, and clearly wanting you to know that I am pointing it out for you, then naturally you want to know why I am doing that: what I want you to do, think, or feel with respect to the tree. You assume that when I point to the tree for you, I believe it will be interesting or relevant for you in some way: perhaps because it is your favorite kind of tree and I want to inform you of its presence here, or perhaps because I have a request about it that I think you would like to fulfill, or perhaps because I want you to share my enthusiasm for it.

To make this crystal clear, let us compare cases with and without a communicative intention (modified from Sperber and Wilson 1986). Thus, suppose that while on a hike we sit down on a rock in the woods, and I lean back because I am tired, which exposes a large tree to your line of sight. No inferences follow. But if I lean back and point to the tree for you with an insistent expression, you naturally attempt to determine why I am doing this. That is, you notice that I have gone to some trouble to point out the tree to you and to express my insistence, and this generates in you a search for some relevance (typically within our common ground): why does he want me to attend to the tree? Since I know that this is the process, I make sure that you know that my pointing out of the tree for you is intentional—so that you will seek to discover the reason for my intentional act toward you: what I want you to know or to do or to feel. That this is a natural part of most human communication is evidenced by the fact that, in most situations, it takes a distinct effort to circumvent it. Thus, if a guest wants more wine in his glass, but thinks it impolite to request it directly of his host, he might simply place his empty glass in a conspicuous location so that she will see it and (he hopes) refill it, but without knowing that he had this in mind all along. The guest wants the host to know about the empty glass, but he does not want her to know that he wants her to know this. Such cases of "hidden authorship"—or, in some cases, simply indifference about the recipient noticing one's authorship—signal an especially deep understanding of the way communicative intentions operate within the communicative act as a whole.

The main point is that this process occurs because both participants know together and trust together the cooperative motivations involved. That is to say, in general, if a human communicator requests help (all other things being equal), the recipient will want to help—and they both know this and trust in this. Similarly, if the communicator offers information, they can mutually assume that he thinks the information will be useful or interesting for the recipient (and that normally means "true" as well)—and so she will accept it. And finally, if the communicator wants to share attitudes, they assume together the prosocial motive of sharing, and the communicator may expect the recipient to share unless there are good reasons against it. The communicator therefore overtly signals his intention to communicate, and they therefore both work together to ensure that the communicative act succeeds.

Importantly, overt expression of the Gricean communicative intention places the communicative act itself—the gesture or the utterance—into the participants' common ground, specifically, into the ongoing joint attentional frame within which they are communicating. Thus, it is most precise to say not just that I want you to know that I want you to attend to something, but that *I want us to know this together*—I want my communicative act to be a part of our perceptually copresent joint attention (I want it to be mutually manifest, in the terms of Sperber and Wilson 1986, or "wholly overt"). Because human communicators make their communicative intention mutually manifest, this makes this intention, in an important sense, public—which triggers a whole other set of processes (Habermas 1987). Specifically, the fact that I have communicated to you overtly, publicly, actually creates not just expectations of cooperation but actual social norms, whose violation is unacceptable.

First, at the level of comprehending the message, if I attempt to communicate with you—I say "Hey, Ethel" and you look at me—when I then produce my gesture or utterance, you cannot just ignore me as though I did not attempt to communicate. Acting occasionally in this way will ruin friendships, and acting consistently in this way will lead to some kind of psychiatric diagnosis and possible removal from mainstream society. And you must at least sometimes attempt to generate communication with others yourself, or the diagnosis will be catatonia and institutionalization will result immediately. Second, at the level of compliance after comprehension, if I make a small request, like "Please pass the salt" at the dinner table (either in speech or gesture), you cannot really reply with "No"—unless you make some excuse for why you cannot comply in this circumstance (and knowing this, I must make reasonable requests). Similarly, if I inform you of some fact I think you will find interesting—"Hey, did you hear Bob Dylan is in town tonight"—you cannot really reply with "I don't believe you," again without some kind of good reason for, in essence, calling me a liar. For my part, if I find out something that we know together you would want to know (we know together that Bob Dylan is your favorite, and so you would of course want to know if he was in town), I must tell you; if I do not, and you find out later, our friendship will be seriously damaged. And if you express to me how important religion is in your life, and I respond that I think it's stupid, I risk damaging our relationship built on common attitudes about the world.

Thus, from the production side, we humans must communicate with others or we will be thought pathological; we must request only things that are reasonable or we will be thought rude; and we must attempt to inform and to share things with others in ways that are relevant and appropriate or we will be thought socially weird and will have no friends. From the comprehension side, we again must participate, or we will be thought pathological; and we must help, accept offered help and information, and share feelings with others, or we will risk social estrangement. The simple fact is that, as in many domains of human social life, mutual expectations, when put into the public arena, turn into policeable social norms and obligations. The evolutionary bases of this normative dimension of human communication, in terms of public reputation, will be elaborated in chapter 5.

The cooperative motives involved here, and the mutual knowledge of these cooperative motives and even norms, mean that the participants in human communication must reason not just practically, but cooperatively. Thus, when apes observe another ape signaling to them, they try to discern what he wants via individual practical reasoning about his goals and perceptions. But they are not trying to understand the message *because* he wants them to, since the two of them do not share an assumption that he is trying to be helpful. The communicator thus does not signal or "advertise" his intention specifically, as humans do in signaling their communicative intention. And in choosing a response, ape recipients do not respond in a certain way *because* the other wants or expects them to; rather, they simply try to do what is best for themselves in the situation given what the communicator apparently wants. In contrast, when humans see that someone is attempting to communicate with them, they want to know what he is attempting to communicate at least partly *because* he wants them to (and they trust his cooperative motives), and they choose a response—for example, complying with a request or accepting offered information or sharing enthusiasm about something—at least partly *because* that is what the other wants them to do. Because human recipients comprehend and respond to communicative bids in certain ways at least partly because that is the way the communicator wants them to (with the communicator relying on this)—and indeed because this way of operating is, if everything is public, normatively prescribed—we call the kind of practical reasoning characteristic of human communication cooperative reasoning.

A final word about the recursivity involved in all of this. First, as noted throughout, the creation of common ground and/or joint attention between two persons requires that each of them sees, knows, or attends to things that she knows the other sees, knows, or attends to as well—and knows that the other knows this about her as well, and so on recursively potentially ad infinitum. Also, the Gricean communicative intention is clearly recursive—at least to several levels. Thus, in Sperber and Wilson's (1986) account, in a declarative speech act I want you to know something (e.g., that your friend approaches), but my communicative intention is that you know that I want this. In this analysis, therefore, communicative intentions are either third or fourth order (depending on how one counts): I want$_1$ you to know$_2$ I want$_3$ you to know$_4$ your friend approaches. Finally, the motivational structure of human communication is also recursive in that we both know together that we both are helpful—so that you are expecting me to expect you (and so on with further embeddings as needed) to be helpful. Most clearly, such recursivity is absolutely required for norms of cooperation in which it is mutually expected by everyone (including oneself) that everyone will be a cooperative communicative partner.

There is much controversy about common ground and related concepts such as mutual knowledge and mutual manifestness—precisely because of their recursive nature. Since people must communicate in real time, infinite computations of this kind cannot be at work in actual practice (Clark and Marshall 1981). And of course the psychological reality is not all of this backing-and-forthing about knowing what others know I know, etc., but rather simply that we both know that we both see, know, or attend to something together: we "share" it, and we have various heuristics for identifying common ground with others. Nevertheless, the underlying recursive levels may become clear when there is some kind of breakdown, as for example, when I think I share something with someone that it turns out I do not. This breakdown may potentially occur at any level of iteration. For example, me saying to you "How beautiful!" will not work (1) if you think I am attending to something I am not, (2) if I think you think I am attending to something I am not, (3) if you think I think you think I am attending to something I am not, and so forth and so on. The fact that breakdowns can occur at different levels—and that people repair such breakdowns differently in each of these cases—provides evidence for the different iterations, at least implicitly, in the participants' understanding.

Overall, a reasonable way of dealing with all of this—or at least the one we will adopt here—is simply to say that the recursive spiral is not infinite but only indefinite; we compute it as far as we need to or are able to, which is typically only several levels up, and of course we mostly do not compute it at all but only note, via some heuristic, whether something is or is not shared with an interactive partner. Or possibly, we simply have a "bird's-eye view" of the interaction, which enables switching perspectives as needed indefinitely (see chapter 7 for a bit more discussion of various alternatives). We will refer to this ability—an absolutely critical skill involved in many aspects of shared intentionality—as recursive mindreading or recursive intention-reading.

3.2.4 Summary

Figure 3.1 depicts all of the different components of the cooperation model of human communication, and something of their interrelations. Beginning in the top left and following the arrows, very sketchily: I as communicator have many goals and values that I pursue in my life: my *individual goals.* For whatever reason, I feel that you can help me on this occasion with one or more of them, by helping me or accepting my offer of information (which I want to make for my own reasons) or sharing attitudes with me: my *social intention.* The best way for me to get your help, or to help you, or to share with you in this situation is through communication, and so I decide to make mutually manifest to us (in our current joint attentional frame) a communicative act; this is my *communicative intention* (perhaps indicated by "for you" signals such as eye contact or with some expression of motive). Given my signal of a communicative intention, I draw your attention to some referential situation in the external world—my *referential intention*—which is designed (along with some expression of motive) to lead you to infer my social intention via processes of cooperative reasoning, since you are naturally motivated to find out why I want to communicate with you (based on *mutual assumptions or norms of cooperation*). You thus first attempt to identify my referent, typically within the space of our *common ground,* and from there attempt to infer my underlying social intention, also typically by relating it to our

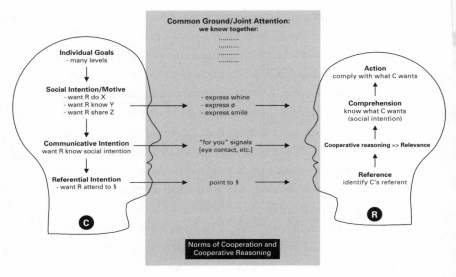

Figure 3.1
Summary of cooperative model of human communication (C = communicator; R = recipient).

common ground. Then, assuming you have comprehended my social intention, you decide whether or not to cooperate as expected.

This fundamentally cooperative process makes human communication utterly different from the communicative activities of all other species on the planet. The communicative power of the processes summarized in this model, as they work together, may be seen by considering a famous pronouncement. In stressing the powers of language over gestures, Searle (1969, p. 38) states:

Some very simple sorts of illocutionary acts can indeed be performed apart from any use of conventional devices at all. . . . One can in certain special circumstances "request" someone to leave the room without employing any conventions, but unless one has a language one cannot request of someone that he, e.g., undertake a research project on the problem of diagnosing and treating mononucleosis in undergraduates in American universities.

But indeed we can make such a request without language. That is to say, if we have linguistic individuals who have been discussing, in language, the fact that "we need someone to undertake a research project on the problem of diagnosing and treating mononucleosis in undergraduates in American universities," then I could, at the right moment in the conversation, point to you, and the meaning of that pointing act would be that "*you* should undertake a research project on the problem of diagnosing and treating mononucleosis in undergraduates in American universities." Of course this cannot happen without linguistic organisms setting up the context linguistically—this much is clear. But the key point for current purposes is simply that when the context—the shared conceptual ground—is set up in enough detail, however that is done, a pointing gesture can refer to situations as complex as one wants.

3.3 Communicative Conventions

And what about modes of human communication that are not "natural" but "conventional"? What about conventionalized gestures (e.g., for greeting and leave taking, for threatening and insulting, for agreeing and disagreeing, etc.—as found in most cultures) and also vocal and signed languages? Are these "codes" that obviate the need for all this complicated psychological infrastructure? Does linguistic communication work totally differently?

3.3.1 Linguistic Communication and the Shared Intentionality Infrastructure

In a word, no. First and most importantly, linguistic and other forms of conventional communication depend fundamentally on the common ground and current joint attentional frame between communicator and recipient just as natural gestures do (Clark 1996). Thus, the vast majority of utterances in everyday speech contain pronouns (*he, she, it, they*) and other context-dependent expressions that require common ground for appropriate interpretation (*that other guy, the place we used to go*, etc.); even the very simplest referring expressions such as *Bill* or *the cat* require common ground to determine which Bill or which cat is intended. Linguistic utterances thus depend, in basically the same way as natural gestures, on common conceptual ground, and indeed the "stronger" the common ground the less language is needed, as the communication of dentists and their assistants (in the examples cited above) amply illustrates.

Further, the communicative intention is also basically the same in both the gestural and linguistic modalities, and the recipient's search for relevance is guided equally in both cases by mutual assumptions of helpfulness. For example, if I enter your office and say out of the blue "Cuba has the best weather in the world," you comprehend the utterance fine, but you are still perplexed as to why I think this information is useful or interesting for you—whereas if we have just been discussing where we might vacation this summer, the reason for the utterance is obvious. Just as in pointing, the assumption that I am attempting to inform you of something I think you will find useful or interesting guides your search for communicative relevance. And the general motives for communicating are basically the same in gestural and linguistic communication as well: requesting, informing, and sharing (though linguistic communication enables some other, less basic motives as well, as elaborated in speech act theory). And we work together collaboratively to establish joint reference and to get the message across in linguistic communication, just as in natural gestures (Clark 1996). In general, then, linguistic communication depends on exactly the same shared intentionality infrastructure that we have been using to explain the surprising communicative power of pointing and pantomiming.

The only substantive difference between natural gestures and communicative conventions in the current context is in the referential intention, what is put "in" the signal to direct attention. But even here, on a very general level, the same description may be applied equally in the two cases. Thus, in both gestural and linguistic communication reference may be divided into the old, given, shared part—the topic, often assumed or indicated only briefly—and the new, newsworthy part— the focus, typically elaborated more fully because it is less shared. For example, if you and I are looking at a cloud together, as topic, I may either point to it or comment on it verbally as it changes shape, to highlight the new aspect. But of course linguistic conventions can be used to make reference to the world in uniquely powerful ways that go well beyond what is possible in natural gestures. This derives mainly from the "arbitrariness" of the communicative devices of a language, which means that we can create a device to indicate pretty much any aspect of experience we can conceptualize—so long as we both know that we share the use of this convention.

3.3.2   *Conventions as Shared Communicative Devices*

Humans create communicative conventions as everyone uses the same device as a means of coordinating attention and action when other ways would be possible as well, so long as everyone did them (Lewis 1969). These "arbitrary" conventions are thus possible only if all individuals have some fairly serious skills of cultural learning, in the form of imitative learning focused on intentional actions (Tomasello 1999), of a type not needed for producing natural gestures. Specifically in the case of communicative conventions, what is needed is so-called role reversal imitation, in which an individual comprehends how a communicator is using some communicative device toward her and then reproduces that use in her own communication back toward others in kind (Tomasello 1999). This creates what de Saussure (1916/1959) called the bidirectionality of the sign, which means that the actual form of the communicative device is conventional or shared among users in that they all know that they all know how to both comprehend and produce these devices for specific communicative ends. Importantly, this sharing of linguistic and gestural conventions depends again on some kind of recursivity—we all know that we all know the convention—in this case at the level of the communicative vehicle or device itself (Lewis 1969).

Linguistic conventions thus basically codify the ways that previous individuals in the community have converged upon to manipulate the attention and imagination of others in specific ways. The arbitrary sound or gesture itself carries no message "naturally," but observing its use reveals—for those with the appropriate cognitive skills and motivations—how those who share the convention use it to direct the attention and imagination of others. The appropriate cognitive skills and motivations are of course none other than (i) the same shared intentionality infrastructure that underlies human pointing and pantomiming, and (ii) a shared learning history with the convention that we all know together (implicitly) that we share—a fact that may be signaled by various kinds of cultural markers (including even use of the convention itself in an appropriate manner). Humans' creation and use of shared communicative conventions thus means that now even the communicative forms themselves depend on processes of shared intentionality.

There is more to be said here, and we will do so in chapters 4, 5, and 6 in which we attempt to provide ontogenetic and phylogenetic accounts of how human communicative conventions (and even grammatical constructions) might have arisen out of natural gestures. Importantly, I will argue in chapter 5 that it would have been impossible evolutionarily to jump from ape vocalizations or gestures to arbitrary linguistic conventions directly without passing through an intermediate stage of nonconventional, action-based, naturally meaningful, cooperative gestures that could act as a kind of natural grounding. In the case of infants during ontogeny, I will argue in chapter 4 that language acquisition is possible only when young children have available to them something resembling the full shared intentionality infrastructure originally built during human evolution as support for natural gestures.

3.3.3 Summary

Table 3.1 summarizes the present account of those aspects of the psychological infrastructure of human

Table 3.1
The psychological infrastructure of human cooperative communication: (1) in the first column things already present in apes, (2) in the second column the new human components, and (3) in the third column how the human version is transformed by recursivity.

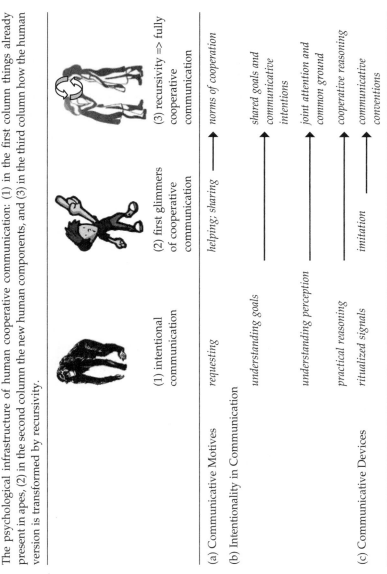

	(1) intentional communication	(2) first glimmers of cooperative communication	(3) recursivity => fully cooperative communication
(a) Communicative Motives	requesting	helping; sharing ⟶	norms of cooperation
(b) Intentionality in Communication			
	understanding goals	⟶	shared goals and communicative intentions
	understanding perception	⟶	joint attention and common ground
	practical reasoning	⟶	cooperative reasoning
(c) Communicative Devices	ritualized signals	imitation ⟶	communicative conventions

cooperative communication, both natural and conventional, that involve shared intentionality. The three dimensions labeled at the left are: (a) communicative motives; (b) underlying intentionality in terms of understanding intentions, understanding attention, and practical reasoning; and (c) form of the communicative device. In the first full column (1) is the state of affairs for great apes in each of these three dimensions: they request things using ritualized signals, and they understand intentions and perceptions and reason practically about them. In the second column (2) are the two new components of human communication, which have been stressed here: the new motives of helping and sharing in communication, and the new ability to imitate actions (much more skillfully than apes, including the ability to engage in role reversal), enabling both iconic gestures and, ultimately, communicative conventions. The third column (3) depicts the way that recursive intention-reading transforms everything: turning helping and sharing into mutual expectations or even norms of cooperation; turning the understanding of goals and intentions into joint goals and Gricean communicative intentions; turning the understanding of attention into joint attention and common ground; turning practical reasoning into cooperative reasoning; and turning imitated signals into bidirectional, shared conventions. The way this transformation due to recursivity works is different in the cases of ontogeny and phylogeny, as we shall soon see.

3.4   Conclusion

My goal in this chapter has been to lay bare the hidden psychological infrastructure of human communication by looking at natural human gestures and how they work. Pointing, in particular, as a complete communicative act, is so utterly simple—an extended finger—that it raises the question of how it could communicate so richly. In the right context, pointing may communicate as richly as language, even directing the recipient's attention to perspectives on things and to absent referents, capacities often attributed uniquely to language. Iconic gestures are used to refer in more specific ways to referents, especially absent referents, and they too may be used to convey highly complex messages. These two types of natural gesture are used by all humans, and only humans.

The "value added" in both pointing and pantomiming comes, in one way or another, from the shared intentionality infrastructure—and so we call our model the cooperation model of human communication. In this model: (i) human communicators and recipients create the joint intention of successful communication, adjusting for one another as needed; (ii) human communicative acts are grounded in joint attention and shared understandings of the situation at hand; (iii) human communicative acts are performed for fundamentally prosocial motives such as informing others of things helpfully and sharing emotions and attitudes with them freely; (iv) human communicators operate in all of this with shared assumptions (and even norms) of cooperation between participants; and (v) human linguistic conventions, as the crowning pinnacle of human discourse, are fundamentally shared in the sense that we both know together that we are both using a convention in the same manner.

Other primates do not structure their communication in this same way with joint intentions, joint attention, mutually assumed cooperative motives, and communicative conventions; rather they simply attempt to predict or manipulate the individual goals, perceptions, and actions of others directly. And as we shall now see, human infants begin to structure their gestural communication cooperatively even before language, and they do so in developmental synchrony with the emergence of their more general skills of shared intentionality as manifest in other collaborative activities.

4   Ontogenetic Origins

It isn't the colour red that takes the place of the word red, but the gesture that points to a red object.
—Wittgenstein, *The Big Typescript*

Often it is easiest to see the components of complex skills and how they work together when we study their emergence in children's early development. An important source of evidence for the cooperation model of human communication, therefore, is how things work ontogenetically. Moreover, it turns out that gestures used as full communicative acts (without language) have been investigated much more intensively, especially in experiments, in infants and young children than in adults. There are infant experiments directly relevant to several key components of our model of the communicative process, and even some that may help us to decide difficult theoretical issues, for example, with respect to the role of joint attention and common ground.

In addition to this general interest in ontogeny as a way of testing our model and its various components, in this chapter we also want to ask three specific questions relevant to the three overall hypotheses as explicated in chapter 1. The first is whether infants' prelinguistic gestural communication has something resembling the full structure of adult cooperative communication, as outlined in the previous chapter. If it does, this would demonstrate that human cooperative communication does not depend on language directly (a fact we cannot determine through observation of normally functioning adults alone), and it would make more plausible the evolutionary hypothesis that human cooperative communication evolved first in the gestural modality.

The second question is whether the emergence of cooperative communication in human ontogeny is connected in some way with the emergence of broader skills and motivations of shared intentionality as manifest in other social and cultural activities, for example, collaborative social interactions in general. If so, this would support the analysis of the previous chapter that human-like skills of cooperative communication are made possible by an infrastructure of social-cognitive and social-motivational skills for shared intentionality more generally. It would also make more plausible the evolutionary hypothesis that human cooperative communication evolved as part of a larger adaptation for collaborative activities and cultural life in general.

The third question concerns language more particularly, specifically the nature of the transition from prelinguistic gestural communication to linguistic communication in human ontogeny. In particular, we would like to know if the early acquisition and use of linguistic conventions depends on the same shared intentionality infrastructure as does infants' early gestural communication. If so, this would support the idea that the acquisition of linguistic conventions depends crucially on social-cognitive skills and motivations originally deployed in early gestural communication. We would also like to know if children's two different types of gesture—pointing and iconic gestures—interact with early language in different ways, as this may give us hints about the evolutionary transition from more natural into more conventionalized forms of human communication.

4.1   Infant Pointing

In the months around their first birthdays, and before they begin acquiring language in earnest, most infants in Western culture begin pointing, with some evidence that this is a widespread, if not universal, pattern cross-culturally (Butterworth 2003). Our central question initially is the degree to which, and the ways in which, infant pointing shares all the social-cognitive complexities of the adult version of this communicative gesture, as just elaborated. Also of interest, of course, are infants' iconic gestures. The problem is that there is relatively little research, especially experimental research, on how infants acquire and use iconic gestures early in development. Our procedure, therefore, will be to explore the cooperation model—explicitly in terms of its different components—in the case of infant pointing, where there is much relevant research. I will report what little is known about how infants acquire and use iconic gestures later, mainly in exploring the transition to linguistic communication.

4.1.1 Infant Pointing in Context

In classic accounts, infants point communicatively for one of two motives: they point to request things (imperatives) and to share experiences and emotions with others (declaratives), with no difference in age of emergence for these two types (Bates, Camaioni, and Volterra 1975; Carpenter, Nagell, and Tomasello 1998). Surprisingly, no one knows where pointing comes from ontogenetically. Specifically, no one knows whether pointing is somehow ritualized by infants from some other behavior, or whether they learn it from others by imitation. Given that many apes come to request things from humans by "pointing" (almost certainly not by imitation), and given that some kind of pointing is very likely universal among human societies, the most plausible hypothesis at the moment is that infants do not acquire their pointing gesture by imitating others; rather it comes naturally to them in some way—perhaps as a nonsocial orienting action that becomes socialized in interaction with others. But there is no directly relevant research here, and it may be that even the fully socialized version requires no learning. Or it may be that even though there is no learning initially, imitation plays a role later as the child notes the correspondence between her pointing gesture and that of others. We simply do not know.

Current theoretical debates about infant pointing and prelinguistic communication center on the question of whether the most accurate interpretation is a cognitively rich or a cognitively lean one. Specifically, the question is whether young infants are attempting in their prelinguistic communication to influence the intentional/mental states of others (Golinkoff 1986; Liszkowski 2005; Tomasello, Carpenter, and Liszkowski 2007) or whether, alternatively, they are simply aiming to achieve certain behavioral effects in others (Shatz and O'Reilly 1990; Moore 1996; Moore and D'Entremont 2001). Related to this is the question of whether infants are attempting in their prelinguistic communication to inform others of things helpfully and to share experience with them emotionally, as opposed to, once again, simply trying to get others to do things they want them to. I will argue and present evidence here for the cognitively rich, and motivationally altruistic, interpretation.

There are surprisingly few systematic studies of infants pointing in their everyday lives. What studies there are have been primarily concerned with children's language development, and so have viewed pointing and other gestures through this lens (e.g., Bates 1979)—to the neglect of other interesting and important aspects of the process. Carpenter et al. (in prep.) had parents make diary observations of eight young infants' pointing in the context of their everyday social interactions. Here are

some especially interesting and instructive examples, produced mostly before the infants had any serious language (other than, in some cases, a few words like *no* and *there*):

Example 13: At age 11 months, J points to the closed window when he wants it open. *Gloss*: Attend to the window; open it.

Example 14: At age 11.5 months, J points to the door as Dad is making preparations to leave. *Gloss*: Attend to the door; Dad's going out of it soon.

Example 15: At age 11.5 months, after Mom had poured water into J's glass at the dinner table, a few minutes later J points to his glass to request that she pour him some more. *Gloss*: Attend to my glass; fill it up.

Example 16: At age 12 months, A points from inside the house out a window in the direction of the sound of an airplane (cannot see). *Gloss*: Attend to the (sound of the) airplane; isn't it cool?

Example 17: At age 13 months, J watches as Dad arranges the Christmas tree; when Grandpa enters the room J points to tree for him and vocalizes. *Gloss*: Attend to the Christmas tree; isn't it great?

Example 18: At age 13.5 months, after finishing eating, L points to the bathroom in anticipation of going to wash her hands. *Gloss*: Attend to the bathroom; it's time to go there.

Example 19: At age 13.5 months, while Mom is looking for a missing refrigerator magnet, L points to a basket of fruit where it is (hidden under the fruit). *Gloss*: Attend to the basket of fruit; it's there.

Example 20: At age 14 months, two different children, J and L, have accidents when a parent is not looking; when the parent comes to investigate, the infant points to the offending object (i.e., the thing he bumped his head on, or the thing that fell down). *Gloss*: Attend to that object; it hurt me/fell down.

Example 21: At age 14.5 months, as Mom is bringing the highchair to the table, L points where it goes. *Gloss*: Attend to that place; put it there.

The main thing to notice in these observations is that, although the particulars differ greatly, the kinds of things that are going on seem very similar to the kinds of things going on in adult pointing. (Note especially J's pointing to the glass to request that it be filled, just as in our adult bar scene, example 1, in the previous chapter). And, as in the adult cases presented in the last chapter, there is great variety in the different underlying social intentions. Thus, in the examples involving requests, these infants pointed not only to objects they wanted— the classic imperative—but also to the object involved when they wanted the adult to perform an action with it, for example, the window to be opened or the glass to be filled with water. And they also pointed to a place at the table when they wanted Mom to put the highchair there. These are all clearly requests, but none of them is concerned with obtaining objects as in classic proto-imperatives, and the pointing itself sometimes indicates the object involved (the window) with the action to be performed being assumed (opening), but sometimes indicates instead a location (the normal place at the table) with both the object and action being assumed (the chair and pushing).

In addition, these infants also pointed for a wide array of other social intentions based on nonrequestive motives. For example, they pointed to the door through which Dad was preparing to leave or the bathroom they were getting ready to visit, to the sound of an airplane, to a sight that was new and interesting for Grandpa (not for the infant), to the place where a missing object was to be found, and to the location where an exciting event occurred just previously. These could all be classified as declaratives, in the sense that the infant's intention is to direct or share attention to something, but in the various observations the infants are directing and sharing attention to very different aspects of the target events—everything from a sound to a hiding location to the place where something happened previously—and they are doing so for a wide variety of different reasons including both anticipating and remembering nonpresent events. Again, this is significantly different from classic declaratives, which typically target an exciting new perceptually present object or event. The references to absent objects or events (the empty glass, the missing refrigerator magnet, the heard plane, the past event) are perhaps especially noteworthy as evidence that the communication is taking place not just on the perceptual level but on the mental level of cognitively represented entities (more on this below).

And this is all happening for the most part before language acquisition has begun in earnest. Nevertheless, despite the superficial similarity to the observations of adult pointing—in the sense of a relatively large distance between social intention and referential intention in a variety of contexts, perhaps based on common ground— we still cannot tell from natural observations alone the nature of the social-cognitive processes involved in these interesting communicative acts. We must therefore supplement these observations with experiments investigating the various social-cognitive and social-motivational processes involved, either directly in studies of pointing or indirectly in studies of related developmental phenomena. We thus look now at evidence, mostly experimental, for each of the major components of the pointing act, as explicated in the cooperation model of human communication, in the earliest pointing gestures of human infants.

4.1.2 Communicative Motives

As noted, infant pointing has classically been hypothesized as emanating from two communicative motives: declarative and imperative. We think the situation is a bit more complex than this. In particular, we think the declarative motive has two important subtypes, and that the imperative motive actually involves a continuum from something like ordering (forcing) to something like suggesting (influencing choice). In addition, in order to integrate communication into the infant's other cognitive activities, we think it is best to conceptualize the different motives more broadly in terms of shared intentionality, specifically, infants' skills and motivations for helping and sharing with others.

In the original formulation by Bates, Camaioni, and Volterra (1975), declarative pointing was analogous to a declarative sentence, such as "The cat is on the mat." Statements of this type have truth-values that indicate how well they fit with the true state of the world. However, in many subsequent analyses, the prototype of declarative pointing is when the infant points to, for example, an interesting animal in the distance, expresses emotions, and alternates gaze to the adult. The infant is interested or excited about the new animal, and seemingly wants to share her excitement with the adult by getting him to look at it along with her and share her reaction to it. This is not much like a declarative statement with a truth-value, since its motive seems very different. We thus believe that we should distinguish between (i) declaratives as expressives, in which the infant seeks to share an attitude with an adult about a common referent, and (ii) declaratives as informatives, in which the infant seeks to provide the adult with needed or desirable information (which he currently does not have) about some referent. Experimental research has established each of these as an independent motive for infants by around their first birthdays.

First, Liszkowski et al. (2004) elicited pointing from 12-month-olds in a situation in which a declarative motive—of the expressive subtype—would be likely (e.g., novel and interesting objects suddenly appearing at some distance). They then experimentally manipulated the adult's reaction in order to test the hypothesis that the infants' social intention in such situations is indeed to share their attitude about the novel event with the adult, and not just to get the adult to look at them or at the event. Specifically, the adult reacted to the infant's pointing by: (i) looking to the event without looking to the infant—on the hypothesis that the infant simply wants to direct the adult's attention to the event, not share attention and interest (Event condition); (ii) emoting positively toward the infant without looking at the event—on the hypothesis that the infant simply wants adult attention to the self (Moore and Corkum 1994; Moore and D'Entremont 2001) (Face condition); (iii) doing nothing—on the hypothesis that the infant is pointing for the self only, or is not attempting to communicate at all (Ignore condition); or (iv) alternating gaze between the infant and the event while emoting positively—on the hypothesis that the infant wants to direct adult attention to the referent, so that they can share attention and interest in the event together (Joint Attention/Share condition).

Infants' reactions to these adult reactions were then noted in an attempt to establish the infants' motive for pointing. Results showed that when the adult simply looked to the indicated referent while ignoring the infant (Event condition), or when the adult simply expressed positive emotions to the infant while ignoring the indicated referent (Face condition), infants were not satisfied. In comparison with the Joint Attention condition, in which infants typically gave one long point, infants in these conditions (as well as in the Ignore condition) tended to repeat their pointing gesture more often within trials—apparently as persistent attempts to establish shared attention and interest. Moreover, infants in these conditions (as well as in the Ignore condition) pointed less often across trials than in the Joint Attention condition—apparently indicating growing dissatisfaction with this adult as a communicative partner since she did not respond by sharing infants' attitude to the referent. Even more directly, using the same basic design, Liszkowski, Carpenter, and Tomasello (2007a) had the adult look at the infant's intended referent, but in different conditions the adult either: (i) expressed interest ("Cool!") or (ii) expressed disinterest ("Uh . . .") in the referent. When the adult expressed disinterest, infants did not prolong or repeat their pointing within trials, presumably because they understood that the adult did not share their enthusiasm, and they also decreased pointing for this adult across repeated trials compared to when the adult expressed interest. These results specifically isolate the infants' motive to share their attitude with an adult in the expressive subtype of declarative pointing, their motive that the adult not just attend to a referent but also align with their attitude about it.

Second, the informative subtype of declarative pointing occurs when the infant's intention is to help the adult (dispassionately) by providing her with information she needs or would be interested in. This motive for pointing is actually much closer to that behind most declarative statements expressed in language. To have this motive infants must have, first, an understanding that others can be knowledgeable or ignorant (see section 4.2.2 for evidence), and second, an altruistic motive to help others by supplying them with the needed or desirable information. In order to test whether 12-month-old infants point with such a motive, Liszkowski, Carpenter, Striano, and Tomasello (2006) placed infants in various situations in which they observed an adult misplace an object or lose track of it in some way, and then start searching. In these situations infants pointed to the needed object (more often than to distractor objects that were misplaced in the same way but were not needed by the adult), and in doing this they showed no signs of wanting the object for themselves (no whining, reaching, etc.) or of wanting to share emotions or attitudes about it. These results suggest that when pointing declaratively infants sometimes want to do something other than share their excitement about a referent with an adult, as occurs in the classic cases; they sometimes simply want to help the adult by

providing her with needed or desirable information—
and these two motives are distinct.

Turning now to imperative pointing, some researchers
have argued that imperatives expressed through pointing are at least potentially quite simple, based on an
understanding of others as causal (vs. intentional or
mental) agents who make things happen (e.g., Bates,
Camaioni, and Volterra 1975; Camaioni 1993). This view
is based at least partially on the well-known facts that
children with autism point imperatively but not declaratively, as do some apes when interacting with humans.
But imperatives actually form a continuum. Some are
based on individualistic motives for inducing or even
forcing the other, as causal agent, to do what one wants;
for example, a young infant might point to a toy with the
goal that the adult retrieve it for her, with the adult understood as a kind of social-causal tool. Other imperatives
are based more on cooperative motives for telling the
other what one wants, as in so-called indirect requests,
and hoping that she, as intentional/cooperative agent,
will decide to help.

Obviously, human infants sometimes produce more
individualistic imperatives to get adults to do things for
them as social tools. But they also sometimes produce
more cooperative imperatives in which they attempt to
go through the intentional/mental states of the recipient—her understanding and motivations—in a way that
more individualistic imperatives do not. It is not totally
clear what kind of evidence would be persuasive that
infants are sometimes using such cooperative impera-

tives. One indirect piece of evidence is that from a very young age infants point in other ways that are clearly cooperative and that clearly go through the intentional/ mental states of the other, that is, they use both expressive and informative declaratives (as demonstrated above) as early as they use imperatives (Carpenter, Nagell, and Tomasello 1998). More directly—although the evidence is only for somewhat older children at 30 months of age— when young children request something from an adult, and the adult misunderstands them but then, by luck, they get what they want anyway, they still attempt to correct the misunderstanding (Shwe and Markman 1997). This suggests that fairly early in development children understand that their request works not by forcing the adult into a specific action, but rather by informing the adult of their desire and then her comprehending this and agreeing to cooperate with it. Precisely when this understanding first occurs in infant development, we do not know.

Our contention is thus that recent research on infant pointing establishes three general classes of social inten-tion or motive, just as in the case of adults: (1) sharing (they want to share emotions and attitudes with others); (2) informing (they want to help others by informing them of useful or interesting things); and (3) requesting (they want others to help them in attaining their goals). As with adults, these three motives all involve in some way or another the cooperative motives of helping and sharing—the two main types of motivation in shared intentionality. Pointing within each of these motives is used for innumerably many particular social intentions, as illustrated most clearly by the diary examples cited in the previous subsection.

4.1.3   The Referential Intention

When infants produce points, there is very good evidence that they intend for the other to attend to a referent in their common ground. This is not a foregone conclusion. Indeed, Moore and colleagues have expressed skepticism that 12-month-olds produce gestures as an attempt to direct the attention of others to external entities. Thus, Moore and Corkum (1994) contend that early (declarative) pointing is mostly aimed at gaining an adult positive emotion to the self, and Moore and D'Entremont (2001) claim that it is the adult's reaction to the infant, instead of to the external entity, that serves as a reinforcer for the pointing behavior. The main evidence for this skeptical interpretation is that infants sometimes point to things for the adult that she, the adult, is already looking at, and so the pointing cannot be an attempt to direct her attention to something new, since they are already both attending to the object.

Liszkowski et al. (2004) directly tested the hypothesis of Moore and colleagues in an attempt to determine whether 12-month-old infants' declarative points are attempts to direct adult attention to a referent, so that they can then share their attitude about it. As noted above, pointing was elicited from infants in a situation in which a declarative motive would be likely, and the adult's reaction was experimentally manipulated. The main finding with respect to reference was that when the adult responded to the infant's pointing by simply emoting directly to her, ignoring the referent, infants showed signs of dissatisfaction by repeating their pointing, in an attempt at message repair, and they pointed less often over trials—again indicating dissatisfaction with the adult's response which ignored the intended referent. Even more directly, using the same basic methodology, Liszkowski, Carpenter, and Tomasello (2007a) had the adult either correctly identify the infant's intended referent or else misidentify it by alighting on a different nearby object (in both cases with positively expressed emotion and gaze alternation). When the adult correctly identified the intended referent, infants simply continued sharing attention and interest with him, but when the adult alighted on the incorrect referent, infants repeated their pointing to the intended referent in an attempt to direct him there. They were not satisfied to share emotions about something other than their original intended referent.

Interestingly and importantly, 12-month-old infants can also refer others to absent entities in their pointing. This is apparent in a number of the diary observations reported above, as 12- and 13-month old infants refer to events that happened in the near past or will happen in the near future. More systematically, Liszkowski, Carpenter, and Tomasello (2007b) exposed infants to targets likely to elicit declarative pointing, and then, after a while, the targets disappeared. The majority of infants—both those who pointed to the visible target and those who did not—pointed for an adult to the location where the visible entity used to be, especially if she had not seen the entity previously. Pointing to absent referents is important because it makes clear that pointing infants are not doing very low-level, behavioristic things like attempting to get the other person to orient bodily to perceptible entities, but rather are attempting to get the other person to orient mentally to some nonperceptible entity they have in mind (see also Saylor 2004).

By around 12 to 14 months of age, then, infants demonstrate an understanding of acts of reference as intentional acts intended to induce the other to attend to some particular external entity or aspect of an entity, even an absent entity, as a part of some larger social act. This process involves much more than simply gaze following, point following, or gaining attention to the self. It involves a communicator's intention to direct a recipient's attention to a particular referent so that the recipient, by identifying this intended referent (and motive) via some relation to their common ground, will make the needed relevance inferences and so comprehend the overall social intention.

4.1.4   Common Ground

We might presume that common ground plays a critical role in infant pointing from the beginning, based on such things as our diary observations involving many different contexts determining many different meanings for the infant's pointing gesture. However, demonstrating a role for common ground requires demonstrating that the context is indeed "shared" or mutually known, and that is (or at least has been) most readily demonstrated in comprehension. This is true for both the social intentions and referential intentions involved.

In terms of social intentions, Liebal et al. (in press) had 14- and 18-month-old infants and an adult clean up together by picking up toys and putting them in a basket. At one point the adult stopped and pointed to a target toy, which infants then picked up and placed in the basket. However, when the infant and adult were cleaning up in exactly this same way, and a second adult who had not shared this context entered the room and pointed toward the target toy in exactly the same way, infants did not put the toy away into the basket—presumably because the second adult had not shared the cleaning-up game as common ground with them. Rather, because they had not just been interacting with this adult, they seemed most often to interpret the new adult's pointing gesture as a simple invitation to notice and share attention to the toy (i.e., as an expressive declarative). Infants in both cases were thus directed to the same referent toy—they understood the referential intention in the same way in both cases—but their interpretation of the underlying social intention was different in the two cases. Most importantly, this interpretation did not depend on their own current egocentric interests, but rather on their recently shared experience (joint attention, common ground) with each of the pointing adults.

In the case of the referential intention, Moll et al. (2008) had an adult direct an ambiguous request to 14-month-old infants by gesturing in the general direction of three objects (the target and two distractors) and asking the child to hand "it" over. In different experimental conditions, the infant had had different experiences with the adult previously, and so had different common ground on which to draw in identifying the referent of the request. Specifically, in the experimental condition, prior to the request the adult and infant had shared the target object excitedly as it unexpectedly appeared and reappeared in several places in a hallway (whereas they had handled the two other objects [distractors] in a more normal fashion). In this condition infants responded to the adult's request by handing him the target object, the one they had shared, more often than the distractors— based on their common ground with him previously. Importantly, they did not do this in either of two control conditions. In one of these a new adult made the request, and so there was no common ground; infants then chose randomly. In the other the adult who made the request had previously experienced the objects individually (in the same excited fashion) while the infant simply looked on unnoticed; so again there was no common ground and the infants chose randomly. Thus, when faced with a request for an unspecified referent object, infants did not assume that the requestor was asking for the object that she, the child, had been excited about (or else they would have retrieved the target also when the different adult requested it), nor did they assume that the requestor was asking for the object that he himself had been excited about (or else they would have retrieved the target also in the condition in which they simply watched the requestor become excited about the target object on their own). Instead, the infants assumed that the adult was requesting the object about which the two of them together, in their recent common ground, had showed excitement.

Infants thus use their shared common ground with a pointing adult—not their own egocentric interests—to interpret both the adult's referential intention and his underlying motive and social intention.

4.1.5 Mutual Assumptions of Helpfulness and Cooperative Reasoning

In general, it would appear that even one-year-old infants expect others to respond to their communicative acts by attempting to comprehend, and they expect others to provide help when it is requested, or to accept offered information, or to share when invited. Whether or not these are mutual expectations has never been directly investigated. But infants seem to make relevance inferences based on cooperative reasoning and common ground—for example, in the Behne et al. (2005) object choice experiment, and the Liebal et al. (in press) and

Moll et al. (2008) studies described above—in the sense that they seem to be doing things communicatively at least partly because they know the adult wants and expects them to. And in difficult cases, infants cooperate with adults in "negotiating" the intended message through queries and repairs about the message itself (Golinkoff 1986).

This interpretation is perhaps given additional credence by evidence that one-year-old infants understand the basics of the Gricean communicative intention that "we know together" or it is "mutually manifest" that I want something from you—based crucially on mutual expectations of helpfulness. First of all, in their natural social interactions, infants from around the first birthday clearly produce communicative acts "for" another person, as they make sure they have the attention of the other, direct the act to them, make eye contact, and so forth (Liszkowski et al. in press). Also, they seem to recognize such ostensive cues when produced by others as designating acts that are "for" them (see Csibra 2003, on infants' recognition of the communicative/pedagogical intentions of others toward them). But the strongest evidence comes from two experiments.

First, in the object choice experiment of Behne et al. (2005), described in chapter 2, there was not only an experimental condition in which infants inferred a toy's location on the basis of an informative pointing gesture, there was also a control condition in which the adult directed his extended index finger toward one of the buckets absentmindedly as he was examining his wrist. He also glanced up to the child so that his superficial behavior was similar to the experimental condition both in terms of his finger extending toward the correct bucket and his gaze alternating between the infant and the correct bucket. What differed was that, unlike in the experimental condition, in this control condition the adult did not make direct eye contact with the infant with the specific intention that she know this was a communicative act; the looking in the control condition was more casual, as if simply checking the child's status—as opposed to marking the pointing as an ostensive act. The 14-month-old infants did not see this more casual protruding finger and looking as a communicative act "for" them, and so they did not make the appropriate relevance inference; that is to say, infants did not see the adult as informing them of the location of the hidden toy, and so they did not find it as they did in the experimental condition. Whatever the specific cues were in this experiment, the general fact is that young infants see a protruding finger in completely different ways depending on whether the adult intends them to see it as an intentional communicative act.

Second is the study of Shwe and Markman (1997), noted above, with somewhat older children at 30 months of age. In this experiment infants requested a desired object from an adult. In the two key conditions, they got the object they wanted, but in one case the adult signaled that she had understood everything correctly whereas in the other case the adult signaled that she thought the child wanted a different (wrong) object sitting nearby— which she said he could not have, so she actually gave him the one he really wanted (by accident, as it were). That is, in this especially interesting condition, the child got what he wanted in terms of the object, but his message was actually not understood correctly. In this case, children corrected these adult misunderstandings nevertheless. This suggests that these children had both the goal of getting the object (as social intention) and the intention of communicating successfully with the adult as a means to that end—which they wanted to accomplish in its own right.

We must recognize, however, that infants' understanding of all of this is still not fully adult-like. Thus, the full-fledged understanding of Gricean communicative intentions by older children and adults include, most conspicuously, an understanding of hidden authorship and concealment—such acts as placing one's empty wine glass for the host to see (and fill), but not revealing that this is what one has done. Adults engage in this kind of hidden authorship quite often in cases involving politeness or other forms of concealment, whereas 1- and 2-year-olds seemingly do not engage in this behavior at all. We thus think that infants comprehend a primordial version of communicative intentions in the sense that they understand when a communicator intends an act "for" someone else's benefit, but that coming to understand the full intentional structure of adult-like communicative intentions involving hidden authorship, concealment, and the like does not emerge until around 3 or 4 years of age. This presumably is based on a process of understanding and controlling the more specific means by which an initially undifferentiated communicative intention may be expressed and understood. This may await more mature skills of differentiating the various perspectives involved in joint attentional interactions in general (Moll and Tomasello 2007b).

It is also unclear whether infants' expectations of helpfulness are truly mutual or shared in the sense that they know that their communicative partners expect these things of them as well—and know that he knows that she also has these expectations, and so forth and so on. One possibility is that infants are simply built to operate in terms of Sperber's (1994) naive optimism—to simply assume a cooperative environment initially based on some simple heuristic, and to assume that everyone else does as well. But at some point infants come to understand more aspects of the process. Most importantly, at some point they come to understand that the other person *ought* to engage communicatively and *ought* to help as requested, and they may become offended if the other person does not act as she is supposed to—and they will begin to operate under politeness norms aimed at regulating these things. Children do not typically operate with these kinds of norms in other domains of activity until later in the preschool period (Kagan 1981), and so perhaps they are operating with something less than adult-like norms initially. But our knowledge of all this is very sketchy.

4.1.6 Summary

The data presented here argue strongly that from almost as soon as they begin pointing infants understand the most important aspects of how human-style, cooperative communication works—they communicate on a mental level, within the context of common conceptual ground, and for cooperative motives—thus displaying something approaching the complete social-cognitive infrastructure of mature cooperative communication. For most infants, pointing emerges at around the first birthday, before language, and so this indicates that in human ontogeny the infrastructure of cooperative communication operates initially not in support of language but in the use of the pointing gesture. Since typically developing children grow up in a language-rich environment from birth, it is perhaps important to note as well that deaf children of hearing parents, exposed to basically no conventional language during their first year of life or more (either spoken or signed), still begin to use the pointing gesture normally and at around the same age (Lederberg and Everhart 1998; Spencer 1993).

Although infants seem to understand something about how communicators achieve their social intention by making their communicative intention mutually manifest, they do not engage in such things as hiding authorship, deception, and so forth, and so they very likely do not understand the internal structure of this complex intention in adult-like ways. Similarly, there is no evidence that they have an understanding of any norms governing the process at the outset. But further research on both of these topics is needed.

4.2 Sources of Infant Pointing

A basic question in all developmental analyses is why some competence emerges when it does in ontogeny—in the case of infant pointing, at around 11 to 12 months of age—since answering this question often provides important information about the underlying cognitive and motivational skills involved and how they interrelate. What we want to know now, therefore, is where infants' skills of cooperative communication, as embodied in the pointing gesture, come from ontogenetically. Our answer will take the form of a kind of dynamic systems model in which the various components outlined in the previous chapter develop somewhat independently, but then come together synergistically in the new function of cooperative communication. This account provides support for the hypothesis that skills and motivations of shared intentionality are critical to the process, as it turns out that cooperative communication does not emerge ontogenetically until these skills and motivations are present, as manifest in infants' collaborative activities with others more generally.

4.2.1   Why Don't Three-Month-Olds Point?

Perhaps surprisingly, the overt behavioral form of human pointing emerges reliably in infant sensorimotor behavior as young as three months of age (Hannan and Fogel 1987). Infants of this tender age often hold their hands in a distinctive shape with extended index finger, sometimes for extended periods of time—and in a way that other primates seemingly do not (Povinelli and Davis 1994). The behavioral form of infant pointing is thus developmentally ready at three months of age. As far as anyone can tell, however, infants at this age are not using this hand shape for any social or communicative function.

One might argue that infants this young do not have the necessary social motivations for communication. But this is not true. In the account in the previous chapter and this one, we posited three basic communicative motives: requesting, sharing, and informing. These motives represent natural human motivations for communicating, and they each have their own evolutionary origin (see chapter 5). As it turns out, they each have their own ontogenetic origin as well, and in at least two of the cases, this is well before any intentional communication.

First, within the first few months of life infants regularly get adults to do what they want them to. When young infants are in need of food or comfort they cry, and this typically results in a helpful adult response. The infant learns that as soon as she begins to cry adults respond, and so crying often becomes ritualized into a kind of incipient crying or whining—a kind of vocal intention-movement. This whining represents the roots of imperative requesting, but with no understanding on the infant's part, of course, of how it works intentionally (e.g., that the adult must perceive the cry and form a goal to act). Whining as incipient crying is the natural basis for the requesting intonation characteristic of young children's gestural and linguistic requests.

Second, infants within the first few months of life also engage with others socially and share emotions with them in face-to-face dyadic exchanges sometimes called protoconversations (Trevarthen 1979; Rochat 2001). Stern (1985) describes a process of affective attunement in which infants and adults tune into the emotions of one another in multiple modalities simultaneously. These rich emotional exchanges are the roots of expressive declaratives, but again with no understanding on the infant's part of how they work intentionally. The emotions expressed in these exchanges, such as excitement and surprise, are precisely those that infants express when they point at something with glee some months later in their expressive declaratives.

Third, and in contrast to the communicative motives for requesting and sharing, the informing motive does not have its roots in earliest infancy. If, as we have argued, the fundamental motivation for informatives is to help others by providing them with information they might need or want, then the most fundamental prerequisites are an understanding of others' goals and an understanding of knowledge or information. Based on current research, 12 months is the earliest age at which infants possess these two prerequisites. Thus, infants seem to understand helping for the first time at around 12 to 14 months of age as they discern the goals of others that they might facilitate (Kuhlmeier, Wynn, and Bloom 2003; Warneken and Tomasello 2007), and it is also at this age that they understand the difference between someone being knowledgeable and ignorant (Tomasello and Haberl 2003). And so, in contrast to the other two motives, the informative motive awaits infants' understanding of others as intentional agents who both help and need help from others—including through the provision of information for ignorant recipients. Offering help to others typically is not accompanied by any exuberant emotional expressions, and so informative pointing and language typically are not either.

If infants can make the appropriate hand shape at three months of age, and have at least two appropriate motives by about this same age, then why are they not pointing for others communicatively? The answer is that to begin directing the attention of others to things for a reason, infants must have something in the direction of the entire social-cognitive, social-motivational infrastructure characteristic of mature human communication, and infants this young do not yet have the necessary skills of either individual or shared intentionality.

4.2.2 The Nine-Month Revolution—In Two Parts

At around 9 months of age, infants begin displaying a whole new suite of social behaviors, based both on their ability to understand others as intentional and rational agents like the self and on their ability to participate with others in interactions involving joint goals, intentions, and attention (shared intentionality). Based on the best available evidence, here is when some of the key prerequisites of understanding individual intentionality emerge:

• By at least 9 months of age infants understand that others have goals, that is, that they want things (e.g., Csibra et al. 1999; Behne, Carpenter, Call, and Tomasello 2005)—and perhaps even younger infants understand this (Woodward 1998).

• By at least 12 months of age infants understand that actors actively choose means for pursuing goals, that is, they form intentions, and they are even able to discern some of the rational reasons why an actor chooses one particular means over another (Gergely, Bekkering, and Király 2002; Schwier et al. 2006).

• By at least 12 months of age, if not before (Woodward 1999), infants understand that others see things (Moll and Tomasello 2004), and by 12 months of age they also understand that actors choose to attend intentionally, for some reason, to some subset of the things they perceive (e.g., Tomasello and Haberl 2003; Moll et al. 2006).

• By at least 12 to 15 months of age infants can determine what others know, in the sense of "are familiar with" (e.g., Tomasello and Haberl 2003; Onishi and Baillargeon 2005).

Once infants understand other persons in these ways, they may begin to engage in some kinds of practical reasoning about others' actions; specifically, they may begin to make inferences about why someone did what she did—as opposed to some other thing she might have done—and what this implies about what she might do in the immediate future.

But this is not enough for cooperative communication. As emphasized in chapter 3, for cooperative communication to work in the way that it does infants also need to be able to create shared conceptual spaces, or common ground, with other persons—a basic skill of shared intentionality. In the normal case, this provides a constrained domain of possible referents for the referential intention, and a constrained domain of possible motivations for the social intention—both necessities for the recipient to make appropriate relevance inferences (and for the communicator to formulate a communicative act that facilitates these inferences). Based on the best available evidence, here is when the key prerequisites of shared intentionality emerge:

• By at least 9 to 12 months of age infants begin participating with others in bouts of triadic joint attentional engagement, creating the kind of common ground necessary for cooperative communication (Bakeman and Adamson 1984; Carpenter, Nagell, and Tomasello 1998).

· Relatedly, by at least 12 to 14 months of age infants can determine which objects they have and have not mutually experienced with another person just previously in joint attention—that is, they can determine not just what we see together (joint attention), but what we know together from previous experience (Tomasello and Haberl 2003; Moll and Tomasello 2007a; Moll et al. 2008).

· By at least 14 months of age infants can construct with others shared goals and intentions in, for example, cooperative problem-solving activities (Warneken, Chen, and Tomasello 2006; Warneken and Tomasello 2007)—and earlier joint intentional interactions might be evidence for shared goals before the first birthday as well (e.g., Ross and Lollis 1987; Ratner and Bruner 1978; Bakeman and Adamson 1984; Carpenter, Nagell, and Tomasello 1998).

And so, from just a few months of age infants have some of the prerequisite capacities for pointing, including the appropriate hand-shape form and at least two appropriate motives. But they do not begin pointing communicatively for many more months because they do not yet understand others as rational agents and they have not yet begun constructing the kinds of joint attentional frames and common ground that enable them to make reference to the world in meaningful ways for other persons triadically. However, as soon as they begin to understand others and interact with others in these ways, at around 9 to 12 months of age, they begin to point for them communicatively. In combination with the evidence that adult-like pointing emerges at 12 months of age (as presented in the previous section), this developmental synchrony suggests that infants' early communicative pointing does indeed rely on precisely these skills and motivations of individual and shared intentionality, as proposed here in the cooperation model of human communication.

Unfortunately, it is not possible by looking at naturally occurring development to specify whether the emergence of infants' communicative pointing at around one year of age is due to their emerging skills of individual or shared intentionality, or to both, because they emerge together ontogenetically. But the data comparing humans to chimpanzees suggests that the skills of shared intentionality, in particular, are critical here for supporting the unique aspects of human-like cooperative communication, and that without these skills human infants who understood others as intentional agents would communicate intentionally, but not cooperatively. Further evidence in this direction is provided by children with autism, who point for others imperatively, but not declaratively—for certain not expressively, and perhaps not informatively (this has never been tested). Importantly, children with autism have some skills for understanding the basics of intentional action—that others have goals and see things— which are capable of supporting imperative pointing, at least of the more individualistic variety (Carpenter,

Pennington, and Rogers 2001). In contrast, children with autism have very poor skills of joint attention (see Mundy and Sigman 2006 for a review) and collaboration (Liebal et al. 2008), and this is very likely why they do not point declaratively. Indeed, there is a very strong correlation in children with autism between skills of joint attention and communication such that children with autism who are capable of engaging more readily in joint attentional behaviors—typically operationalized in terms of coordinating visual attention—are the ones who subsequently acquire more sophisticated skills of gestural and linguistic communication (see Mundy and Burnette 2005 for a review).

4.2.3 Summary

A highly simplified depiction of the developmental process—a very crude dynamic systems model—is presented in figure 4.1. Our knowledge here is still very primitive, however, and providing detailed answers to the question of how infants acquire their various communicative activities awaits further research investigating more precisely how the different skills and motivations involved actually pattern temporally—with experiments to determine causality—in human ontogeny. The key points for now are only two. First, each of the three main motives for infant pointing must be accounted for separately, on its own ontogenetic terms, as each represents a fundamental mode of social interaction that must have

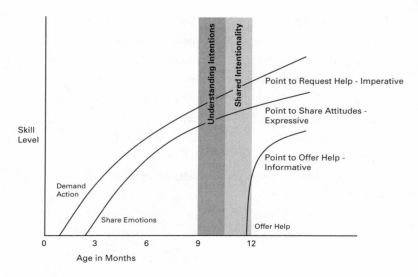

Figure 4.1
Developmental emergence of cooperative communication in pointing.

its own evolutionary basis, with advantages for both communicator and recipient (see chapter 5). And second, despite the developmental readiness of many other components, young infants do not begin to engage in cooperative communication by pointing until their skills of shared intentionality emerge at around the first birthday (these skills are thus the "control parameter" constraining age of emergence).

It is important as well, in this context, that in the current account we do not credit 12-month-olds with the full structure of mature cooperative communication. In particular, they seem not to have fully mastered all aspects of the Gricean communicative intention or norms of cooperation. These are aspects of shared intentionality that do not emerge in other arenas of children's cognitive development until three or four years of age as well, thus providing still further evidence that children's skills of cooperative communication depend crucially on their skills of shared intentionality more generally.

4.3 Early Pantomiming

We have so far avoided talking about infant gestures other than pointing. This is mainly because there is much less relevant research, and so we know much less about their nature and acquisition. But they are nonetheless very important for our story, especially in the transition to language. Of particular importance, of course, are iconic gestures (pantomiming) as they may be said to be in some sense symbolic or representational in a way that pointing is not. In addition, iconic gestures are categorical—the communicator wants the recipient to imagine something "like this"—in a way that pointing normally is not.

4.3.1 Conventional and Iconic Gestures

As argued in the previous chapter, in addition to directing others' attention to things deictically, for example, by pointing, one may also attempt to induce others to imagine things by gesturing iconically, that is, by pantomiming. But that is only if one is being creative. Many human gestures are simply conventional. For example, the gestures for "OK," for greeting and leave taking, for various obscene messages, and so forth, are not related to their referents iconically in any obvious way (although they may have been at one time histori- cally). In studies of infants' earliest gestural communica- tion during the second year of life, the nondeictic gestures cataloged are almost exclusively conventionalized ges- tures learned by imitation from adults. For example, Iverson, Capirci, and Caselli (1994) report such things as shaking the head "No," waving "Bye-bye," raising the palms "All gone," raising arms high for "Tall," blowing for "Too hot," flapping arms for "Birdie," panting for "Doggie," and so forth. Acredolo and Goodwyn (1988) report a systematic study of such "baby signs," also in the second year of life, with much individual variability. In general, the use of such conventionalized gestures is much less frequent, by several orders of magnitude, than use of pointing gesture alone (Iverson, Capirci, and Caselli 1994; Camaioni et al. 2003).

Several lines of evidence suggest that infants acquire and use these conventionalized gestures in basically the same ways they acquire and use linguistic conventions. First, infants acquire both of these kinds of conventions at basically the same age (Acredolo and Goodwyn 1988), suggesting that they depend on the same social-cognitive infrastructure, and infants acquiring conventionalized sign languages, such as American Sign Language, acquire their first conventional signs at the same age as well (Schick 2005). Second, in experiments, novel arbitrary gestures for objects are acquired just as readily as are novel words for objects (Namy and Waxman 1998; Woodward and Hoyne 1999). And third, the frequency with which children experience such gestures and the way the adult introduces them in naming games affects their acquisition, in much the same way that these same things affect the acquisition of linguistic conventions (Namy, Acredolo, and Goodwyn 2000; Namy and Waxman 2000)—which suggests similar learning processes in the two cases.

A substantial number of conventionalized gestures are iconic in some way, but it is not clear whether infants notice or use this—which again makes them more like arbitrary linguistic conventions (Tomasello, Striano, and Rochat 1999). Thus, children learning conventional sign languages are exposed to both iconic and arbitrary gestures (i.e., signs), but there is no preference or age advantage for learning iconic signs (Folven and Bonvillian 1991; Orlansky and Bonvillian 1984). Also, in experiments, 18-month-old infants show no preference for learning iconic over arbitrary gestures for objects (Namy, Campbell, and Tomasello 2004). Very young children's comprehension of iconicity in gestures or any other medium has yet to be convincingly demonstrated.

And what about truly creative iconic gestures at this early age? There is almost no research, but Carpenter et al. (in preparation) have reported diary observations of what were almost certainly spontaneously created iconic gestures by infants in the months immediately after the first birthday. These were rare, but all infants observed produced one or more of these on several different occasions.

Example 22: At age 13 months, A playfully pantomimes biting to indicate an action he was not supposed to do on a particular object. *Gloss*: Attend to my biting; that's what I'm going to do to that object.

Example 23: At age 14 months, A tilts his head to the side to indicate to Mom what she should do to dump a bucket off her own head. *Gloss*: Attend to my action; do that!

Example 24: At age 14 months, A "fingers" his chest, looking and smiling at Mom whose shirt has strings he likes to play with. *Gloss*: Attend to my action; I like those strings (or doing this to those strings).

Example 25: At age 17 months, A pantomimes crumpling a ball of paper to ask that it be done. *Gloss*: Attend to my action; do that!

Deaf children who have not been exposed to any conventional language, spoken or signed, use such iconic gestures fairly frequently, but exactly how they come by these gestures (i.e., the degree to which they are learned from adult models) has not been extensively studied (Goldin-Meadow 2003b). In any case, to produce such creative iconic gestures, infants need to have some skills of imitation, simulation, symbolic representation, or pretense, in the sense that they must enact a familiar action not for real, in order to bring about its normal effect, but rather only in pretense, in order to communicate something related to that absent action. Importantly, to gesture iconically infants must also connect the ability to enact an action outside its normal context (simulation, pretense, representation) with an understanding of the Gricean communicative intention. This is because, as noted in chapter 3, if the gesturer does not connect his simulating act to some indication of a communicative intention, then the potential comprehender could simply think he is acting bizarrely or engaging in pretend play instead of trying to communicate about some absent situation (again, see Leslie's 1987 argument for the need to "quarantine" pretend acts from real acts). Creative iconic gestures thus involve some kind of symbolic representation, produced for purposes of interpersonal communication, in a way that pointing to present entities does not.

There is almost no research on the comprehension of iconic gestures by young children just beginning to learn language, but presumably this requires all of the infrastructure used to interpret pointing gestures in terms of joint attentional frames, three layers of intentions and practical reasoning, assumptions of cooperativeness, Gricean communicative intentions, and so forth, in addition to the ability to make some kind of symbolic mapping. In ongoing research we have found that young children have much difficulty understanding these creative iconic gestures, not only when they are used to request objects (as in Tomasello, Striano, and Rochat 1999, noted above), but also when they are used to simulate for infants what action they need to perform to solve a problem (Haimerl et al. in prep.). The research of DeLoache (2004) suggests that young children have special difficulties with symbolic representations when the medium is physical, for example, a scale model for the spatial layout of a real room.

In all, despite the relative lack of research, it is clear that infants in the second year of life use conventionalized gestures much less frequently than they use the pointing gesture, and spontaneously invented iconic gestures are rarer still. What this means is that pointing—drawing attention to a perceptually present entity—seems to be a much simpler and more natural means of communication for young children than is the use of iconic gestures, and indeed early conventionalized gestures are in many ways more similar to linguistic conventions than they are to iconic gestures. One possible implication of these facts for human evolution is that the most primitive form of human cooperative communication—in the sense of being the first or original—is the pointing gesture, with iconic and conventionalized gestures requiring extra skills in addition, especially of imitation and symbolic representation.

4.3.2   Iconic Gestures, Pretense, and Language

A critical developmental fact is this: over the second year of life nondeictic gestures (conventionalized and iconic) actually go down in frequency in comparison with pointing (Iverson, Capirci, and Caselli 1994; Acredolo and Goodwyn 1988). The explanation most often given is that children are learning language during this time, and conventionalized and iconic gestures compete with linguistic conventions in a way that pointing does not— perhaps because iconic and conventionalized gestures and language, but not pointing, involve some kind of symbolic representation and even categorization of a referent.

Experimental evidence for this conclusion comes from several experimental studies. First, Bretherton et al. (1981) found that early in the second year infants prefer to indicate objects with a gesture, whereas later in the second year, after they have begun acquiring more language, they prefer a linguistic convention. Second, Namy and Waxman (1998) found that infants learn arbitrary gestures and words for objects equally well early in the second year, but they learn words much more readily than arbitrary gestures by around the second birthday, again after language acquisition has begun in earnest. In contrast to this decline of iconic and conventionalized gestures, the pointing gesture increases in frequency over the second year of life, and as infants begin learning language pointing is integrated into the process; for example, many of infants' earliest complex communications involve combinations of a conventional word and a pointing gesture, each indicating a different aspect of the referential situation (Ozcaliskan and Goldin-Meadow 2005).

These data imply that the pointing gesture serves a basic function different from that of linguistic communication, whereas iconic and conventionalized gestures compete with language for the same function. But, interestingly, infants do continue to do something like iconic gesturing for noncommunicative purposes during this same developmental period: they begin to engage ever more frequently in pretense or symbolic play. Thus, when a young child pretends to drink from an empty cup, she is in some sense iconically representing the real act; she is just not doing this for communicative purposes. It may then be that humans' biological predisposition to iconically represent absent entities and actions for communicative purposes in the gestural modality is supplanted by vocal language in normal ontogeny, but this ability manifests itself instead in children's pretense activities in which they symbolically represent absent entities and actions for playful purposes. Indeed, when a young child pretends to drink from an empty cup and looks playfully to the adult's face, one could say that in addition to pretense for the self this is also an iconic gesture to share this representation with the adult communicatively.

Children continue to engage in pretend play throughout childhood, and end up as adults in all kinds of artistic endeavors such as theater and representational art. But in terms of communication, the nondeictic gestures of older children and adults seem to change their way of working as they become adapted to serve complementary functions to language. Thus, both McNeil (2005) and Goldin-Meadow (2003a) argue that in face-to-face linguistic communication language is used for the more propositional aspects of communicative messages, whereas accompanying gestures are used for the more imagistic aspects, for example, to outline the shape of something named or to imaginatively traverse a path talked about. Interestingly, very young children (before 3 years or so) mostly do not use these kinds of supplementary gestures as they talk—at least not in the way adults do—although this has been very little studied.

It may thus be that humans' evolved abilities to represent the world iconically in gestures for purposes of interpersonal communication manifests itself in ontogeny today in several different ways as a result of the emergence of vocal language. Infants produce some iconic gestures to communicate very early, but then as language emerges the use of these abilities is "diverted" to playful pretense, mainly for the self but sometimes for others. The use of gestures as supplements to language in face-to-face communication undergoes a gradual and fairly long development in which children must learn to partition their communicative message between vocal language and gestures in supplementary ways (some of which may be different for different languages; McNeill 2005). These are all extremely important facts evolutionarily, as they suggest to us, among other things, that when humans began to use vocal conventions they replaced not pointing, but pantomiming.

4.4   Shared Intentionality and Early Language

In chapter 3, I argued that the everyday use of language depends on the shared intentionality infrastructure in basically the same way as pointing and other natural gestures. Of special importance is some kind of joint attention or common ground between communicator and recipient, which serves as the background of shared understanding against which linguistic conventions are chosen and comprehended. The necessity of common ground is even more evident in the case of language acquisition: how is the young child to comprehend when an adult utters "Gavagai" if not with reference to their shared common ground? The critical role of the shared intentionality infrastructure in language learning and use, including joint attention and common ground, is the central premise of the social-pragmatic theory of language acquisition, as espoused by Bruner (1983), Nelson (1985, 1996), and Tomasello (1992b, 2003).

4.4.1   Acquiring Linguistic Conventions

Soon after infants begin pointing and using iconic and conventionalized gestures, at around their first birthdays, they also begin comprehending and using linguistic conventions. As surprising as it may seem, most extant theories of language acquisition have no systematic account of why infants begin with language acquisition at precisely this age. In the words of Bloom (2000, p. 45): "In the end, nobody knows why word learning starts at about 12 months and not at six months or three years." But that is true only for theorists who think of language acquisition as associating words with things, or perhaps words with concepts, with no consideration of the cooperative infrastructure of shared intentionality (Tomasello 2004). If all infants had to do to learn a linguistic convention or word was to associate reliably a sound with an experience ("mapping" is the typical metaphor), then indeed infants should begin acquiring language at 6 months of age—since they are perfectly capable of such associations at this age (Haith and Benson 1997). In the social-pragmatic theory of language acquisition, however, the close developmental synchrony between gestural and linguistic communication is expected because both gestures and language are learned and used within the same interpersonal nexus of shared intentionality—and that emerges, as documented, at around 9 to 12 months of age.

Quine (1960) captured the problem most poignantly in his famous parable (though Quine himself was addressing a somewhat different philosophical issue): A stranger visits an unknown culture. A rabbit runs past. A native of the culture utters what is presumably a piece of language: "Gavagai." Assuming that the stranger knows this is a communicative act, the question is still: how is she to know whether the native is attempting to direct her attention to the rabbit, to its leg, to its color, to its fur, to running, to a potential dinner, and so forth? The answer is that without any forms of shared experience or common ground with the native speaker (which are, for purposes of the parable, specifically excluded), there simply is no way. Quine (1960, p. ix), himself, says: "Language is a social art. In acquiring it we have to depend entirely on intersubjectively available cues as to what to say and when."

Specifically in the case of language acquisition children may achieve the necessary common ground in one of two basic ways. The first is inside of collaborative interactions with others, which have joint goals that generate top-down joint attention. To illustrate, let us imagine a variation on Quine's parable. Suppose that there is a cultural practice in the native's village of catching small fish for dinner in a certain way: first one must get a bucket (usually found inside a particular hut) and a pole (usually found outside the same hut), and one must take these to the stream, and each person must stand on a different side of the stream holding one end of the pole with the bucket in the middle so that water goes in it, and so on. And let us assume that the stranger is in the process of becoming enculturated into this practice through repeated participation. Now one evening when dinnertime comes, and preparations begin, the native picks up the pole from outside the hut and points for the stranger through the door to inside the hut—perhaps saying "Gavagai." To the degree that the stranger understands the practice, she will know that the native wants her to fetch the bucket inside so that they can go fishing—and so the word *gavagai* almost certainly means either "bucket" or "fetch," or perhaps something more generic like "that" or "there." But if upon arriving at the stream, the native starts indicating to the stranger that she should fetch other things, also using the word *gavagai*, and not using this word to point out things when they do not need to be fetched, our stranger can begin to crack into the native language.

Much of children's early language acquisition is like this. Bruner (1983) presented evidence that virtually all of children's earliest language is acquired inside routine collaborative interactions with mature speakers of a language—in Western culture, such things as eating in the high chair, going for a ride in the car, changing diapers, feeding ducks at the pond, building a block tower, taking a bath, putting away the toys, feeding the dog, going grocery shopping, and on and on. In each one of these practices the infant, like our stranger, first learns to participate and form with the other shared goals, and this enables her to understand what the other person is doing (in terms of his goals and intentions) and why he is doing it (in terms of why one plan was chosen, in the current situation with its particular contingencies, and not another). This in turn determines to a large extent the domain of joint attention and where the other person's attention is focused at any given moment in the activity, and so what he is very likely talking about with some novel term. Future uses of the same term in other contexts will serve to narrow down the possible intended referents and messages even more.

Soon children become able to learn new words in all kinds of collaborative interactions. For example, Tomasello, Strosberg, and Akhtar (1996) had an adult and an 18-month-old infant play a finding game. In the context of this game, at one point the adult announced her intention to "find the toma." She then searched in a row of buckets all containing novel objects (rejecting some by scowling and replacing them) until she found the one she wanted (indicated by a smile and the termination of search). Children learned the new word *toma* for the object that the adult's smile indicated, no matter how many rejected objects intervened in the process—thus ruling out any simple process of association based on spatiotemporal contiguity. Indeed, Tomasello, Strosberg, and Akhtar (1996) found that in the context of a similar finding game, 18-month-old infants could identify the adult's intended referent even when they themselves never saw it—because it was an object they knew to be locked inside the toy barn the adult was currently trying to get into (see Tomasello 2001 for other similar studies). To learn the new word in these situations, the child basically had to understand the intentional structure of the shared finding game and to reason practically, indeed cooperatively, about the adult's actions in it.

The second way to establish joint attention for word learning is bottom-up; for example, a strange animal might simply appear to a father and child during their walk in the park, and the father might then name it. One might assume that infants would simply learn the name of the new animal in such situations egocentrically, attaching it to whatever is salient for them alone. But this is not what happens. From very early in development, young children understand that in using a novel piece of language the adult is inviting them to share *her* attentional focus. Thus, Baldwin (1991) waited until an 18-month-old child was focused on one object, and then she looked at another object and named that one. Children learned the word not for the object they were already focused on, but rather for the one the adult was inviting them to attend to. Similarly, and even more strikingly, Akhtar, Carpenter, and Tomasello (1996) had a child, her mother, and an experimenter play together with three novel objects. The mother then left the room. A fourth novel object was bought out and the child and experimenter played with it. When the mother returned to the room, she looked at the four objects together and exclaimed to the child "Oh, wow! A modi! A modi!" Understanding that Mom would most likely be excited about the object she was seeing for the first time, 24-month-old children learned the new word for that object (even though they themselves were equally familiar with all four objects). To learn the new word in these situations, children had to determine not just what was salient for the adult, but what the adult thought would be salient for them—actually, what the adult thought they would think she would think was salient for them, and so on. They needed to imagine the necessary common ground.

When joint attention is measured very generally as joint visual focus on potential referent objects, it is found to correlate quite strongly with young children's initial acquisition of words (Tomasello and Farrar 1986; Carpenter, Nagell, and Tomasello 1998; see Tomasello 1988, 2003, for reviews of related findings). Specifically, the way mothers use language inside joint attentional frames facilitates their children's acquisition of words, whereas the way mothers use language outside these frames has no effect. We may thus think of joint attentional frames as "hot spots" for language acquisition. Interestingly, however, this correlation seems to decrease over the second year of life (Carpenter, Nagell, and Tomasello 1998). This may be for two reasons. First, infants may be learning to acquire new words more flexibly by "eavesdropping" on third parties' use of language to one another (Akhtar, Jipson, and Callanan 2001)—perhaps by imagining themselves in the interaction, which they comprehend, whether they are participating or not, from a "bird's-eye view" (Tomasello 1999). Second, joint visual attention may become less important for language acquisition, as children become able to use language itself for establishing joint attention. Thus, at some point, children do not need to determine where the adult's visual attention is focused when she says to them "Give me that modi you're playing with"—as they know the meaning of the language around the unknown word, and this establishes the joint attentional frame within which the novel word is understood.

In any case, these theoretical considerations and empirical findings all point to the same conclusion. Young children do not learn their initial linguistic conventions by simply associating or mapping arbitrary sounds onto recurrent experiences in an individualistic manner. Rather, they acquire their initial linguistic conventions by attempting to understand how others are using particular sounds to direct their attention within the space of their current common ground—sometimes supplied top-down by the joint collaborative activity in which they are currently participating, and sometimes by other forms of bottom-up common ground as well. This is of course the same basic process that supports infants' initial comprehension of pointing and other gestures. Without some kind of meaningful social engagement with the adult using the novel piece of language, children just hear noises coming from the mouths of others; they do not experience others directing their attention in meaningful ways. They then must imitatively learn the convention by engaging in role reversal imitation in which they use the acquired piece of language toward others in the way that others have used it toward them.

4.4.2 Using Linguistic Conventions

Young children produce their earliest referential language typically between 14 and 18 months of age. In the vast majority of cases, children have previously been communicating for some weeks or months using gestures. In the study of Carpenter, Nagell, and Tomasello (1998), all 24 infants had used some kind of communicative gesture, typically pointing, before they began producing any referential language. Although it is theoretically possible that children might begin to use language within the context of some kind of common ground before producing any gestures, it is a significant fact that the vast majority gesture first, thus setting up the shared intentionality infrastructure of language for use with prelinguistic gestures.

Infants' earliest motives for communicating linguistically are the same as for pointing: informing, requesting (including requesting information), and sharing attitudes.[1] Often, infants use early pieces of language in the same way as adults by simply reversing roles with them in the same or similar situations. For example, Ratner and Bruner (1978) observed a young child just after his first birthday playing a game of "hide the puppet" with his mother. In repeated rounds of the game, the mother tended to say "All gone" at the same moment in the game, just after the puppet had disappeared. The child's first production of "All gone," not surprisingly, simply involved doing what the mother had done, at the same juncture, previously. Children also name objects for adults by reversing roles in the naming game that the adult at some earlier point originated. But children also learn pieces of language from adults for making reference to

---

1. Three more specific functions that young children quite often acquire early in their language development as well—and which typically do not occur with pointing—are expressions of gratitude ("Thanks"), greeting ("Hi" and "Bye"), and apologizing ("Sorry"), however imperfectly they may understand these functions.

the world, but then use them for different purposes than the adults from whom they learned them. For example, many parents ask their children of food "Do you want some more?," but when children start using parts of this expression they use it to request "More!" The child thus learns the referential device from the adult model, but then uses it for her own purposes.

Children's early use of both pointing and language show the same complementarity between what must be expressed in the referential act itself and what may be left implicit in common ground; that is to say, pointing and linguistic utterances have the same "information structure." Thus, in most cases pointing presupposes the joint attentional common ground as "topic" (old or shared information), and the pointing act is actually a predication, or focus, informing the recipient of something new, worthy of her attention. In other cases, pointing serves to establish a new topic, about which further things may then be communicated. Both of these are functions served by whole utterances in linguistic communication (see Lambrecht's 1994 predicate focus and sentence focus constructions). When infants first begin talking—when they are still confined to only one- or two-word utterances—they typically choose to refer to complex situations by using the most "informative" term available. For example, if a new object enters the scene, or an already present object begins engaging in a new activity, beginning language learners tend to refer to the new element in the situation (Greenfield and

Smith 1976). More recent evidence demonstrates that from as early as the second birthday, children choose the new element on the basis of its newness not for themselves but for the listener (Campbell, Brooks, and Tomasello 2000; Wittek and Tomasello 2005; Matthews et al. 2006).[2] In addition, many of children's early utterances are combinations of gestures (mostly pointing) and words, dividing up in various ways the topic and focus functions (Tomasello 1988; Ozcaliskan and Goldin-Meadow 2005; Iverson and Goldin-Meadow 2005), which suggests a common infrastructure for gestures and language as well.

4.4.3 Summary

Many animals can associate sounds with experiences, and human infants can do this from a few months of age. If association or "mapping" were all that is involved in acquiring a linguistic convention, then language would be everywhere in the animal kingdom, and it would start at three months of age in humans. But the fact is that animals and young human infants do not

---

2. Interestingly, when young children choose inadequate referring expressions leading to misunderstandings, what is most useful in helping them learn to choose expressions more adequate to the recipient's perspective is the adult signaling in a salient way her noncomprehension—rather than, for example, the adult simply demonstrating examples of adequate referential acts, which are less helpful since they are not connected to child misunderstandings (Matthews, Lieven, and Tomasello 2007).

acquire or use linguistic conventions. The reason is that "arbitrary" linguistic conventions can be acquired only in the context of some kind of conceptual common ground with mature speakers, often in collaborative activities with joint goals and joint attention, and this only becomes possible in human ontogeny at around one year based on species-unique shills and motives for shared intentionality.

4.5 Conclusion

In this chapter I have tried to make the case that infant gestural communication, especially pointing, has something approaching the full adult structure, with perhaps a few sophistications still to come. In doing this, I provided empirical support for many of the components of the cooperation model in general, as well as for three specific hypotheses.

First, the full cooperative infrastructure is basically in place before language acquisition has begun in earnest, as demonstrated by the various experimental studies of 12-month-olds' pointing reviewed here. Of course, children are bathed in language from birth, and one might suppose that they are influenced by that in some way even though they are not producing language themselves. But the early pointing of deaf infants who have been exposed to no systematic vocal or signed language is essentially the same as that of hearing infants (Lederberg and Everhart 1998; Spencer 1993). And so we claim that in ontogeny the first manifestations of uniquely human forms of cooperative communication emerge in prelinguistic gestural communication—especially in the pointing gesture—and that they do not depend on language production or comprehension.

Second, although pointing and other gestures typically emerge before language, they emerge only after the constitutive skills of individual and shared intentionality. Indeed, we noted that infants have at least two motivations for pointing from very early in infancy—requesting things from adults and sharing emotions with them—and they also have the pointing hand shape as well. But infants' first pointing gestures come only as they are beginning to understand others as intentional agents and to participate with them in joint attentional interactions. This ontogenetic pattern—along with several experimental studies—provides strong support for many of the hypothesized components of the cooperation model of human communication, including the crucial role of joint attentional frames and other forms of common ground.

Third, infants' first acquisition and use of linguistic conventions also provides support the cooperation model. The problem of referential indeterminacy arises precisely when an act of reference is removed from the kinds of shared intentionality contexts within which language acquisition normally occurs. When children experience an adult using a linguistic convention outside of such contexts, it is true: they acquire nothing. But when children experience an adult using a linguistic convention within such inherently meaningful contexts, they are quite often able to understand what is being communicated independent of language and so to acquire productive use of that convention. They then use it in ways that are not so different, from a functional point of view, from the way they use pointing and iconic gestures—and, indeed, early language and gestures are often used together. Early linguistic conventions tend to supplant not pointing, which often supplements language, but rather iconic gestures, which operate in a similar manner to language in being both symbolic and categorical.

5   Phylogenetic Origins

If I want to show a person the way I point my finger in the direction he is to follow, and not the opposite one. . . . It is in human nature to understand pointing a finger in this way. And thus the human language of gestures is in a psychological sense primary.

—Wittgenstein, *The Big Typescript*

If the claim is that human communication is fundamentally cooperative, we have a problem. Specifically, we have a problem in explaining its evolution because, as is well known, in modern biology the evolution of cooperation requires special treatment if there is any hint that the individual is subordinating its own interests to those of others altruistically, for example, in acts of helping. We therefore must explain why human recipients are so motivated to comply with communicators who request help from them, and why human communicators are motivated to actually offer help to recipients by informing them of things freely for their benefit. Why do individuals who do these altruistic things leave more offspring?

Our proposal is that human cooperative communication was adaptive initially because it arose in the context of mutualistic collaborative activities in which individuals helping others were simultaneously helping themselves. This is not quite as obvious as it first sounds, as cooperative communication today may be used for all kinds of selfish, deceptive, competitive, and otherwise individualistic ends—and so these could theoretically have been contexts in which human-style communication originated as well. But the current proposal is that in the beginning skills of cooperative communication originated and were used only in activities that were collaborative all the way down (and so structured by joint goals and attention, which provided the necessary common conceptual ground). Only later was cooperative communication co-opted for use outside of collaborative activities and for noncooperative purposes such as lying.

The intimate relation between collaborative activities and cooperative communication is most readily apparent in the fact that they both rely on one and the same underlying infrastructure of recursively structured joint goals and attention, motivations and even norms for helping and sharing, and other manifestations of shared intentionality. This common infrastructure is most clearly evident in the fact that great apes have noncooperative forms of both group activities and intentional communication, underlain by skills for understanding individual intentionality, whereas human infants develop cooperative forms of both collaboration and communication underlain by skills and motivations for shared intentionality (and before language). We thus believe that our evolutionary account is more than just another "just-so story," as the common infrastructure of shared intentionality underlying both the collaborative and communicative activities of contemporary human beings provides us with a tangible stamp of their common evolutionary origin.

To go beyond cooperative communication in mutualistic contexts, we will also need at some point to invoke processes of indirect reciprocity in which individuals care about the reputation they have among others in the social group, since having a reputation as a good helper and cooperator contributes in important ways to social success. This will be necessary especially to account for humans' tendency to simply inform others of things helpfully even outside of contexts in which they themselves receive a mutual benefit. We will also need, at some later point, to invoke processes of social identification, affiliation, and conformity to account for the sharing motive, whose function, in the current hypothesis, is to increase common ground with others and the sense of social belonging—which provide the kind of within-group homogeneity necessary for natural selection to work on the level of the cultural group. These processes of social identification are also necessary to account for the fact that human communication is governed by social norms that dictate how things ought to be done (e.g., granting reasonable requests, not lying, etc.), if one is to be a fully functioning member of the social group.

Finally, we begin in this chapter and continue in the next to provide an account of how human skills of linguistic communication build on this already existing platform of cooperative communication evolutionarily to provide humans with the most flexible, open-ended, and powerful form of communication on the planet. For this we also will need, in addition to the shared intentionality infrastructure, skills of cultural learning and imitation, including role reversal imitation, to enable the creation of group-shared communicative conventions. We will argue that arbitrary communicative conventions—first gestural and then vocal, with a period of overlap—could only have arisen by building on action-based gestures (i.e., pointing and pantomiming) which were already meaningful "naturally."

5.1   The Emergence of Collaboration

The current hypothesis is that human cooperative communication emerged as part and parcel of the evolution of humans' unique forms of collaborative activity. We cannot here attempt to explain the evolution of humans' hyper-cooperativeness in general (see Richerson and Boyd 2005 for an excellent overview), but what we can show is that human collaborative activities differ from great apes' group activities in precisely the same way that human cooperative communication differs from great ape intentional communication. Specifically, human collaborative activity and cooperative communication both rest, in a way that great ape group activity and intentional communication do not, on such things as recursive intention-reading and the tendency to offer help and information to others freely.

5.1.1 The Group Activities of Chimpanzees

Chimpanzees, as representative of great apes (and the ape species on whom there is by far the most research), are very social creatures, and engage in a number of complex group activities, for example, in group hunting. But our question here is whether they also engage more specifically in collaborative activities, defined more narrowly as multiple individuals pursuing a joint goal—and all knowing together that they are doing so—with interrelated, complementary roles. This kind of collaboration requires, in our analysis, skills and motivations for shared intentionality, including as the basic social-cognitive prerequisite, recursive mindreading.

In their natural habitats, chimpanzees sometimes hunt in small parties to capture small animals such as monkeys. Most impressively, male chimpanzees in the Taï forest hunt together in small groups for red colobus monkeys (Boesch and Boesch 1989; Boesch and Boesch-Achermann 2000; Boesch 2005). In the Boeschs' account the animals have a common goal and take complementary roles in their hunting. In this account, one individual, called the driver, chases the prey in a certain direction, while others, so-called blockers, climb the trees and prevent the prey from changing direction—and an ambusher then moves in front of the prey, making an escape impossible. Of course, when the hunting event is described with this vocabulary of complementary roles, it appears to be a truly collaborative activity: complementary roles already imply that there is a joint goal, shared by the role-takers. But the question is whether this vocabulary is appropriate.

From our perspective, a more plausible characterization of this hunting activity is the following (see Tomasello et al. 2005). One chimpanzee begins by chasing the monkey, given that others are around (which he knows is necessary for success). Each other chimpanzee then goes to, in turn, the most opportune spatial position still available at any given moment in the emerging hunt. In this process, each participant is attempting to maximize its own chances at catching the prey, without any kind of prior joint plan or agreement on a joint goal or assignment of roles. This kind of hunting event clearly is a group activity of some complexity in which individuals are mutually responsive to one another's spatial position as they encircle the prey. But wolves and lions do something very similar, and most researchers do not attribute to them any kind of joint goals and/or plans (Cheney and Seyfarth 1990a; Tomasello and Call 1997). It is also relevant that in other chimpanzee communities, the group hunting seems to be much less coordinated (e.g., Ngogo: Watts and Mitani 2002; Gombe: Stanford 1998)—perhaps owing to differences in the local ecologies in terms of how easy it is to hunt successfully alone, to find alternative food sources, and so forth.

This cognitively leaner interpretation is supported by studies that have investigated chimpanzees' abilities to collaborate in experimental settings. The basic facts are these:

• In Crawford's (1937, 1941) classic studies, sometimes cited as demonstrating collaboration, chimpanzee pairs did not synchronize their actions until they received extensive human training. This training included separating the individuals and teaching them each to pull on command, which jump-started the synchronization of actions later when they were put back together and the command was given so that both pulled simultaneously—by accident, as it were. When subjects were later given a slightly different transfer task, all pairs reverted to uncooperative behavior. (See Savage-Rumbaugh, Rumbaugh, and Boysen 1978 for a study involving even more extensive human training.)

• In more successful experiments with less or no training, most chimpanzee coordination involves individuals learning to refrain from acting (i.e., waiting) until the other is in place and ready to act (Chalmeau 1994; Chalmeau and Gallo 1996; Melis, Hare, and Tomasello 2006a,b).

• There are no published experimental studies— and several unpublished negative results (two of them by myself and colleagues)—in which chimpanzees collaborate by playing different and complementary roles; the only successes have come in tasks with identical parallel roles such as simultaneous pulling.

• In the successful studies involving parallel roles, almost no communication among partners is observed (Povinelli and O'Neill 2000; Melis, Hare, and Tomasello 2006a,b; Hirata and Fuwa 2006)—although there was some tugging at a recalcitrant partner in Crawford's (1937) study. Also, in chimpanzees' group hunting in the wild, little if any intentional communication among participants is observed (i.e., none that anyone has suggested serves a coordinating function).

These results suggest that human-like collaborative activity—group activity with an intentional structure comprising both a joint goal and complementary roles—is something in which great apes do not participate. In general, it is almost unimaginable that two chimpanzees might spontaneously do something as simple as carry something heavy together or make a tool together.

One potential explanation for why chimpanzees and other apes do not collaborate with one another in human-like ways is that they do not understand the goals and perceptions of their partner as an individual actor in the situation (Povinelli and O'Neill 2000). Because the goals and perceptions of others are not readily observable, and so require inferences, we ourselves at one time thought that only humans understood them and how they work together in goal-directed action (Tomasello and Call

1997). But recent research, much of it cited above in section 2.4.1, has changed all of that. Apes understand that others have goals and perceptions and how these relate to one another in intentional action, perhaps even rational action. So this is not the reason they do not collaborate in human-like ways. Rather, as might be expected, we believe that whereas apes understand what the other is doing as an individual intentional agent, they have neither the skills nor the motivations to form with others joint goals and joint attention or otherwise participate with others in shared intentionality.

A recent experiment supports this interpretation. Warneken, Chen, and Tomasello (2006; see also Warneken and Tomasello 2007) presented 14- to 24-month-old children and three human-raised juvenile chimpanzees with four collaborative tasks: two instrumental tasks in which there was a concrete goal, and two social games in which there was no concrete goal other than playing the collaborative game itself (e.g., the two partners using a kind of trampoline to bounce a ball up in the air together). The human adult partner was programmed to quit acting at some point in the tasks as a way of determining subjects' commitment to the joint activity. Results were clear and consistent. In the problem-solving tasks, chimpanzees synchronized their behavior relatively skillfully with that of the human, as shown by the fact that they were often successful in bringing about the desired result. However, they showed no interest in the social games, basically declining to participate. Most importantly, when the human partner stopped participating, no chimpanzee ever made a communicative attempt to reengage her— even in cases where they were seemingly highly motivated to obtain the goal—suggesting that they had not formed with her a joint goal. In contrast, the human children collaborated in the social games as well as the instrumental tasks. Indeed, they sometimes turned the instrumental tasks into social games by placing the obtained reward back into the apparatus to start the activity again; the collaborative activity itself was more rewarding than the instrumental goal. Most importantly, when the adult stopped participating in the activity, the children actively encouraged him to reengage by communicating with him in some way, suggesting that they had formed with him a shared goal to which they now wanted him to now recommit. Overall, the children seemed to collaborate just for the sake of collaborating, whereas the chimpanzees were engaged in a more individualistic manner.

Further support for this interpretation comes from a recent longitudinal study in which the same three human-raised chimpanzees were assessed on a whole suite of social-cognitive skills (Tomasello and Carpenter 2005; see also Tomonaga et al. 2004). It was found that the chimpanzees were very similar to human infants on the more individually based social-cognitive skills involving the understanding of goals and perceptions. But in a series of simple cooperative tasks in which a human played one role and the chimpanzee a complementary role—for example, the human held out a plate and the chimpanzee placed a toy on it—when the human forced a role reversal chimpanzees basically either did not reverse roles, or else they performed their action without reference to the human. In a similar series of tasks, human infants not only reversed roles, but when they did so they looked expectantly to the adult in anticipation of her playing her new role in their shared task (Carpenter, Tomasello, and Striano 2005). Our interpretation is that human infants understand joint activity from a "bird's-eye view," with the joint goal and complementary roles all in a single representational format—which enables them to reverse roles as needed. In contrast, chimpanzees understand their own action from a first-person perspective and that of the partner from a third-person perspective, but they do not have a bird's-eye view of the interaction—and so there really are no roles, and so no sense in which they can reverse roles, in "the same" activity.

In terms of joint attention, the most systematic comparative study is that of Carpenter, Tomasello, and Savage-Rumbaugh (1995; see also Bard and Vauclair 1984, for some similar observations). They observed human 18-month-olds as well as chimpanzees and bonobos in interaction with an adult human and some objects, with a focus on objectively defined looking patterns. In this situation, all three species interacted with objects and simultaneously monitored the adult human's behavior reasonably frequently. However, human infants spent far more time than apes looking back and forth from object to adult, and their looks to the face of the adult were, on average, almost twice as long as those of the apes. The infants' looks were also sometimes accompanied by smiles, whereas apes do not smile. These differences gave the impression that the apes' looks to the adult were "checking" looks (to see what the adult was doing or was likely to do next), whereas the infants' looks to the adult were "sharing" looks (to share interest); the apes knew that the other had goals and perceptions, but they did not have the ability or desire to share them. These apes interacted with others around objects, but they did not engage with them in shared endeavors with shared goals and experiences. Tomasello and Carpenter (2005) found something very similar when they had a human attempt in various ways to encourage three human-raised chimpanzees to share attention with her in the context of play with objects. The chimpanzees sometimes looked at the interacting human to check what she was doing, but they did not look to her as a way of sharing interest in and attention to some external entity. They also did not attempt to initiate joint attention by communicating gesturally, and, in an experiment, they did not use shared experience with the human to determine what was novel, and thus surprising, for that adult (as do human infants: Moll et al. 2006).

Based on these results and others (see Tomasello et al. 2005 for a review), it seems clear that human infants create with others joint goals and complementary roles in collaborative activities in a way that our nearest primate relatives do not. The sine qua non of collaborative action is a joint goal and a joint commitment among participants to pursue it together, with a mutual understanding among all that they share this joint goal and commitment (Bratman 1992; Gilbert 1989). Joint goals also structure joint attention, since acting with a partner toward a joint goal, with mutual understanding that we are doing this, quite naturally leads to mutual attention monitoring. And so, one important reason that nonhuman primates do not participate in collaborative activities in human-like ways, or participate in joint attentional interactions in human-like ways, is that although they have human-like skills for understanding individual intentionality, they do not have human-like skills and motivations of shared intentionality.

It is a very important fact for our story here that when chimpanzees engage in group hunting they do not communicate intentionally about the ongoing activity in any observable way—either to set a goal or to coordinate roles. In other contexts chimpanzees use their intentional gestural signals to get others to do what they want them to, and they also point imperatively for helpful humans to get them to fetch things for them, and they comprehend the requests of others to some extent. To make and interpret requests requires skills for understanding individual intentionality, that is, skills for engaging in practical reasoning about an intentional agent who perceives things and has goals. Similarly, when multiple chimpanzees are simultaneously attempting to catch a monkey they understand one another as intentional agents and react to each other as such. But since they are, in an important sense, competing in this activity—or, at least, behaving individualistically—they do not engage in any intentional communication. If my most immediate goal is that I capture the monkey unbeknownst to you, then I will not be doing much communicating.

The basic fact is that chimpanzees' (and presumably other apes') competitive nature makes it very difficult for them to share the food after the monkey is captured—and how can there be a joint goal of capturing a monkey when everyone knows there will be a fight over sharing it at the end? It is true that when a group of chimpanzees captures and kills a monkey, the participants in the hunt typically all get meat—more than late-arriving chimpanzees who did not participate in the hunt (Boesch and Boesch-Achermann 2000). However, recent research by Gilby (2006) elucidates the basically individualistic mechanisms involved in this "sharing." Gilby notes, first of all, that chimpanzees who possess meat after the kill often attempt to avoid others by stealing away from the kill site, by climbing to the end of a branch to restrict the access of other chimpanzees, or by chasing beggars away (see also Goodall 1986; Wrangham 1975). Nevertheless, meat possessors are typically surrounded by beggars, who do such things as pull on the meat or cover the possessor's mouth with their hand. The possessor typically allows the beggars to take some of their meat, but what Gilby documents quantitatively is that this is a direct result of the begging and harassment: the more a beggar begs and harasses, the more food he gets. The logic is that if the possessor actually fights the harasser for the meat actively, it is very likely that he will lose all or some of it to either the harasser or others nearby in the melee—so the best strategy is for him to eat quickly all that he can, and allow others to take some meat to keep them happy (the so-called tolerated theft, or harassment, model of food sharing). Tomasello et al. (2005) suggest the further possibility that hunters obtain more meat than latecomers because they are the first ones immediately at the carcass and begging, whereas latecomers are relegated to the second ring.

This account of chimpanzee group hunting is supported by a recent experimental study as well. Melis, Hare, and Tomasello (2006a) presented a pair of chimpanzees with out-of-reach food that could only be obtained if they each pulled on one of the two ropes available (attached to a platform with food on it) and did so simultaneously. Two findings are of particular importance here. First, when there were two piles of food, one in front of each participant, there was a moderate amount of synchronized pulling. However, when there was only one pile of food in the middle of the platform, making it difficult to share at the end, coordination fell apart almost completely. Second, Melis et al. identified in pretesting individual pairs who were particularly tolerant of one another and fed together relatively peacefully. There was much more synchronized pulling from these pairs than from less tolerant pairs. These findings demonstrate especially clearly that chimpanzees can only coordinate synchronized activities when there is likely to be no squabbling over the food at the end.

It is perhaps also relevant here that although chimpanzees sometimes help humans and one another (Warneken, Chen, and Tomasello 2006; Warneken et al. 2007), they do not help others in situations in which they themselves have a chance to obtain food—even when it would be easy for them to do so at no cost (Silk et al. 2005; Jensen et al. 2006). This raises the possibility that chimpanzees might be able to engage in collaboration in non-food-related activities. It is not so easy to think of what these might be, as collaboration is only useful for things in which it is difficult to be successful on one's own. The best possibility would seem to be coalitions and alliances in intragroup fighting, but in the vast majority of cases what actually happens is that a fight starts between two individuals, and their friends join in to help them after the fact (see Tomasello and Call 1997 for a review). The best gloss for this activity is thus helping, not collaboration, as there is no evidence that the same-team combatants have created a joint goal (although they each may have "the same" goal separately) and coordinated plans or roles toward that joint goal.

And so, chimpanzee group hunting would not seem to be a highly facilitative context for the emergence of cooperative communication because it is not a truly collaborative enterprise in the narrow way we have defined collaboration here, as joint goals with coordinated plans/ roles (but see Boesch 2005 for a defense of the view that it is truly collaborative). Indeed, if one chimpanzee helped another play his "role" in the hunt by informing him, for example, that the monkey was coming his way, the communicator would actually be decreasing his likely intake of meat at the end, as the informed individual would very likely use this information to maximize his own meat intake. It is perhaps also important that bonobos do not hunt in groups in the wild, suggesting that the chimpanzee version and the human version may have arisen independently, based on different underlying psychological processes (since if the common ancestor to all three species hunted cooperatively—if group hunting was homologous in *Pan* and humans—bonobos should also).

5.1.2   *The Collaborative Activities of Humans*

As compared with other primates, humans engage in an extremely wide array of collaborative activities, many of these on a very large scale with non-kin and many under the aegis of social norms in the context of symbols and formal institutions. And different cultural groups collaborate in different activities: some in hunting, some in fishing, some in house building, some in playing music, some in governing, and on and on, which testifies to the flexibility of the underlying cognitive skills involved. Thus, while most primates live in social groups and participate in group activities, humans live in cultures premised on the expectation that its members participate in many different kinds of collaborative activities involving shared goals and a division of labor, with contributions by all participants and a sharing of the spoils at the end among all deserving participants. Humans even create cultural practices and institutions whose existence is nothing more or less than the collective agreement of all group members that it should be so—and these may be governed by social norms with real punitive force. As just one example, while nonhuman primates have some understanding of familial relatedness, humans assign social roles such as "spouse" and "parent" that everyone recognizes and that carry social and legal obligations to cooperate in specified ways—or else suffer sanctions.

With respect to hunting in particular, much research has been done on various hunter-gatherer groups to document the ways they forage for certain kinds of game and/or plants that are not so easily captured by single individuals (e.g., large game, some fish, underground plants, and so forth; see Hill and Hurtado 1996 for a review). Typically in these activities, a small group establishes the joint goal of capturing a certain prey or extracting a certain plant, and then they plan their various roles and how they should be coordinated ahead of time—or else those roles are already common knowledge based on a common history of the practice. The participants almost always share the catch with others, not only in their immediate families but also more broadly in the social group at large—and indeed they are typically under strict social norms to do so, as those who do not share are harshly sanctioned.

This propensity to share the fruits of collaborative labor in a "fair" way is extremely strong in humans; people in almost all cultural groups have internalized norms for sharing and fairness (see Fehr and Fischbacher 2003 for a review). For example, humans from both industrialized societies and hunter-gatherer groups have played the so-called ultimatum game under experimental conditions (see Henrich et al. 2005)—always under anonymous conditions and only a single time. In brief, it goes like this. An individual is given a relatively large sum of money (in some studies comparable to a month's pay). The individual is told that she can offer some of this to an anonymous other person from the same group, and then that person has the opportunity to either accept the offer—so that they each get their share—or reject it so that no one gets anything. What people typically do is to offer the other person about half the money. They do this at least partly to be "fair" in some general sense, but also because they surmise, correctly, that the other person will reject unfair offers (typically less than 30–40 percent). Exactly how this works varies from culture to culture, but in all cultures there is at least some obligation to share important goods with others (there are even some cultures in which the offers are much more than half, and these are nevertheless often rejected—presumably because they create an obligation in the recipient to repay later in kind). When people are told they are playing against a computer, they do not share or reject unfair offers but rather try to maximize their own take.

In terms of the actual social coordination involved in collaborative activities, thinkers from Schelling (1960) and Lewis (1969) on have noticed that human cooperative coordination quite often depends on recursively understood common ground in an especially critical way. Thus, if you and I get separated at some large outdoor gathering, we very likely will end up back together because we both can figure out what is a likely meeting place that the other would go to, for example, the car. To do this successfully, I have to think where you will likely go, but you are also thinking where I would likely go, so then I have to think where you think I would go, and on and on, again, ad infinitum. In other words, we both have to know that the other's thinking is contingent on our thinking if we are to attain our joint goal of finding one another. Importantly, in the current approach any time we create a joint goal, this must involve a kind of negotiation that inherently involves such mental coordination— because I only want to engage in the collaborative activity if you do also (and you feel the same about me), and so we must both assess the other's propensities, which depend on their assessment of our propensities, and so on. There are many other kinds of social interactions, including competitive interactions, that involve some form of intention-reading or mindreading, but they do not have the recursive structure of pure coordination of this kind.

Human infants begin collaborating with others with joint goals and coordinated plans, as noted above, soon after their first birthdays, at about the same time they begin communicating cooperatively. In the Warneken and Tomasello (2007) study, infants as young as 14 months of age seemed to form joint goals (see also Ross and Lollis 1987), and in the Carpenter et al. (Carpenter, Tomasello, and Striano 2005) study infants as young as 12 months of age sometimes reversed roles in a simple collaboration. Graefenhein, Behne, Carpenter, and Tomasello (submitted) found that somewhat older children (around 3 years of age) were even sensitive to the normative dimension of the process. That is, these children reacted more strongly when the adult quit cooperating if they and the adult had begun the collaborative activity with an explicitly acknowledged commitment ("Let's go play that game, OK?), as opposed to cases in which the play activity had arisen by the adult joining the child unbidden. In all of these studies, infants and young children attempted to regulate the collaboration by communicating.

And what about cooperative communication? If, as I have been arguing, human cooperative communication is "designed" to operate in, and indeed to facilitate, mutualistic collaborative activities, then what should it look like? What should be its design features? One feature would certainly be that it takes advantage of the fact that collaborators are already acting together with joint goals and joint attention in the space of common conceptual ground—which of course it does. Another would be that it is often used to help others by informing them of things that would be interesting or useful to them (since that helps me)—which of course it is. And indeed, given the joint attention and common ground created by collaborative activities (involving recursive mindreading), participants should actually expect the other to be helpful, and expect the other to expect them to be helpful, and so on—which of course they do. In contrast, great ape intentional communication comprises almost exclusively requests aimed at individualistic goals in which others are used as social tools—which fits well with their basically individualistic motives in group activities such as hunting. This is of course not to say that modern humans cannot use their skills of cooperative communication for individualistic, competitive, and selfish ends—they can and they do—but even lying requires collaboration to get the deceptive message across and a sense of trust on the part of the recipient (or else the lying could not ever work), and so even here we see the cooperative infrastructure. Interestingly and importantly, whereas chimpanzees can conceal themselves from others (Melis, Call, and Tomasello 2006), there is still no experimental evidence that they can actively mislead others—perhaps because, to repeat, lying requires cooperative communication.

5.1.3   *Summary*

Thus the present hypothesis about the origins of co-operative communication is more than just another "just-so story" of what some human behavior "is good for." It is more because cooperative communication actually shares an infrastructure of shared intentionality with collaborative activities, and indeed it seems difficult to imagine how joint goals and attention, not to mention mutual assumptions of helpfulness and the communicative intention, could have arisen in contexts in which we were all operating solely for our own benefit or in competition. If human cooperative communication had arisen initially to enable more complex forms of competition and deception, then we would not expect to see a common cognitive infrastructure with collaborative activity, nor would we expect to see as its most basic motivation the desire to help others by providing them with information they need (which, to repeat, is actually a prerequisite assumption if lying is to succeed in fooling the recipient).

5.2   The Emergence of Cooperative Communication

We do not have a specific and detailed evolutionary story to tell here, but there are certain logical or at least plausible ordering relationships among the various components of human communication as we have laid them out so far. Our task now, therefore, is to propose some orderings of things that can take us from great ape intentional communication, based on the understanding of individual intentionality, to human cooperative communication, based on skills and motives of shared intentionality— using evolutionary processes known to be involved in the evolution of cooperation. The sequence we propose is organized around three basic processes by which cooperation is known to evolve, as tied to our three basic motives of human cooperative communication:

• to explain the granting of requests and the initial motive to help by informing, we invoke mutualism (the request is granted or the information is offered because it helps us both);

• to explain offering help by informing outside of mutualistic contexts, we invoke reciprocity and indirect reciprocity (help is offered because it adds to my reputation for co-operativeness so that others will want me as a cooperative partner—and help me in return); and

• to explain sharing emotions and attitudes, we invoke cultural group selection (emotions and attitudes are shared as a way of increasing common ground and solidifying group membership).

In the current account, most of this took place evolutionarily within the context of collaborative activities, for all of the reasons outlined in the preceding section, and within the gestural modality, for all of the reasons outlined in chapters 2 and 3—although at some point we must account for cooperative communication outside of collaborative contexts and the shift to the vocal modality.

5.2.1 Mutualistic Collaboration and Requesting Help

Our starting point is great ape group activities, which, as I have just argued, are not truly collaborative in the sense of being structured by joint goals, and great ape intentional gestural signals, which are used to spur others to desired actions but generally not within group activities. Our overall model for an initial move in the direction of human collaboration and cooperative communication is the two-stage model proposed by Hare and Tomasello (2005)—based on an analogy to processes of domestication.

First, since our nearest ape relatives are not so inclined to share the spoils of group activities, or indeed to share food freely in any situation, step one in the direction of human-like collaboration and cooperative communication is for individuals to become more tolerant, generous, and less competitive with one another, perhaps especially in feeding contexts. An interesting possibility is that this first step is represented by modern-day apes interacting with cooperative humans. In the study by Hirata and Fuwa (2006), for example, chimpanzees who did not solicit other chimpanzees to engage in a group activity quite readily solicited a presumably more helpful human. And recall that apes raised by humans learn to spontaneously point (and do other things) for those humans to request things from them imperatively, which they do not do with other apes (see section 2.3). Even within the species, chimpanzees solicit as a partner in group activities individuals whom they have learned are more helpful and tolerant (Melis, Hare, and Tomasello 2006a). All of this suggests that in human evolution greater tolerance among conspecifics would have been enough to begin moving in the direction of true collaboration as well as imperative pointing—with no further cognitive skills necessary beyond those of modern-day great apes.

The second step is that these individuals, who are coordinating actions with one another more regularly and tolerantly, would then be in a position for natural selection—given the appropriate ecological conditions—to specifically favor cognitive and motivational machinery supporting more complex collaborative interactions. As Bateson (1988, p. 12) puts it:

Once evolutionary stability of co-operative behavior was achieved . . . features that maintained and enhanced the coherence of the highly functional co-operative behavior would then have tended to evolve. Signals that predicted what one individual was about to do, and mechanisms for responding appropriately to them, would have become mutually beneficial.

What might be selected for in these tolerant, peacefully co-feeding individuals is the ability to create joint goals and joint attention. Thus, if at some point group hunting chimpanzees became more tolerant and less competitive about sharing the food at the end, then it does not matter who captures the monkey because the food will be shared in the end in any case. When we all expect to share the food in the end and we all know this together, then we can have—if the necessary cognitive abilities have evolved—a mutually known joint goal that "we" capture the monkey. And when individuals are pursuing a joint goal, each knows that what is relevant for her is also relevant for the others jointly—at least potentially. Joint attention can also arise from the bottom up, as it were, as when a strange animal appears on the horizon, we each see it, and then look to one another to confirm our shared interest—which does not derive from a current collaborative activity (though in many cases it derives from some past shared activity or experience). But the current proposal is that joint attention started (and starts today in human infants) top down in collaborative activities with joint goals.[1] Mutualistic collaboration is thus the birthplace of the common conceptual ground necessary for inferentially rich cooperative communication of the human kind.

In terms of communication specifically, as we are working toward our joint goal in mutualistic collaboration, it is to each of our advantages that we help the other—and we are also likely to understand attempts to request and offer help communicatively as we are in the common ground of the collaborative activity. In this context, the communicator's tendency to request help

1. Interestingly, it would seem difficult to get any kind of recursive processes going in the auditory domain alone—since auditory stimuli are broadcast to everyone simultaneously. In the visual domain, I see something, and to know whether you also see it I have to look at you (unlike audition). I also have to look at you to see if you see me seeing it, and so forth and so on. Thus, nocturnal animals with no vision, following this line of thinking, would never evolve joint attention.

and the recipient's tendency to simply help might naturally arise as a way of facilitating progress toward a joint goal. Note that chimpanzees do offer help to conspecifics on occasion, which means that the evolutionary process would have had something to work with as an initial state in the evolution of requesting help from others as a fundamental communicative motive. But they do not offer help in most group activities, or inform others helpfully in any activities, which means that the evolutionary process still has work to do. Note also that in mutualistic collaborative activities the difference between requesting help and offering help by informing is minimal. That is, if we are moving a log together toward a joint goal, if there is an obstacle in the way I can request that you remove it to help us, or I can inform you of its presence which I assume will lead you to want to remove it to help us. If we are outside of mutualistic contexts, the difference between requesting help (I want you to move that stone because it will help me toward my goal) and helping by informing (I want you to notice that stone because it is impeding you toward your goal) is much greater.

An analogy here might be instructive. It is an interesting morphological fact that of all the primates only humans have highly visible eye direction (because of white sclera; Kobayashi and Koshima 2001), and indeed even human infants tend to follow the eye direction over the head direction of others, whereas great apes tend to follow the head direction over the eye direction of others (see also Tomasello et al. 2007). Why should this be?

There must be some advantage to the human individual that she "advertise" her eye direction for others, and this would seem to assume a predominance of situations in which the individual may count on others using that information collaboratively or helpfully, not competitively or exploitatively. We may think of communicative behaviors that serve to advertise the internal states of individuals in the same way. For example, we may think of cooperative requests as "advertisements" of my internal state of wanting, which can only be adaptive in situations in which it is to my benefit for others to know about my wanting—prototypically when they have their own reasons for wanting to help satisfy my desires, as in mutualistic collaboration. It is thus in these kinds of contexts that human beings might have developed the tendencies and skills to simply inform others of their desires, or to inform others of things that might be useful to them both.

In terms of the communicative devices themselves, the most obvious candidate for requesting help, and perhaps even offering help, in mutualistic collaborative activities is pointing. Mutualistic collaborative activities take place in the here and now and are structured very powerfully, in a top-down manner, by joint goals and joint attention. Pointing should thus be sufficient in most instances to get the job done. We could even communicate successfully about the missing tool by pointing in the direction where it probably resides currently. Iconic gestures are probably not possible at this early stage because they require a Gricean communicative intention to mark them as something other than vacuous actions in the wrong context (see below). However, if individuals at this point were capable of some skills of imitation, then naturally occurring intention-movements (e.g., "pushing" someone toward the location where they should be operating from) could not only be created by ontogenetic ritualization, as in apes, but perhaps could be imitated as well.

And so, our proposal is the relatively uncontroversial one that human collaboration was initially mutualistic—with this mutualism depending on the first step of more tolerant and food-generous participants. The more novel part of the proposal is that mutualistic collaboration is the natural home of cooperative communication. Specifically, skills of recursive mindreading arose initially in forming joint goals, and this then led to joint attention on things relevant to the joint goal (top-down) and eventually to other forms of common conceptual ground. Helping motives, already present to some degree in great apes outside of communication, can flourish in mutualistic collaboration in which helping you helps me. And so communicative requests for help—either for actions or for information—and compliance with these (and perhaps even something in the direction of offering help by informing) were very likely born in mutualistic collaboration. At this point in our quasi-evolutionary tale, then, we have, at a minimum, pointing to request help and a tendency to grant such requests—with perhaps some offers of help in the form of useful information—in the immediate common ground of mutualistic collaborative interactions.

5.2.2 Indirect Reciprocity and Helping by Informing

Human beings help one another (including by informing) and request help from one another in many situations outside of mutualistic collaboration. And so we have to account for this generalization from the original adaptive situation. But offering help and responding positively to requests for help outside of mutualistic contexts involve something in the direction of altruism, one individual subordinating its interests to another's, and this requires special explanation. Again, I cannot even begin to give a full account of the evolution of human altruism, so here I offer just a few thoughts on how it might have gone in the case of cooperative communication.

Chimpanzees already do some helping (Warneken and Tomasello 2006; Warneken et al. 2007). What this is based on is not exactly clear, although there are some suggestive data for direct reciprocity—helping the individual who helped you—in chimpanzees' natural interactions (de Waal and Lutrell 1988). But it is unlikely that this direct reciprocity is wide-ranging or robust, and it almost certainly is not present when food is involved. In a field study, Gilby et al. (2006) found that sharing meat after a hunt was not associated with the recipient "repaying" the donor later reciprocally with either sex or support in fights (although see Watts and Mitani 2002). And, again, in the studies of Silk et al. (2005) and Jensen et al. (2006)—although not testing reciprocity directly—individuals did not help others get food, even if their history with those others was as parent, child, or ally.

In any case, helping outside of collaborative interactions would seem to require some kind of reciprocity. Given the limitations of direct reciprocity, a good candidate is indirect reciprocity, in which individuals choose to help or cooperate with others who have good reputations for helping and cooperating in general (Nowak and Sigmund 1998; Panchanathan and Boyd 2003). Evidence that chimpanzees do indeed form judgments about others relevant to their reputations was provided by Melis, Hare, and Tomasello (2006b). In that study, chimpanzees needed a partner to help them obtain food, and there were two potential partners available (both novel to them in this context). One partner turned out to be a poor partner—a dominant male who usually attempted to monopolize the situation—and the other turned out to be a good partner. After only a small amount of experience with each of these partners, chimpanzees began choosing the better partner almost exclusively. This shows that noncooperators pay a price for their selfishness and competitiveness by being excluded from attractive opportunities for mutualistic collaboration (and the individuals who shun them basically pay no price for this—it is not costly punishment and so there is no second-order problem of altruism here).

That fact that individuals choose partners for mutualistic collaboration based in some sense on their reputation means that individuals who understand this may now seek to enhance their reputations by public acts of helping and cooperation, assuming that they understand that others are observing and assessing them. Therefore, in the context of nonmutualistic activities in which the individual does not benefit at all, she might still offer help to others, including by offering information she thinks will be helpful or relevant to them, in order to enhance her reputation as a helpful person—whom others will want to cooperate with in the future. Another possible ultimate cause of helping by informing is so-called showing off (by means of a costly signal of fitness; Zhavi and Zhavi 1997) in which, in the context of sexual selection, I show my social power by exhibiting my knowledge of useful things. Of special importance in this regard might be informing others of things relevant to the reputations of others in the group (gossiping; see Desalles 2006). Another important adaptive context for informing may have been pedagogy (Gergely and Csibra 2006), especially of one's own offspring as this then brings benefits of inclusive fitness (kin selection) to the informing act. But still, even though these were probably important derivative functions, the common cooperative infrastructure of human collaboration and communication suggests that collaborative activities were the original home of human cooperative communication.

Once we get beyond requesting and into informing, communication about things displaced in time and space becomes much more of a need. Although human pointing enables the communication of much more complex messages than ape attention-getters, it is obviously still limited in a number of ways. Most critically, the common conceptual ground, which is the fundamental source of pointing's communicative power, is also a source of its limitations. Thus, if you and I have much experience together at a watering hole and sometimes see a gazelle there, and today you see me returning from that direction and pointing excitedly back there, you will probably assume there is now a gazelle there; I have succeeded in referring to an absent entity by pointing. But, of course, if we do not share that previous experience, I cannot point to the absent referent; pointing is essentially impotent in situations in which the participants have little or no common ground, especially where large inferences are required. Thus, pointing will not be a very effective form of communication for teaching novices or young children how to do things. If I am engaged in a complex procedure of extracting tubers from underground with a stick, and I need your help in removing the dirt, if you have done this with me before I may simply point to the dirt covering my access point; but if you have never experienced this activity before, it is unlikely that a simple point will convey to you what you are supposed to do. For this same basic reason, pointing is unlikely to be a very effective means of communication between strangers. The almost complete dependence of pointing on common ground between communicator and recipient is thus both its strength and its weakness.

Iconic gestures rely on common ground in the same basic way, but a bit less so because more information is potentially in the gesture itself. And so I may gesture to my novice partner iconically how she is to dig out the dirt I want her to dig out, even if she has never done this before in this context (though she still needs to see my gesture as communicative and as relevant to our current activity). I may depict for a friend antelope movements and sounds to indicate its presence at the watering hole (perhaps pointing there too), even if we have never before seen one there together. And iconic gestures should be more effective than pointing, in many contexts, with strangers. But there is a reason why iconic gestures emerge later in human ontogeny and are absent in apes. To use an iconic gesture one must first be able to enact actions in simulated form, outside their normal instrumental context—which would seem to require skills of imitation, if not pretense. But even more importantly, to comprehend an iconic action as a communicative gesture, one must first understand to some degree the Gricean communicative intention; otherwise the recipient will suppose that the communicator is simply acting bizarrely, trying to run like an antelope or to dig a hole for real when the context is clearly not appropriate (the act must thus be "quarantined" from interpretation as a real action, in a sense similar to that proposed by Leslie 1987 for pretense). Iconic gestures thus presumably derive from ape intention-movements—incipient real actions—but add a representational dimension based on simulation/ imitation and the recipient's comprehension of the communicative intention. The reward for mastering iconic gestures is the ability to communicate more effectively about a wider range of situations to people with whom one shares less experience (Donald 1991).

From a functional perspective, when people start actually wanting to be helpful so as to enhance their reputations, and they can count on others wanting to be helpful as well, they start informing them of things freely. Indeed, even individualistic imperatives can turn into cooperative imperatives: I do not tell you what to do, but I merely inform you of my desire because I know you will want to help me fulfill it. Importantly, it is in these ultrahelpful contexts that the Gricean communicative intention emerges. The sequence might go something like this (C = communicator, R = recipient):

· C's goal is that R know something: either some helpful or interesting information (in an informative) or his own internal states (in a cooperative request).

· R understands that C wants her to know something, and she wants to be cooperative and accept this information because she trusts that it will be something that either is helpful to her directly (if it is an informative) or else will provide her with the opportunity to be helpful herself (if it is a cooperative imperative) and thus to enhance her reputation by granting C's request.

• C recognizes that R wants to understand and respond to his desire for her to know something, at least partly because she trusts his cooperativeness; and so now in addition to letting her know that he wants her to know something, he emphasizes to her that he wants her to know that he wants her to know something—in the expectation that, given her helpful attitude, her knowing that he wants this will make her try harder to understand and comply.

This kind of reasoning—what I have called cooperative reasoning—is fundamentally different from practical reasoning either about one's own actions or about those of others individually. In the words of Levinson:

There is an extraordinary shift in our thinking when we start to act intending that our actions should be coordinated with—then we have to design our actions so that they are self-evidently perspicuous. (1995, p. 411)

One can easily imagine that the communicative actions described in the first step of this sequence (essentially Sperber and Wilson's 1986 "informative intention") actually held at one point early in human evolution—again, especially in mutualistic contexts. I want you to see that food so you will get it, since we are going to share it in the end (and I do not really care one way or the other if you know that I want you to see the food); for example, I pull a branch of berries down in front of your face. But once the communicator appreciates that the recipient really cares about what he wants, then he can exploit this by making sure that she knows that he is trying to inform

her either of some interesting information or his internal
states; for example, if you do not notice the berries in
front of your face, I might vocalize or otherwise draw
your attention to me and the fact that I have pulled these
berries in front of your face intentionally for a reason
(mutually assumed to be a cooperative reason—so you
should try to discern it). None of this is possible until
both participants know together that they both want to
be helpful. It is also interesting to note that it is highly
unlikely, as noted above, that this sequence would have
played out initially in iconic gestures. I can easily direct
your attention to something in the immediate environment without highlighting my authorship so much, for
example, as apes do by pointing, and then rely on nature
taking its course as you see and react to that thing as
predicted. But when I gesticulate at you, for example by
pantomiming an antelope, I cannot inform you without
at the same time letting you know that I want to inform
you—no informative intention without a communicative
intention—because unless you recognize my communicative intention the action will just be bizarre and communicate nothing.

Complying with the requests for help of others and
indeed offering help to others thus likely began in mutualistic collaboration, where compliance is always adaptive because it benefits the self, and then generalized to
nonmutualistic situations owing to their positive effects
on the reputation of the helper. Two interesting related
phenomena are these. First, humans quite often—and

almost always in certain situations—express gratitude by thanking someone who has helped them. This specialized communicative function evolved because it benefits the reputation of both participants. When I thank you for a favor I have advertised to anyone in the neighborhood that you are a helpful person, and I have also made it clear that anyone who helps me can expect to get this kind of good publicity—people want to help grateful recipients who advertise their altruism to others. Second, another important dimension of politeness is not ordering people to do things (as in individualistic imperatives), but rather simply expressing one's desire (as in cooperative imperatives), perhaps even very indirectly, and letting them volunteer—after which they may be thanked because they did it of their own free will and not under order (Brown and Levinson 1978). One interpretation of this behavior is that in asking you a favor one incentive I am offering is that you will be allowed to do it freely (so you get credit for it as a voluntary act) and then I will thank you publicly in return. In a sense, in expressing gratitude and in asking for favors only indirectly, one is making sure that the one doing the favors gets a reputation benefit for having done them. The combination of such processes with social norms leads to emotions such as guilt, publicly expressed as apologies, when one person does not help another as she should have.

We thus have now, in our quasi-evolutionary story, humans who respond to requests and offer helpful and interesting information to others relatively freely, even outside of mutualistic contexts—using both pointing and iconic gestures to do so. A critical question now is how such behaviors might have generated sanction-carrying social norms governing this helpfulness. This is a very difficult question, far beyond my competence and purview. But for now, I can at least point to the fact that in a group of individuals capable of recursive mindreading and also concerned with their reputations—so that everyone knows together that everyone is worried about their reputation—mutual expectations of helpfulness could easily arise. Mutual expectations are not norms because they have no punitive force, but they are one step in that direction. And so we can posit at this point the kinds of mutual expectations of helpfulness so crucial for displaying one's communicative intention and having it recognized with appropriate relevance inferences from others—but with normative force coming from another direction, to which we now turn.

5.2.3   Cultural Group Selection and Sharing Attitudes

All of the studies of great ape social learning and imitation that include human children as a comparison find that quantitatively, if not qualitatively, children learn from others in a much more detailed fashion (see Whiten et al. 2004 for a review). One possible reason for this is that humans focus to a greater extent than apes on the actual actions performed (as opposed to the results, or desired results, in the environment). This more action-based approach might possibly have come as a result of humans' need to learn from others imitatively in human-specific situations, such as complex toolmaking, and would presumably be helpful in creating iconic gestures that simulate real events.

However, there is another dimension to imitation not typically highlighted in experimental studies, and this is the so-called social function of imitation (Uzgiris 1981; Carpenter 2006). It is well known in social psychology, for example, that one way of expressing solidarity with others in a group is to behave like them, dress like them, talk like them, express attitudes like theirs, and, in general, to be like them. The gist of this idea is captured very nicely by the moment in the movie *ET* in which the children face the child-sized alien in their bedroom, and the little girl stares at him and slowly raises her index finger. When the friendly beast looks back at her and slowly raises his index finger in return, the children (and the audience) gasp in recognition: he is like us (and so could potentially be one of us)! The reverse side of this, of course, is that human groups discriminate against others that are not like them, and they go to great pains to devise ways for marking explicitly who is one of them and who is not. Most obviously, anyone who does not speak our language is not one of us, but also anyone who does not dress like us, or eat like us, or paint his face like us, or worship like us, or all kinds of other things. To an unprecedented degree, human groups mark themselves to make sure of group membership, even having group-specific greetings—a unique kind of speech act—that serves, in part, to solidify group membership. On the psychological level, the way that human infants come into this in-group/out-group way of living is by imitating those around them and even conforming to them, so as to be like them—even leading to regional accents in languages. But more than just being like others, humans also want to be liked by others, and one way of cultivating affiliation and liking is by sharing emotions and attitudes about the world in various kinds of gossip, narrative, and expressive speech acts within the social group. In both the case of wanting to "be like" others and to "be liked by" others, failures lead to negative emotions: shame or guilt if I behave in deviant ways that violate a social norm, and loneliness or isolation if no one likes me—which presumably evolved precisely to help ensure attention to and compliance with social norms of both helpfulness/reciprocity and also conformity/solidarity/affiliation.

This imitation/conformity/solidarity/affiliation dimension of things has two important consequences for the evolution of human cooperative communication, and they concern very different aspects of the process. First, the desire to cultivate affiliations with others forms the basis for one of the three basic motives in the cooperation model of human communication: the desire to share emotions and/or attitudes with others. Although it may not seem sharply distinct from the informing motive in

general—one could say that when I express my enthusiasm for a painting, I am simply informing you of my
attitude—studies with human infants (reviewed in the
previous chapter) show that my goal in expressing my
enthusiasm is not, as in the case of informatives, to
provide you with information that you want or need, but
rather to elicit from you an expression of attitude that
aligns with mine. When we feel the same about some
common experience, this makes us feel psychologically
closer. To appreciate the importance of this process, one
need only imagine what would happen if one's spouse
one day began expressing contempt for all of one's best
friends and most beloved objects and activities in the
world. Similarly, when people are asked to explain love
affairs begun without personal contact on the Internet, a
common response is that "we share so much," "we like
the same things," and so forth. A well-established finding
in social psychology is that people tend to affiliate with
others who share their perspective and attitudes about
things (Schachter 1959). And much of the reminiscing in
personal narratives characteristic of families or friends
reuniting after separation serves to cement relationships
as well, with an especially important part being the
shared evaluations of the past events as they are narrated
("It was so cool when we . . . ," "It was so sad when
he . . ."; Bruner 1986). It is thus possible that sharing emotions and attitudes serves a kind of group identity function for humans and that this is a uniquely human function.
And so the proposal is that expressive-declaratives,

so important in early infant communication and affiliation, represent a distinct social intention for sharing emotions, and indeed, one could even look at expressive-declaratives as particularly proactive efforts to expand common ground with others, as a way of affiliating with them in ever deeper ways.

The second consequence of the imitation/conformity/solidarity/affiliation dimension of things for communication concerns the establishment of norms. Pressure from the group for the individual to conform is the essence of social norms; the ultimate threat is being ostracized or even physically excluded from the group. And so we noted above that on the basis of mutual understanding in a group that everyone wants to help and is also concerned with their reputation for helping, humans might have evolved mutual expectations about helpfulness in communicative situations. But when we add in pressure to conform with group expectations (if asked, I simply must pass the salt), we get full-fledged norms such as norms of helpfulness in communicative situations, with accompanying social sanctions for violations (e.g., loss of reputation, shunning). Our formula for norms, at least in the case of communication, then, consists in mutual expectations about behavior and a concern for reputation plus pressure to conform to group expectations—or else! It is interesting to note, in this regard, that whereas humans have norms for helpfulness in communication—apparent in obligations for informing in certain situations (e.g., informing you that your car lights are on if I discover this)—such norms do not govern expressive-declaratives. There is no social sanction for not expressing oneself to others or for not agreeing with such expressions—only a personal loss in terms of diminished opportunities for friendship and affiliation.

Interestingly and importantly, great apes seem to have none of this. That is to say, there is no good evidence that apes imitate others only for social conformity and/or solidarity; they do not use expressive-declaratives in their communication (even with humans); and their communication does not seem to be governed by any social norms (nor does any other aspect of their lives). And so, although great apes share with humans the ability to learn instrumental actions from others socially, perhaps even via imitation in some instances, the social function of imitation and the resulting pressures to conform to group norms would seem to be uniquely human. It is certainly possible that this dimension of things evolved in the normal way, working on individuals. But I myself am convinced—for reasons that would take us too far afield to recount—that humans evolved this "wanting to be like others" dimension of things as a way of maximizing within-group conformity and between-group difference, in the context of multilevel selection on the group as a whole: so-called cultural group selection (Richerson and Boyd 2005). This very controversial process is probably not critical to our story here, but if groups are indeed possible units of selection in evolution—especially in the context of cultural processes for conformity within groups and differentiation between groups—it would help to explain why humans, and only humans, have developed systems of linguistic communication that are effective *not* with all members of their species, as for all other organisms, but only with those who have grown up in their same cultural group.

Finally, let us return to the Gricean communicative intention. We saw above that the functioning of the Gricean communicative intention can be understood only in light of various kinds of mutual understandings and expectations among communicators, that is, specifically, when everyone knows together that everyone expects helpfulness and cooperation, and when everyone knows together that everyone is concerned with reputation. But there are not just expectations, but actual norms governing the process. One important function of the Gricean communicative intention—above and beyond the communicator alerting the recipient that she wants something from her—is that it essentially makes everything public, what some theorists call "wholly overt." This means that the norms apply and cannot be avoided. If somehow we take things out of the public space, by not expressing a communicative intention, then the norms do not apply. Consider again our example from chapter 3 concerning hidden authorship. If I place my empty wine glass in a conspicuous position, hoping my host will see it and fill it, but (for reasons of politeness) making sure he does not see me do it and so does not view it as an overt request, no norms apply. If my host sees my empty glass, and even if I notice him see it (and even if he looks in the mirror and notices me noticing him see it), still no norms apply. But if I signal him overtly by brandishing the empty glass in his direction, in most cases this would trigger a norm—we know together that he has seen the empty glass and presumably has inferred from the brandishing act toward him that I want a full glass, and so he *must* deal with it in some way, or pretend that he did not in fact see my act. Or consider an analogous example. My colleague and I know together that she has to fetch her child at 5:30 every day, and we are talking in the hall at around that time. She very subtly glances down at her watch. I see this. If my seeing it is not made public, I can keep talking and ignore it. But if she glances down at her watch ostensively—wanting us to notice this together—I cannot ignore it, but must deal with it in some way.

A major function of the Gricean communicative intention, then, is to place my communicative act in the public space so that all the norms apply. When I address you, if you acknowledge this address, you must engage with me communicatively. If I do not address you, but simply hope you will notice something and act in a certain way, then you do not have to engage with me. If you engage with me, and I ask you a favor or inform you of something publicly, then you must comply or accept—or give a reason why you will not. Of course, you could pretend that you did not understand the message, but when comprehension becomes public then the norms of helpfulness apply. On the more positive side, when something is in the public space it is relevant to my positive reputation as well. Thus, when I engage you and you accept, you are ratifying that you are playing the same game that I am. When I ask you a favor and you comply, your reputation benefits. When I offer useful information, my reputation benefits. And so, by making the communicative act public the Gricean communicative intention structures human communication so that all of the norms and their sanctions are in force. Anyone who doubts the complexities that can result from this form of publicly expressed communication need only consider the incredible intricacies resulting from considerations of politeness in cooperative communication (see, e.g., Brown and Levinson 1978).

Again, it almost goes without saying that all of this is uniquely human. There is no evidence that nonhuman primates create anything resembling a public space in which considerations of reputation and normative sanctions are at play. One other interesting aspect of this normative dimension is that it is used to sanction antisocial uses of the powerful new tool of cooperative communication. That is to say, skills of cooperative communication—and all of the assumptions of cooperativeness underlying them—create the possibility of lying. Lying usually works because recipients assume that communicators are being helpful, including truthful, unless there is a specific reason to believe otherwise. The social group attempts to correct this "unintended consequence," this flaw in an otherwise beautiful tool, by making public strong social norms against lying so that anyone caught lying (for no good reason) suffers a significant reputational decrement. Thus, whereas great apes can conceal things from others (Melis, Call, and Tomasello 2006), there is no evidence that they can actively mislead or lie to others—because they do not communicate cooperatively with the mutual expectation that both participants are attempting to be helpful, including truthful.

5.2.4 Summary

What we have done here is to use the three basic processes that evolutionary biologists use to explain the emergence of cooperation (other than kin selection) and apply them to the three basic motives human cooperative communication. Thus, to explain the granting of requests we invoked mutualism, to explain offering help by informing we invoked indirect reciprocity, and to explain the sharing of emotions and attitudes we invoked cultural group selection. We tried to explain how humans' motivations for helping and sharing in communication—the basic motives of shared intentionality—might have arisen as part and parcel of an adaptation for collaborative activities more generally. We thus proposed that the basic cognitive skill of shared intentionality—recursive mindreading—arose as an adaptation for collaborative activity specifically (given an initial adaptation in the direction of tolerance and generosity with food), leading to the creation of joint attention and common ground.

The combination of helpfulness and recursive mindreading led to mutual expectations of helpfulness and the Gricean communicative intention as a guide to relevance inferences, which could then come under social norms created by still another uniquely human propensity, in this case to be like and to be liked by others in this social group, as opposed to those other social groups. The initial communicative device in this scenario early on would almost certainly have been pointing (and some intention-movements), and then iconic gestures came into being only after the emergence of the Gricean communicative intention was there to "quarantine" it from misinterpretation. Where exactly in this process humans began to conventionalize their communicative devices is not known.

5.3   The Emergence of Conventional Communication

This rather complicated, though still somewhat sketchy, account was mainly about the social-cognitive, social-motivational infrastructure of human cooperative communication and how it evolved. But it would seem that we are still a long way from how humans today communicate with one another using one of the world's 6,000+ languages. But we are not so far, actually. The main point of these lectures is that most of what makes human communication so powerful is the psychological infrastructure that is present already in species-unique forms of gesturing such as pointing and pantomiming, and language is built upon, and relies totally upon, this infrastructure. Without this infrastructure, communicative conventions, like *gavagai*, are only sounds, signifying nothing.

Whereas pointing and pantomiming may be considered "natural" communication because they direct attention and imagination in ways that all humans can understand among one another, even with no previous contact, "conventional" communication uses arbitrary signs, and these require shared social learning experiences among all the members of the group (who all know, in principle, that they share these learning experiences). And this highlights a key theoretical point. Communicative conventions are defined by two separable characteristics (Lewis 1969). First and most critically, we all do something in the same way because that is the way everyone is doing it (and we all know this together): it is shared. Second, we could have done it differently if we had wanted to: it is, at least to some degree, arbitrary. But arbitrariness is a relative notion, and could indeed be seen on a continuum. Are certain obscene gestures "arbitrary," or are they iconic representations of real actions? Many such gestures were at one time iconic, and then became more arbitrary over historical time—but they were conventional, in the sense of shared, throughout. In any case, our proposal here will be that first came shared conventions, and then there was a kind of "drift to the arbitrary" over historical time. In this view, the most arbitrary forms of conventional communication—that is, linguistic communication in the vocal modality—could never have evolved *de novo*, but had to have evolved from, or by overlapping with, more naturally meaningful gestural conventions.

5.3.1 The Drift to the Arbitrary

Our model at this point, before the advent of communicative conventions, might be something like a modern-day, 12- to 14-month-old prelinguistic human infant: communicating regularly by pointing and occasionally using iconic gestures when pointing is not feasible. Perhaps combinations of these were at some point possible as well, such as pantomiming an antelope while pointing to the out-of-sight location where it is presumably grazing.

For the evolution of language, iconic gestures are especially important as they involve symbolic representation, typically of displaced referents, and indeed in the previous chapter we provided evidence that in children's development linguistic symbols supplant not pointing, but iconic gestures. Nevertheless, iconic gestures, like pointing, have communicative limitations as well, especially as compared with language. If I pantomime for you the act of digging to suggest to you, a novice, what you should now do (assuming you understand it as a communicative act), comprehension relies to some degree on your familiarity with digging in general and your assessment of what is needed now in the current situation. If I could simply tell you what to do with a conventional language, it might still depend on your past experience and your current assessment of the current situation to some degree, but much less so. But of course communicative conventions rely on a previous common history of social learning, and so it is also fair to point out that when we do not share that social learning history—as, for example, when two people who speak different languages attempt to communicate—iconic gestures actually are superior to conventional communicative devices, which are useless in this situation.

In any case, human groups at some point went beyond iconic gestures that needed to be invented anew on every occasion, and moved to communicative conventions. Conventions are ways of doing things that are somewhat arbitrary—there are other ways they could be done—but it is to everyone's advantage if everyone does it in the same way, and so everyone just does what everyone else is doing because that is what everyone is doing (Lewis 1969). This arbitrariness means that one cannot invent conventions on one's own. One can invent communicatively effective iconic gestures, but arbitrary communicative conventions require that they be "shared," so that everyone can rely on everyone else in the group knowing how the convention is used communicatively—which is obviously, again, at least a partial product of recursive mindreading. We have argued previously that the form of social learning required here is not just imitation, but role reversal imitation, in which each initiate to the convention understands that she can use the convention toward others as they have used it toward her, and vice versa—so that both producer and comprehender roles are implicitly present in both production and comprehension (Tomasello 1999).

But we are still left with the problem of how conventions get started in the first place. Invoking a process of explicit agreement—as in various kinds of social contract theories—is not really a viable option, as agreement presupposes an already existing means of communication, more powerful than the one to be invented, in which to formulate the agreement. But among organisms who already possess the cooperative communicative infrastructure we have laid out here, and who are also capable of collaboration and role reversal imitation, conventions can arise "naturally" as a result of a combination of shared and unshared experiences. Here is the kind of scenario that must have occurred at the dawn of arbitrary communicative conventions. First came some kind of cooperative iconic gesture. For example, perhaps a female of the genus *Homo* wishes to go digging for tubers. To get others to come with her, she pantomimes digging for them in exaggerated fashion in the direction in which tubers are normally found. The cavemates understand this gesture naturally, that is, they understand that this digging gesture is intended to depict a real instrumental action of digging. It is possible that some of them might then learn this gesture from her, by role reversal imitation, thus creating a shared communicative device that is conventional in the sense of being shared, and at least partially arbitrary in the sense that other gestures for this same function could certainly have been used.

But now let us assume the following extension of the scenario. Some individuals not familiar with digging, perhaps children, observe this "Let's go digging" gesture, and for them the connection between the ritualized digging gesture and the act of digging for tubers is opaque (though they do see that it is intended to be communicative); they think it is just intended to initiate leaving generally. They might then imitatively learn the gesture to initiate leaving (for something other than digging) on some future occasion—so that the original iconic grounding of the gesture is now completely erased. (This is not unlike the way that some motivated linguistic forms, such as metaphors, become opaque ["dead metaphors"] across historical time as new learners are not exposed to the original motivation.) One can possibly imagine in addition some kind of general insight at some later point that most of the communicative signs we use have only arbitrary connections to their intended referents and social intentions, and so, *voilà*, we can if we want make up new arbitrary ones as needed.

Another important outcome of this process is a kind of standardization of signs. That is, when iconic gestures are motivated, "the same" action or event is typically depicted in different ways depending on context; for example, opening a door is pantomimed in one way whereas opening a jar is pantomimed in another. This is typical of individually created home signs, for example (Goldin-

Meadow 2003b; see next chapter). However, as the iconicity becomes opaque for new learners the possibility arises for a stylized depiction of opening that is highly abstract and resembles no particular kinds of opening with particular objects. This is typical of many signs in conventionalized sign languages, and of course opens the way for the totally arbitrary and abstract signs characteristic of the vocal modality.

The first uses of communicative conventions were presumably as holophrases. This term has been used to mean different things (see Wray 1998), but here we simply mean a one-unit communicative act. But actually, from the communicative point of view, even in this simplest of cases, there is more than this going on. First of all, as should be clear from our previous arguments, the meaning conveyed by a one-unit utterance may be as complex as you wish—depending on the joint attentional context within which it is used. To return to our boyfriend's bicycle example from chapter 1, in such a context I communicate the same message whether I point, or say "There!," or say "There's your boyfriend's bicycle!" A single unit in the communicative signal says nothing about the complexity of what is communicated, as what is communicated depends not only on what is in the communicative signal explicitly but also on what is in the common ground implicitly. The second important consideration is that holophrases actually have two components. As outlined in chapter 3, the communicative act always comprises both an attention-directing, referential aspect, and a potential expression of motive. And so, if I want you to give me some water, I might say "Water" with a demanding intonation, whereas if we are walking down the sidewalk and I want to warn you of a puddle, I might say "Water!" with a surprised and warning tone of voice and/or facial expression. The holophrase, just like the pointing gesture, thus always has these two components—reflecting reference and motive—even if in some contexts the motive is assumed and so not expressed with any distinctive tone of voice or facial expression. The fact that from a functional point of view even holophrases are inherently composite might be seen as a kind of initial wedge into grammar.

The move to communicative conventions is thus, paradoxically, a natural one. No one intends, certainly not initially, to invent any conventions. Communicative conventions happen naturally as organisms who are capable of role reversal imitation and who already know how to communicate in fairly sophisticated ways—cooperatively, with gestures—imitatively learn one another's iconic gestures. Then individuals who are not privy to the iconic relation observe the communicative efficacy of the gesture and use it on that basis only, without any iconic motivation—at which point it has become, for these new users, arbitrary. This is what has been called a "process of the third kind," a sociological result of human intentional actions, but not something that any one person actually intended (Keller 1994; more on this in chapter 6).

5.3.2   The Switch to the Vocal Modality

We have so far remained fairly neutral about whether the earliest communicative conventions—after nonconventional pointing and pantomiming—were in the gestural or the vocal modality. But actually the first communicative conventions absolutely could not have arisen in the vocal modality, at least not given the starting point of nonhuman primate vocalizations. There are two essential points.

The first point is the same one documented at length in chapter 2. Nonhuman primate vocalizations are tethered quite tightly to emotions and so are not produced intentionally. Like almost all animal communication, they are essentially "coded" communication in the sense that individuals are born producing species-specific vocalizations and reacting to them in species-typical ways. Mother Nature has left almost no room for intentionality, cooperation, or inferences, beyond recipients associatively learning what often happens in conjunction with a vocalization (e.g., leopards tend to appear with certain bird alarm calls). And so for vocalizations to participate in intentional and ultimately cooperative communication, vocalizing individuals would first need to gain intentional control over them.

Human beings did of course at some point gain control over their vocalizations. But this brings us to the second problem. Vocalizations are not as good a medium for referential communication as are action-based gestures.

Thus, in terms of attention directing, it does not come naturally to any primates, including humans, to direct the attention of others by vocalizing to external targets. Indeed, what primates do naturally upon hearing someone vocalize is locate the vocalizer himself and identify his emotional state, and perhaps in some circumstances look around to locate the cause of his emotional state. What comes naturally to some primates, namely humans, is to direct others' attention visually in space through some form of action such as looking or pointing, based ultimately on the tendency of all primates to follow the gaze direction of others. In terms of directing imagination to absent referents, nonconventionalized vocalizations are again extremely limited. We might mimic some environmental sounds associated with important referents and so indicate them indirectly (e.g., the sound of a leopard—or a sound mimicking my normal emotional reaction to leopards), but again this would seem much less natural and productive than action-based pantomiming in the visual channel.

An interesting exercise might be to imagine two groups of young children who have never before communicated with anyone. Each is isolated on its own desert island, "Lord of the Flies" style. One group of children has their mouths bound with duct tape and the other has their hands tied behind their backs. (Apologies to all Human Subjects committees everywhere—I promise that the children are otherwise very well taken care of and that their parents have given informed consent before their bondage.) What kinds of communication might arise in each of these two groups? Well, we actually know quite a bit about what might happen in the case of the children unable to use their mouths, because deaf children born to parents who do not know any sign language actually develop with their parents and siblings quite sophisticated systems of action-based gestures that use pointing and pantomiming, so-called home sign (Goldin-Meadow 2003b). And if such children come together later, they develop even more sophisticated, conventionalized gestural sign systems with grammatical properties (as in Nicaraguan Sign Language; see next chapter). In the case of the children unable to use their hands, we do not know what would happen, of course. But it is difficult to imagine them inventing on their own vocalizations to refer the attention or the imagination of others to the world in meaningful ways—beyond perhaps a few vocalizations tied to emotional situations and/or a few instances of vocal mimicry. This is because humans have no natural tendencies in the vocal modality—analogous to following gaze directionally in space or interpreting actions as intentional in the gestural/visual modality—to serve as natural starting points. And so the issue of conventionalizing already meaningful communicative acts never arises. Incidentally, my own guess is that the children with their hands tied would probably end up trying to direct attention with their eyes and/or heads and to pantomime with their bodies.

The point of this fanciful, if perhaps a bit grotesque, exercise is simply to underscore that given the nature of the vocal medium, and especially its functions in the lives of primates in general, it is very difficult to even imagine the evolution of meaningful, human-like, cooperative communication—much less communicative conventions—exclusively in the vocal modality. But it is not difficult at all to imagine this happening in the action domain, and indeed we do not need to imagine it because, as noted, it sometimes does happen with deaf children born in special circumstances (there are also a number of well-documented cases of adult humans in special circumstances such as noisy factories, or for communication among different linguistic communities in such activities as trade, inventing gesture sign systems; Kendon 2004). Perhaps the fundamental reason underlying this difference is that for primates in general, and human beings in particular, we automatically follow gaze direction and we automatically see behavioral actions as intentional and inherently meaningful, including when they are directed to us. If the essence of human communication is its intentionality, then human action is the ultimate source of its meaning. It is not that this could not conceivably happen in the vocal modality in some other organisms; it is just that given how vocalizations work in primates—especially their close tie to emotions and their tendency to draw attention to themselves, their source, not to external referents—it is almost inconceivable.

And so, to get to human cooperative communication, in all its cooperative peculiarities, we must start with an action-based infrastructure. This must be based ultimately on the human propensity for gaze following and for pointing directionally to induce gaze following, and for interpreting the actions of others in intentional terms (and also on collaborative actions as the main source of the cooperative infrastructure). And so the question naturally arises: why did humans end up switching to the vocal modality? When humans today communicate they most often use both language and gesture, but language does most of the referential work (perhaps in combination with pointing) and gestures supplement this with imagistic signs conveying information not easily codified in language (McNeill 2005; Goldin-Meadow 2003a). However, there is no doubt that vocal language is predominant and even has a grammatical dimension (and sometimes a written version), which naturally occurring gestures do not. How did the vocal modality assume such preeminence?

In the history of thought on this question, there has been no shortage of hypotheses, as all of the classic gesture origins theorists have had something to say on the matter. One could thus posit, for example, the superiority of the vocal modality because: it enables communication at a longer distance; it enables communication in dense forests; it frees the hands so that one may be communicating and manually manipulating things simultaneously; it frees the eyes to be scanning for predators and other important information while communication is taking place auditorily; and on and on. Any or all of these may have played a role. What we would simply like to contribute as an additional possibility here, consistent with the account we have been giving in this chapter, is that communication in the vocal modality is more public than communication in the gestural modality. In discussing primate communication in chapter 2, we noted that primate vocalizations are broadcast indiscriminately so that everyone nearby hears them, and that gestures are directed to individuals. Having gone through a period of using gestures to direct communicative acts to individuals, the switch to the vocal modality might have meant that communicative acts are still directed at individuals—and indeed the communicative intention may be seen as a metasignal for communicating that this is "for you"—but at the same time the vocal medium enables anyone nearby to eavesdrop, as it were (this being preventable only by special acts such as whispering). This means that vocal acts are by default public, and so are relevant for reputation-making and the like.

Finally, our proposal for how the transition came about more specifically is that in the beginning the earliest vocal conventions were emotional accompaniments, or perhaps added sound effects, to some already meaningful action-based gestures—or at least some already meaningful collaborative actions. There was thus at least some redundancy, at least from the point of view of the recipient, in what the communicator was attempting to communicate with the gestures and the vocalizations. As humans gained more voluntary control over their vocalizations, they could have also used some vocal icons (e.g., making the sounds of a leopard), though like visual icons those could only have arisen after the emergence of the Gricean communicative intention. But at some point, in some situations, the vocalization came to be functional on its own—perhaps under pressure to communicate at longer distances, or for the communication to be in the public space, and so forth.

As one example, an especially interesting class of words, universal in all languages, is that of so-called demonstratives, which are often accompanied even today by pointing. In English, these are words such as *this* and *that* or *here* and *there*. The special nature of these words may be seen (as Wittgenstein 1953 first noted) by thinking about how children might learn them. For words such as nouns and verbs we may, given the appropriate joint attentional frame, point to something and name it for a child and she will learn the name. But how might we use pointing to teach children the words *this* and *that* and *here* and *there*? The answer is we cannot really. How does one point at *that* or *there*? The problem is that if we point to something in an attempt to teach these special words, the pointing is both part of the ostensive act intended to teach (to direct attention to the appropriate referent) as well as the meaning itself—a peculiar situation that, miraculously, does not seem to confuse children at all. They must in some way understand the redundancy involved.

In any case, demonstratives are clearly special because they are present in all known languages; they almost always embody a spatial component of distance from the speaker (as in *this* versus *that*); they are very often accompanied by pointing gestures; and they in all cases seem to be primitive, as they do not derive from other types of words (Diessel 2006). And so demonstratives may be the most basic communicative acts in the vocal modality— they often are used quite early in development by infants—quite plausibly because of their redundancy with the pointing gesture.[2]

Iconic gestures, of course, contain more referential specificity in the communicative act itself than do pointing gestures. Thus, without context, pointing to an animal running past could be intended to refer to almost anything, whereas pantomiming running or pantomiming a rabbit—while still fundamentally indeterminate without common ground—narrows things down quite a bit. I can only point and intend to indicate a rabbit that is not currently perceptible in very special circumstances, but I can pantomime an absent rabbit with the same intention quite easily. As noted in chapter 3, iconic

---

2. It is noteworthy that the crucial distinction between demonstratives and contentful words was first proposed by Bühler (1934/1990), whose theory of language highlighted the critical importance of the current interactive context in which we are speaking, the "deictic center," and its relation to the referential scene about which we are currently speaking. He thus proposed that, though small, demonstratives represent a separate class of items because they relate to this deictic center in a fundamentally different way than the contentful elements of language.

gestures are typically used for two basic functions: (i) to indicate an action, and (ii) to indicate an object associated with the enacted action (or, less often, the object depicted in a static display). We may then posit that the elements of language that correspond to iconic gestures are the referentially contentful words such as verbs (prototypically for actions) and nouns (prototypically for objects). On almost everyone's account verbs and nouns are the most fundamental types of content words in a language, as they are the only two classes that are plausibly universal, and most of the other types of words in a particular language can be shown to be historically derived from nouns and verbs (or else demonstratives; Heine and Kuteva 2002). The proposal would thus be that initially humans used some vocalizations while pantomiming actions or objects in a naturally meaningful way. These became conventional as others learned the vocalizations socially, conventionally, making the pantomime unnecessary—with vocalizations having some of the advantages listed above such as freeing the hands, long-distance communication, making things public, and so forth.

In terms of our quasi-evolutionary story, then, we may go all the way back to ape attention-getter and intention-movement gestures, then move through the human use of pointing and pantomiming as natural communicative acts (based on new skills and motivations of shared intentionality), and end in human communicative conventions for directing attention (demonstratives) and inducing the recipient to imagine intended referents (content words such as nouns and verbs and their derivatives).

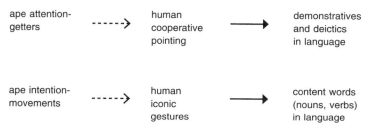

These two lines of correspondence simply reflect that in action-based gestures there are really only two things that humans can do to refer others' attention to things, at least naturally: we can direct their visual attention in space (as in the top row), or we can do something to evoke absent objects and events in the imagination (as in the bottom row). Human linguistic conventions simply provide us with special ways of doing these things based less on current common ground and more on a shared history of social learning.

We have not focused at all here on asking when particular things happened during human evolution; we have chosen, rather, to focus simply on the ordering of events. But one additional fact about human vocal-auditory competence is especially noteworthy. Recent genetic research has established that one of the key genes responsible for articulate human speech (the FOXP2 gene) came to fixation in the human population no more than 150,000 years ago with modern humans (Enard et al. 2002). It is difficult to imagine any function other than articulate speech, as used in modern languages, for the incredibly fine-grained motor control that this gene seems to enable. And so this very recent date of 150,000 years (right before modern humans starting spreading out all over the globe) might be taken as indicating a point in human evolution where good articulators— which presumably facilitate the use of a vocal language— were at a competitive advantage. We are not concerned here about a specific timeline for all of this, and so for now the important point is simply that these genetic data provide additional evidence that humans began using the vocal modality as their major modality of communication only very late in the process.

5.3.3 Summary

The argument is simply that one cannot jump straight to conventional communication. When we visit a foreign country with a very different language we can get lots of things done by the "natural" communicative acts of pointing and pantomiming, especially in collaborative activities such as transporting something together or in institutionalized activities occurring in shops or railway stations where common ground is solid. But we do almost nothing communicative in the vocal medium, other than express a few emotional reactions to things, and we basically never invent new vocal communicative conventions. We could theoretically invent new and arbitrary communicative conventions with our foreign friends even in the vocal modality, but only if there was a transition period in which these arbitrary devices were used redundantly with other communicative devices that were more naturally meaningful. Or perhaps, if there was a significant amount of time involved, arbitrary communicative conventions could arise among foreigners implicitly across a transmission chain in which the originators used naturally meaningful gestures and later learners reproduced that use without understanding its natural basis (typically because of some missing aspect of common ground). These are really the only two possibilities for the origin of communicative conventions, and they both involve an intermediate step of natural communication.

Our overall account, then, is an evolutionary sequence in which we go from (1) collaborative activities, to (2) "natural" action-based cooperative communication (first within collaborative activities and then outside them), and then to (3) conventional communication—with perhaps some parallel developments in the latter two as natural forms of communication began being conventionalized (and so became partially arbitrary) and also supplied a grounding for totally arbitrary vocal conventions.

5.4 Conclusion

If one paints with very broad strokes, it is possible to characterize much animal social behavior as cooperative, as one might even say that herd animals cooperate by staying close together, thereby discouraging predators.

But the human version of cooperation has unique characteristics, most clearly manifest in human cultural institutions from marriage to money to government, which exist because and only because of the collective practices and beliefs of human groups (Searle 1995). The cognitive bases for these special types of cooperative activity are the various skills and motivations for shared intentionality (Tomasello and Rakoczy 2003). Our proposal is thus that the cooperative structure of human communication is not an accident or an isolated human characteristic, but rather one more manifestation of humans' extreme form of cooperativeness. But exactly how this is so, and how it came to be this way, is far from straightforward.

Our story here has thus been both complicated and speculative. A graphic summary—from ape gestures to human linguistic conventions—is provided in figure 5.1. To recapitulate briefly, modern-day great apes—representing our model of the starting point—have many of the necessary components for human cooperative communication: they gesture flexibly to one another with imperative motives, they understand intentional action and engage in practical reasoning about it, they direct attention in the service of social intentions, they have some motives for helping others in some contexts, and they engage in complex group activities. But they do not seem to have skills and motivations of shared intentionality, and so their communication is not fully cooperative and inferential, in the sense that the recipient does not

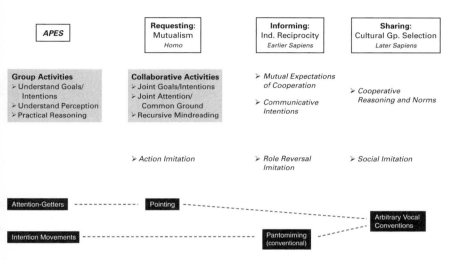

Figure 5.1
Evolutionary foundations of human cooperative communication.

attempt to infer the relevance of the communicator's referential act to his social intention, and so the communicator does not display his communicative intention for her ostensively—and there is no common conceptual ground, nor any mutual expectations or norms governing the process.

Human skills and motivations of shared intentionality emerged initially within mutualistic collaborative activities in creatures we will simply call *Homo* (second column in figure 5.1). But mutualistic collaborative activities could not emerge until humans first became more tolerant and generous in sharing the spoils of group activities (e.g., meat of the prey in group hunting), and then evolved a new piece of cognitive machinery: recursive mindreading. This critical component created joint goals, which then created joint attentional frames relevant to the joint goal, which then served as the common conceptual ground giving meaning to pointing and other cooperative communicative acts. In the context of mutualistic collaboration toward a joint goal, the tendency to request help and to supply help in return, as the initial motive of human cooperative communication, could flourish because in this context helping my partner helps me. And then helping could generalize to other contexts based on indirect reciprocity, which provided the second cooperative motive of offering help by informing so as to enhance reputation—as characteristic of a creature we will call *Early Sapiens* (third column in figure 5.1). Mutual assumptions of cooperation and the resulting Gricean communicative intention, in which the communicative act is put into the public space, resulted from recursive mindreading combining with these two cooperative motives of requesting and offering help and information. The third major motive, sharing attitudes, very likely came from a completely different source involving motives to be like groupmates and to be liked by groupmates—in a creature we will call *Later Sapiens* (fourth column in figure 5.1). This motive, combined with mutual expectations, led to norms governing many human activities, including cooperative communication.

In the context of this evolutionary pathway, great ape attention-getters transformed into human pointing (bottom row in figure 5.1). After this first step, ape intention-movements could then evolve into human iconic gestures for use in situations in which the common ground, or joint attentional frame, of the communicators made pointing a less than ideal mode of communication—given that the iconic gesture could be seen as communicative, based on an understanding of the Gricean communicative intention. Communicative conventions then emerged as outsiders imitated the iconic gestures for their perceived communicative ends but without all of the original common ground—leading, over time, to a kind of "drift to the arbitrary," then generalized to the creation of conventions. The switch to the vocal modality probably occurred for many reasons, one of which may have been that vocal communication puts things more readily into the public space. But the switch had to have used naturally meaningful, action-based gestures as a kind of temporary bridge, as "arbitrary" communicative conventions cannot arise without in some way piggybacking on already meaningful communicative activities.

6   The Grammatical Dimension

To imagine a language means to imagine a form of life.

—Wittgenstein, *Philosophical Investigations*

We have structured our evolutionary account of human cooperative communication around the emergence of the three major motives involved: requesting, informing, and sharing. We have also speculated on some of the processes by which naturally meaningful, action-based gestures used for these purposes could have at some point turned into full-blown communicative conventions, culturally created and learned. But at every step along the way, including even the spontaneous gestures of great apes, individuals also use sequences of gestures and/or conventions to communicate, and we have so far given no systematic account of these. What we need is an account that will enable us, in the end, to explain the emergence *not* of Language (with a capital L), but the emergence of 6,000 different human languages with 6,000 different sets of communicative conventions—including grammatical conventions for structuring multiunit utterances into coherent messages. Of course there will be universals—it is everywhere the same species with the same cognitive tools trying to do many of the same things—but there are particularities as well, and indeed the fact that humans do not have one single means of communication for all members of the species is already an evolutionary novelty that must be explained.

Our general approach is once again to focus on the three major motives of human cooperative communication: requesting, informing, and sharing. The basic idea is that the purpose for which one communicates determines how much and what kind of information needs to be "in" the communicative signal, and therefore, in a very general way, what kind of grammatical structuring is needed. Thus, since requesting prototypically involves only you and me in the here and now and the action I want you to perform, combinations of natural gestures and/or linguistic conventions require no real syntactic marking but only a kind of "simple syntax" in a grammar of requesting (even though with modern languages we may formulate quite complex requests). But when we produce utterances designed to inform others of things helpfully, this often involves all kinds of events and participants displaced in time and space, and this creates functional pressure for doing such things as marking participant roles and speech act functions with "serious syntax" in a grammar of informing. Finally, when we want to share with others in the narrative mode about a complex series of events with multiple participants playing different roles in different events, we need even more complex syntactic devices to relate the events to one another and to track the participant across them, which leads to the conventionalization of "fancy syntax" in a grammar of sharing and narrative.

Although the basic steps in this sequence of different kinds of grammatical structuring must have taken place before human beings dispersed across the globe, after this dispersal different groups of humans conventionalized different ways of fulfilling the functional demands of simple, serious, and fancy syntax. This structuring was embodied in grammatical constructions—complex patterns of multiunit utterances—which were conventionalized in different groups via grammaticalization and other cultural-historical processes. The way these processes operate depends crucially on processes of shared intentionality and cooperative communication in combination with other cognitive processes and constraints. As in the case of the origin of communicative conventions in general, the origin of grammatical conventions thus highlights the ongoing dialectic between biological and cultural evolution.

With regard to modality, the evolutionary hypothesis is, again, that even when grammar is involved most of this story played out in the gestural modality. This is supported by the fact that conventional sign languages with full grammars seem to arise quite rapidly and easily when certain sociological conditions hold (e.g., deaf people interacting in certain kinds of communities). The most well-publicized recent examples are Nicaraguan Sign Language (Senghas, Kita, and Özyürek 2004) and Bedouin Sign Language (Sandler et al. 2005), which have each developed complex grammatical structures in only a few generations. The upshot is that while most linguists typically think of sign languages as unusual expressions of the human capacity for vocal language, it is also possible that the human capacity for language evolved quite a long way in the service of gestural communication alone, and the vocal modality is actually a very recent overlay. If humans were actually adapted for communicating in complex ways gesturally, with voluntarily controlled articulate speech being a recent evolutionary modification, this would go a long way toward explaining the naturalness of complex human communication in the gestural modality.

6.1   The Grammar of Requesting

Based on the account given in chapter 5, at some point after humans started down their own evolutionary path—labeled the *Homo* stage in figure 5.1—they began engaging in mutualistic collaboration. This created some joint attentional frames and common ground within which they could request things from others in more elaborate ways than, for example, apes pointing for humans—and the recipients were likely to comply. They also had some skills of imitation at this point, and so some of their intention-movements may have been socially learned as well. But, on our hypothesis, at this moment in evolutionary time human communication was not yet fully cooperative—they were requesting but not informing, and so there were no indirect, cooperative requests that asked others to do things displaced in time and space (as fully linguistic creatures can do).

Here we would like to explore what the grammatical structuring of communication at this stage might have looked like. We do this by looking at several extant situations that are comparable to *Homo* in several dimensions—"linguistic" apes, deaf children using home sign, and nascent language learners—though we should emphasize at the outset that none of them is comparable in all dimensions. Our goal will be to characterize a kind of grammar of requesting with a simple syntax adapted for getting others to do things in the here and now. Maximally, this will involve gesture combinations that create new meanings, but without any syntactic marking, as this would serve no function in communication whose reference is confined to me and you in the here and now and the action I want you to perform (to repeat, we focus here only on these immediate requests and not on indirect and other more cooperative requests that are possible after a complex language has been developed). But before this, we begin by specifying, very briefly, our starting point in apes' natural gestural sequences, which have no grammatical structure at all.

6.1.1   Great Ape Gesture Sequences

In their natural communication with one another, chimpanzees and other great apes quite often produce sequences of gestures in a single context, toward a single social goal. In the systematic study of Liebal, Call, and Tomasello (2004), about one-third of all gestural communicative acts of chimpanzees contained more than one gesture. These sequences contained pretty much all possible combinations of intention-movements and attention-getters, from the visual, auditory, and tactile modalities (see Call and Tomasello 2007 for similar findings with the other great ape species).

Almost 40 percent of these gesture sequences consisted of simple repetitions of the same gesture more than one time. The other sequences were sequences of different gestures—raising the possibility of some kind of grammatical structure in the sense of creating new meanings not possible with single gestures, or even in the sense of different gestures playing different roles in the communicative act. However, systematic analysis of these sequences provided no evidence for such grammatical structure. On the basis of several different analyses, what seemed to be happening was that the communicator used one gesture, and then when the recipient failed to respond in the desired way, he produced another one right afterward—perhaps in some cases even in anticipation of a lack of response. In no analysis could investigators discover any new messages communicated by a sequence that could not have been communicated by one of the individual gestures alone. As noted in chapter 2, there was also no structuring based on manipulating the attention of the other; that is, it did not happen that chimpanzees preferentially used an attention-getter as the first gesture to secure the recipient's attention and then followed this with an intention-movement of some kind (i.e., nothing resembling topic-focus structure either).

It is of course possible that investigators have not been looking for grammatical structure in ape gesture sequences in the right way. But based on all available analyses, the gesture sequences of great apes seem to contain basically no relational or grammatical structuring of any kind—and there are no reports of anything resembling grammatical structure in the vocal communication of any great ape species either. We thus use the term "sequence" and not "combination," which we will reserve for multiunit messages with at least some kind of structuring creating a new meaning.

6.1.2 Great Ape "Language" with Humans

There has been much controversy over the grammatical structure, or lack thereof, of the signed utterances produced by language-trained great apes. (Note again that attempts to teach apes new vocalizations of any kind have all failed.) Much of this controversy is due to lack of systematic, quantitative data. However, there are now two studies of the gestural productions of these special animals that have the kind of data needed: one with five chimpanzees using a sign language, and one with a bonobo named Kanzi using an artificially created system. These studies both used systematic samples of naturally occurring communicative interactions, with two independent observers for a significant portion of these, enabling quantitative estimates of interobserver reliability.

First, in a recent study, Rivas (2005) systematically analyzed four corpora from five chimpanzees over a seven-year period—consisting of the well-known Washoe and friends—trained in something like American Sign Language (ASL) by the Gardners, Fouts, and collaborators. There were 22 hours total of taped interaction involving the various chimpanzees with one of several human caretakers (with a variety of types of interobserver reliability estimates for the different measures taken—all of which were reasonably high). Excluding immediate imitations and unintelligible sequences, there were 2,839 communicative acts. The apes both "pointed" (and also used some other natural gestures such as begging) and used ASL signs, sometimes in combination.

The first result, as noted in chapter 2, was that of the acts that had a clear communicative function (and excluding responses to questions), 98 percent were requests for objects or actions; the remaining 2 percent were classified as "naming," which mostly came in the context of a kind of naming/recognition game with a picture book. In a subset of utterances called "unprompted," because they initiated an interaction, 100 percent of the acts were requests. Because the utterances were almost all requests, the action words in the two-unit and three-unit utterances were almost exclusively about very concrete physical actions that the animals liked such as eating, drinking, and playing games such as chase, and the objects were almost always things that the humans controlled and the apes coveted. These desired actions/objects typically were signed first in the sequence, followed by some kind of "wild card" or requestive sign or an indication of the person that should fulfill the request. We thus get such things as "FLOWER there(point)," "TOOTHBRUSH gimme(beg gesture)," "BALL GOOD," "GUM HURRY," and so forth—all as requests. The conclusion of Rivas (2005, p. 413) is that this ordering is best interpreted as "the expression of an acquisitive motivation": "The objects and action signs are produced first because these are the more important or salient signs of the (usually request) utterances, specifying what is requested. The request markers THAT/THERE/YOU/GOOD/HURRY are produced last because they are less important (not specifying what is requested) and function to add emphasis or to spur the human into action."

The second main result was that the utterances had no real grammatical structure and indeed were mostly very short: 67 percent were one-unit utterances, 20 percent were two-unit utterances, and 13 percent were more than two-unit utterances. Because all of the utterances during the sampled period of time were analyzed, it was

possible to see that there were many "unrelated combinations" that made little sense, such as "DRINK GUM" and
"CLOTHES EAT." There were other sequences, however,
that seemed to embody the kinds of semantic relations
characteristic of young children's requests, such things as
"action + object" ("EAT CHEESE"), "action + location"
("TICKLE there(point)"), and so forth. It may be that in
these sequences the chimpanzees were simply indicating
two different aspects in a single requestive situation,
without relating them to one another explicitly. But it
would seem reasonable to suppose, as in the case of
young children, that at the very least, the apes are indicating multiple things in the situation and so are expressing
meanings richer than those they could have expressed
with a single sign alone. We should thus credit them with
at least some minimal grammatical competence, some
first glimmerings on the road to human syntax. Nevertheless, there were no sequences anywhere in any of the
data in which sign order or any other syntactic device
actually marked a systematic difference in meaning of
any kind or a particular syntactic role in the utterance as
a whole—the criterion that most linguists would adopt
for truly grammatical structure. If "EAT CHEESE" does
not mean something different from "CHEESE EAT," then
word order is not being used as a significant syntactic
device.

In the other main, quantitatively based study of the
gesture sequences of language-trained apes, Greenfield
and Savage-Rumbaugh (1990) examined data from a five-

month period of daily observations of the bonobo Kanzi when he was five years old. The overall corpus consisted of 13,691 utterances, of which 1,422 (10.4 percent) were sequences involving either two lexigrams (from a keyboard with a made-up set of lexigram symbols) or a lexigram and a gesture. Excluding communicative acts for which interpretation was unclear (second observer not present to take context notes) and responses to test questions, the final corpus of sequences consisted of 723 two-element utterances (longer utterances were excluded, so their structure is unknown). About 5 percent of the data was checked for interobserver reliability, which was quite good.

As in the Rivas (2005) study, the proportion of requests was extremely high, approximately 96 percent of all two-element utterances (function of the other 4 percent unknown). Also as in the Rivas study, almost all of the actions requested were concrete, dyadic actions such as bite, chase, carry, grab, hide, hug, slap, tickle, and keep-away (a game). Like Rivas, Greenfield and Savage-Rumbaugh found that almost a quarter of Kanzi's productions did not have much structuring, being classified as "miscellaneous," "no relation," or else as "conjoined actions, entities, or locations." Over one-third of the two-unit sequences consisted of pointing and naming. More interestingly, almost one half of the utterances were classified as representing two of the three elements agent-action-object or else an entity plus an attribute or location (note that no reliability analyses were done on this classification). The majority of these last types were a sequence of a lexigram and a gesture (mostly pointing or related directional gestures). Kanzi's preferred ordering, which was not a reflection of the caregiver's behavior, was first to indicate the lexigram and then to gesture, as in "KEEP-AWAY that(gesture)" and "JUICE you(gesture)." This ordering seems very similar to that of Washoe and friends in which the desired object or action is indicated first, followed by some further instigating sign. The lexigram-lexigram sequences showed no particular ordering preference. Of the seven action words used in such sequences, five of them were used with an order preference: two for preceding the involved object and three for following it. But note again that, even where there might be an ordering preference, it was not the case that different orders meant different things.

Interestingly, Kanzi has shown impressive competence in comprehending many types of English sentences used as requests (his caregivers typically spoke to him in English along with their gesturing and use of lexigrams). This includes the ability to recognize that different lexigram orders indicate requests to do different things (all of the testing was done in terms of his response to requests; Savage-Rumbaugh et al. 1993). However, it turns out that a number of other nonprimate species, such as dolphins and parrots (Herman 2005; Pepperberg 2000), have also shown essentially the same ability to recognize correlations between sign orders and particular types of requested actions, and so the ability to attribute significance to ordering patterns in learned signs is not confined to apes. In none of these animals is there a corresponding competence with sign order in the *production* of communicative acts, and so their comprehension skills might be based on many different kinds of cognitive and/or learning skills, some of them having very little to do with communication in particular.

The communicative abilities of these "linguistic" apes are indeed amazing, in the sense that they are learning novel communicative gestures and signs and using them effectively with another species—the clearest and most impressive examples of such flexible skills ever documented. And they might even be using sequences to communicate in more elaborate ways than they could with single-unit communicative acts alone—a very simple kind of grammar. This might indicate that these apes have the ability to, in effect, parse a conceptual situation into two different elements, such as event and participant, that is not so different from the way humans do it. It is possible that this distinction between events and participants derives from skills of imitation (demonstrably better in human-raised apes than in typical apes, and better still in human children; see Tomasello 1996) in which event categories are formed as a result of the judgment that I want to perform "the same" action I just saw (i.e., imitation = same action, different participant). However, from the point of view of syntactic structure more rigorously defined, it is fair to say that not much is here. In neither of the two systematic, quantitative studies is there any evidence for grammatical structure in the sense that different orders of signs (or any other device) function to mark participant roles or in any way to change meaning.

The simple explanation for why "linguistic" apes do not use syntactic devices in their communication with humans (even if they may comprehend the contrastive use of order when signed or spoken to) is that all their communication is designed for the requestive function. This exclusive focus on requests in the here and now of current interaction means that there are almost no functional demands on the gestural or sign production of these apes for syntactically marking the roles that different actors play in an event (syntactic marking), for identifying more explicitly the different actors involved (as in noun phrases), for designating the time of an event (as with tense markers), for marking a topic (as with topic markers), for designating speech act function (as with intonation or special constructions), or for doing any of the other things that we will call, a bit later, serious syntax in the grammar of informing. They have thus created, in this species-atypical environment, a kind of grammar of requesting quite well adapted to their particular communicative needs: they typically sign what they want in a single sign, followed by some indication of the person they want to do it, the object they want it done on, or some kind of wild card request marker as a spur to the human requestee.

6.1.3 Deaf Children Using Home Sign

Greenfield and Savage-Rumbaugh (1990) claim that what
Kanzi does with his gestures and lexigrams is comparable to what is done by deaf children growing up without
any kind of conventionalized language model (because
their parents have chosen not to expose them to a conventional sign language; Goldin-Meadow 2003b). These
children develop with the adults around them a way of
communicating based on a combination of pointing (and
other deictic gestures) and pantomiming. The children
learn some of their pantomimes from their parents, but
others they invent (which, interestingly, is not really feasible in a spoken language based on totally arbitrary
signs)—and there is pressure for these all to be iconic so
that other people outside the family may comprehend
them as well. The multisign utterances the children experience from adults are degenerate in a number of ways,
mainly because the parents are speaking as they gesture,
and their speech quite often preempts their gestures for
certain functions. Nevertheless, the children end up with
multisign utterances that seem to have at least some
grammatical structure—demonstrably more than that of
their parents and, as we will argue here, demonstrably
more than those of "linguistic" apes.

Because we began with signing apes and their grammar
of requests, the first thing to note is that much of these
children's language consists of *comments* on things,

informing others of things that they presumably are interested in and would like to know—including narratives displaced in time and space. Although no exact percentages of different kinds of utterances are reported, in one systematic coding of all the utterances of a sample of ten of these children (age 1 to 4 years) during 30 to 60 minutes of play, roughly one-third of their multisign utterances seemed to be simple comments (not requests) referring to actions involving transfer of objects or people (e.g., *move* or *come*), another one-quarter referred to transforming objects (e.g., *twist* or *break*), and many others had to do with transporting objects (e.g., *carry*); only a small minority had to do with playing games or performing concrete actions (Goldin-Meadow and Mylander 1984). This contrasts markedly with the language-trained apes' fixation on requesting games and concrete, dyadic activities such as chasing and hugging. The lack of overlap in the kinds of actions that apes and home-signing children talk about may be seen clearly in table 6.1, where out of almost 100 action words altogether, only two (*eat* and *go*) are used by individuals of both species. This difference is quite plausibly attributed to the different social goals the two species are pursuing in their use of communicative devices.

Nevertheless, it is still the case that the utterances of these children are relatively short. The majority consist of only one gesture, and approximately 85 percent of their multiunit utterances contain only one iconic sign, typically combined with pointing, with the mean number of

Table 6.1
Action signs used by home signing children (Goldin-Meadow and Mylander 1984), apes, and both (number of individuals, out of 6, in parentheses). (Thanks to Esteban Rivas for help compiling the chimpanzee list.)

Action Signs of Children	Con't.	Con't.	Action Signs of Apes	Action/Object Signs of Apes	Action Signs by Children and Apes
act on (1)	go out (1)	shoot (2)	bite (1)	brush (3)	go (2/3)
beat (3)	go up (2)	sip (1)	carry (1)	comb (2)	eat (2/4)
blow (3)	hammer (1)	spray upward (1)	chase (4)	dirty (2)	
bounce (1)	hit (2)	squeeze (1)	cry (1)	drink (4)	
chew (2)	hold (2)	strum (2)	go (3)	flower/smell (3)	
circle (1)	hold/spray (1)	suck (1)	go-there (1)	food/eat (4)	
climb (2)	jump (1)	take off (2)	go-you (1)	hear/listen (2)	
cradle (1)	leave thru (1)	take out (1)	grab (1)	light (1)	
cut (2)	lick (1)	tie (1)	groom (3)	oil (2)	
dance (1)	lift (1)	tilt (1)	hide (1)	paint (1)	
depress (1)	lift in (1)	transfer (1)	hug (4)	see/look/glasses (1)	
dive (1)	lift out (1)	turn (1)	keep-away (1)		

Table 6.1
(continued)

Action Signs of Children	Con't.	Con't.	Action Signs of Apes	Action/Object Signs of Apes	Action Signs by Children and Apes
do (1)	march (1)	twist (5)	open-room (1)		
don (2)	move (6)	twist off (1)	peekaboo (2)		
drive (1)	move back-forth (1)	walk (2)	peekaboo/smell (1)		
eat (2)	pedal (1)	wash (1)	slap (1)		
fall (1)	pet (1)	wing (1)	smell (2)		
float (1)	puff at (1)	wriggle (1)	swallow (1)		
fly up (2)	pull (1)		tickle (3)		
give (6)	pull off (1)				
go (2)	ride (1)				
go around (2)	roar (1)				
go away (1)	scamper (1)				
go down (1)	scoop (1)				

NB: Classification of ape signs done by original researchers (not Rivas 2005), and may be an artifact of correspondence with human signs.

gestures per utterance being between 1 and 1.4 for all but one of the children (including pointing)—and with very little development on this dimension over a several-year period of observation. Goldin-Meadow (2003b) provides evidence that these relatively modest productions are underlain by what she calls predicate frames, as on different occasions children explicitly indicate objects playing different roles in a given action or event; for example, with the iconic sign for cutting, the same child on different occasions will indicate the cutter, the thing cut, or the instrument used in the process. This would seem to be an especially clear indication of very productive event-participant parsing, perhaps based on humans' especially powerful skills of action imitation, or even role reversal imitation (again, imitation = same action, different participant).

Children using this home sign, as it is called, structure their utterances in simple ways. Most importantly, they sometimes use a device quite common in conventional sign languages to indicate the "patient" of an action, namely, as they make the iconic sign for the action they move their hand(s) in the direction of the patient of the action—a kind of iconic depiction of the "acting on" relation to mark the patient. It is not clear how often this device is used; the description in Goldin-Meadow (2003b, p. 111) only says "at times, the children orient their gestures toward particular objects in the room." Speakers of conventional sign languages of course do such things obligatorily, and they do many more of them for different functions (Padden 1983). In terms of sign order, only some of the children show consistent ordering patterns, and these essentially involve first pointing to an object and then producing the iconic gesture for the action (the one child who produced sufficiently many transitive actions for analysis put the patients relatively consistently after the action gesture)—basically the opposite of the ordering pattern favored by the linguistic apes. There is little evidence, however, that different orders are intended to signify any differences of meaning contrastively. Another possible manifestation of grammatical struc- ture—systematically investigated for only one child—is that when a given iconic sign seems to be used for indi- cating an object as opposed to an action (e.g., for the object *brush* instead of the action *brushing*), it is given in more abbreviated form—though still in only a minority of cases, possibly suggesting some notion of word classes in the direction of noun and verb (Goldin-Meadow 2003b, p. 130).

It is true that both the bonobo Kanzi and young chil- dren using home sign produce many one-element utter- ances, a fair number of two-element utterances, and only a small minority of longer utterances. In both cases the prototypical multielement utterance is one sign (lexigram or iconic) and one more or less natural gesture, typically pointing. But there are two fundamental differences. The first is that Kanzi (and the other apes) produce almost exclusively requests (with the very few nonrequests mainly being some kind of naming or recognition), whereas the home signers produce in addition many informative utterances—which means they talk about a whole range of topics, such as objects and their movements and properties, that the apes do not normally talk about. It is possible that this difference accounts for the difference in their preferred ordering patterns. That is, because they are requesting, the apes indicate the desired object or action first, followed by some kind of indication of the person they want to do it, the object they want it done on, or some kind of requestive marker, whereas home signers tend to indicate first what they are talking about (e.g., by pointing to it) and then predicate something interesting about it (nascent topic-focus structure, perhaps). The second difference is that because the home signers are making their signs iconically in space, they have the possibility of using space to modulate meanings in systematic ways, and some of them have begun to do this. Kanzi does not have this possibility in his lexigram system, and it is not clear whether these kinds of things are modeled for apes in ASL, or whether they are looked for when observing apes using ASL-like signs. But, again, when all one is doing is requesting, there is not much need for indicating the subject or direct object of an action.

And so these home-signing children are not confined to a grammar of requesting, but actually seek to inform others of things helpfully quite often. But they still produce utterances with very simple syntax, mostly of the probabilistic, and not normative, variety. They are cognitively normal in all other ways—including the possession of skills and motives for shared intentionality—so why are they not more grammatically sophisticated? The obvious reason is that they are not learning a full-blown conventional language that has developed in a community of users. And they do not even have other people who also use home sign naturally, without speech, and with whom they could conventionalize some things; when children such as these do have such a community, they begin to use utterances with much more grammatical structure, as we shall see shortly.

6.1.4   Children's Earliest Language

Typically developing, speaking human infants point and use other kinds of gestures before they begin acquiring their spoken language. As documented in chapter 4, children learning a vocal language in the normal way tend to increase their amount of pointing as they are acquiring a language, but decrease their use of iconic and conventional gestures, presumably because language is usurping their function. What this means is that many of children's earliest one-word utterances, their holophrases, are actually combinations of pointing and language (as well as intonational marking of motive). And it seems that such gesture-word combinations are forerunners of children's early syntax.

Two recent studies document how this happens. Assuming that children's early acts of pointing accompanying language indicate objects, Iverson and Goldin-Meadow (2005) defined two types of gesture-language combinations. In one, what we may call redundant combinations, the child points at an object and simultaneously names it; in the other, called supplementary combinations, the child points at an object and simultaneously predicates something about it, for example, pointing to a cookie and saying "Eat." What these researchers found was an astoundingly high correlation between young children's use of supplementary gesture-word combinations and their early word-word combinations (rs = .94), whereas children's use of redundant gesture-word combinations did not correlate at all. Ozcaliskan and Goldin-Meadow (2005) extended these findings to even more complex linguistic productions (see also Capirci et al. 1996). The interesting thing to note here is that supplementary gesture-word combinations manifest something like the kind of simple syntax that we see in linguistic apes and home-signing children: utterances composed of a pointing gesture to an object and some kind of iconic or arbitrary sign for an action, property, or other kind of predicate—without any syntactic devices involved at all (indeed pointing and words are typically produced simultaneously so that ordering is not even an issue).

In their earliest multiword utterances, young speaking children quite often do something a bit different—but still not totally different. Beginning at around 18 months of age, most children produce word combinations in which one element is a constant and the other element is a variable. Prototypically, a relational or event-word is used with a wide variety of object labels (e.g., "More milk," "More grapes," "More juice," or "Ball gone," "Dog gone," "Grapes gone"). Following Braine (1963), we may call these pivot schemas, which represent a widespread and productive strategy for children acquiring many of the world's languages, sometimes including productive utterances never before heard from adults, for example, the famous "Allgone sticky." Although it has not been documented to nearly the same extent, the early grammatical combinations of deaf children learning a conventional sign language show many of the same properties (Schick 2005). One way of conceptualizing these early pivot schemas, and also the predicate frames of home-signing children, is as fairly direct manifestations of their growing conceptualization of event-participant structure, such that basically any participant may fill basically any of the different participant roles. This conceptualization of events may depend on something like role reversal imitation in collaborative activities in which the child conceptualizes the event, as argued above, from a bird's-eye view with all participant roles, including its own, in the same representational format. This might be another reason why apes tend to talk about simple concrete actions in requestive form: they do not really understand events from a bird's-eye view and so do not really form anything like pivot schemas or predicate frames with open slots.

But even so, young children's pivot schemas are not really syntactic. That is to say, whereas in many early pivot schemas there is a consistent ordering pattern of event-word and participant-word (e.g., *More _* or *_ gone*), a consistent ordering pattern, to repeat, is not the same thing as productive syntactic marking used contrastively to indicate what role a word is playing in a larger combinatorial structure. The same basic analysis also holds for children's earliest period of acquisition of languages that employ case marking: children acquire their early nouns in one or another case form, but they do not have contrastive control over the different case forms of the same noun. This means that although young children are using their early pivot schemas to partition scenes conceptually with different words, they are not using such things as word order or case marking productively to indicate the different roles being played by different participants in that scene (see Tomasello 2003 for a review).

Young speaking children—and also young deaf children learning a conventional sign language—thus are not confined to a grammar of requesting, but they still begin without any serious syntax. In this case the reason would seem to be simply that it takes some time to discern the grammatical structure embodied in the particular utterances heard in a normal speech community. This is an important fact in any debate about the evolutionary origins of grammar. Young children acquiring a spoken language naturally, even though they have all of the cognitive and social-cognitive capacities and motivations they need as well as a mature linguistic community around them, do not start with syntactically structured utterances, but rather start with a kind of simple syntax that does not yet employ productive syntactic devices.

6.1.5 *Summary*

If we are thinking evolutionarily, other than apes' natural communication none of the situations we have examined here is representative of any early stage of human evolution. The "linguistic" apes are growing up in modern human environments, and the human children all have cognitive abilities that early humans very likely would not have had, including especially skills of role reversal imitation and shared intentionality. And so our model of the evolution of grammar at its earliest point will have to be some combination of these different situations (sketchily characterized in table 6.2). The communicative devices our imaginary *Homo* would have had at this time for potential combination (see chapter 5) would have been pointing and conventionalized intention-movements (since full-blown iconic gestures await the emergence of the communicative intention—see section 5.2.2).

What makes our task a bit easier is that, beyond great apes' natural gesture sequences, in all the other situations individuals produce true combinations and with a similar kind of simple syntax—in the sense that they partition the referential situation into multiple elements, often events and participants. Interestingly, although both

Table 6.2

	Joint Attention	Imitation	Pointing	Other Signs	Motives	Community of Speakers
Homo	yes	yes	yes	Intention-Movements	Request	yes
"Linguistic" Apes	—	?	yes	ASL/Lexigrams	Request	yes
Home Signers	yes	yes	yes	Iconic	All	—
Young Children	yes	yes	yes	Words + Iconic	All	yes

pointing and pantomiming may be used on their own to refer to either objects or actions, in their combinations all the individuals here typically use pointing to indicate objects (participants) and pantomiming (or signs) to indicate events. Given the ubiquity of some such distinction in the world's signed and spoken languages, we may posit that event-participant organization (as some kind of basis for verbs and nouns?) comes naturally to both apes and humans.[1] We may thus propose that our early *Homo* produced not just gesture sequences but gesture combinations that partitioned the referential situation into different elements—prototypically events and participants—but without any syntactic marking of those elements for their role in the utterance as a whole.

6.2   The Grammar of Informing

Given *Homo* individuals who have what it takes to combine multiple gestures to request things from one another, in the context of collaborative activities and joint attention, what happens to their multigesture combinations when they (i.e., *Earlier sapiens*) go beyond request-

---

1. When the spontaneously produced speech of mature speakers is examined in terms of intonation units—often the speech between pauses (typically containing four or five words and lasting a few seconds)—it is found that they prototypically contain single phrases (clauses) indicating a single event or state and one or a few participants (Chafe 1994; Croft 1995), suggesting the naturalness of simple event-participant organization in the language use of mature speakers as well.

ing and begin to inform one another of things helpfully, even outside of collaborative activities (due to processes of indirect reciprocity)? Informing prototypically involves events and participants beyond me and you in the here and now, as they concern things about which the recipient is currently ignorant. Communicating about this wider range of events and objects creates at least three new communicative challenges:

Identifying: as we move beyond requests, the communicator must have ways for making reference to absent or unknown objects and events, even using multiple items as a single functionally coherent constituent, but still grounding the referential act for the recipient in their shared common ground;

Structuring: as we move beyond requests, the communicator must have ways to syntactically mark such things as who did what to whom (including third parties) in the indicated event or state of affairs;

Expressing: when motives other than requests are possible, the communicator must distinguish those (and possibly other speaker attitudes) for the recipient.

6.2.1 Conventional Syntactic Devices

There are many different ways for meeting each of these challenges in both the gestural and the vocal modalities. First, in modern signed and spoken languages there are many ways of identifying specific participants and events for the recipient when they exist outside of me and you in the here and now. In both modalities, however, the key is that the communicator uses me and you in the here and now—that is, the current joint attentional frame, common ground, Bühler's (1934/1990) deictic center—to ground his acts of reference in what they both perceive or know together. Thus, if he can, the communicator will point to something perceptually present or indicate an entity with a sign designed for things already in current joint attention (e.g., with *she* or *it*). But for nonpresent entities and events, most of the contentful words/signs in both modalities are category terms that cannot by themselves single out particular referents; if I say or sign "cat" or "bite" these do not pick out any individual referents from our common ground, or from anywhere else, without further specification. The communicator thus must give search directions for finding individual referents: objects must generally be located in space, including conceptual space, and events must generally be located in time, including imagined time (Langacker 1991; Croft 1991). I thus say or sign things like "the cat" (the one in our current joint attention) or "my cat" or "the cat that lives in the vacant house on the corner," to single out one among all members of that category—there is a whole referential hierarchy depending on how salient the intended referent is within our current common ground (see Chafe 1994; Gundel, Hedberg, and Zacharski 1993). And I say or sign such things as "will bite" or "was biting" to indicate which particular event, or imagined event, I am referring to by locating it in time relative to now. The fact that multiple items work together in a certain pattern to effect a single coherent communicative function (e.g., referring to a single object or event) means that they form a single constituent in larger constructions—creating hierarchical structure.

Second, in modern sign languages there are a number of ways for structuring things to make clear who did what to whom, the most common being simply order (Liddell 2003)—and of course order is used quite frequently in spoken languages as well. In almost all of the languages of the world, both gestural and vocal, the actor/subject is referred to before the patient/object in the utterance, presumably because in the real world causal sources typically move and are active before the things they act upon or affect. This ordering principle thus has at least somewhat natural sources, but to be productive it needs to be conventionalized in opposition to other alternatives. In addition, sign languages sometimes also use space for this same function; for example, to indicate me giving you something, I move the sign for giving from me to you iconically (and the opposite for you giving to me)—another device with an obvious natural source. Signers may also, as noted above, indicate the patient of a designated action by pantomiming the action in the direction of a perceptually present object, a device sometimes referred to as agreement (to highlight its affinity with such things as subject-verb agreement in spoken languages). To indicate who is doing an action, signers may also shift their own body in space to act from the spatial perspective of someone present in the situation indexically, again a natural iconic device. Both types of languages also sometimes use conventional signs, words, or markers (e.g., prepositions, case markers) for indicating the role a participant is playing in an event.

Third, in both modalities the communicator gives some expression to his motive (and sometimes other attitudes) as additional information to help the recipient infer his social intention. In both modalities these tend to be natural expressions of emotion, although to serve as contrastive markers they must be conventionalized for such use. Thus, a question is asked with a certain kind of facial expression in sign languages, and/or a certain intonation in spoken languages, possibly related in deep history to natural expressions of puzzlement and/or surprise. Not-so-polite requests may be given with a demanding facial expression or tone of voice, possibly related in deep history to expressions of anger. These expressions of motive—with a natural basis in human emotional reactions in both signed and spoken languages—have become conventionalized, each in their own way contrastively, in both modalities.

In the previous chapter, what we called natural communication was communication based on action-based gestures adapted to humans' natural tendency to do such things as follow gaze direction (i.e., pointing) and interpret the actions of others intentionally (i.e., pantomiming). Individuals are able to understand these gestures without any particular learning history (assuming they have the shared intentionality infrastructure of cooperative communication with communicative intentions, common ground, and so forth), just as one may understand such gestures naturally in a shop or railway station in a foreign country. Conventionalization removes the naturalness and replaces it, so to speak, with a shared learning history: everyone who grew up in this community knows what this arbitrary communicative convention is typically used for because we all had similar learning experiences with it (and all know this together).

Syntactic devices and constructions are like this too, despite attempts to make them into contentless, algebraic "rules" (e.g., Chomsky 1965; Pinker 1999). Each of the different languages of the world, both spoken and signed, has its own syntactic and other grammatical conventions for structuring utterances so as to solve the various problems raised by informative communication. Indeed, each of the different languages of the world has a variety of prepackaged constructions that combine various types of signs/words and grammatical markers for use in recurrent communicative situations; for example, the English passive construction (e.g., "The dog was injured by the car," in which the subject is the patient of the action) is composed of a certain arrangement of certain constituents (each of which is its own constructional pattern as well) for a specific communicative function. This more functional view of grammar does not deny that there might be very general processing or computational principles that in some way shape or constrain the kinds of grammatical patterns that human beings may conventionalize, or that things may start with "natural" principles like indicating first the agent of an action. But what grammar consists in most immediately is a set of conventional devices and constructions—conventionalized differently in particular languages—for facilitating communication when complex situations outside the here and now need to be referred to.

6.2.2 *Nicaraguan Sign Language*

An extremely interesting illustration of the transition from simple syntax to serious syntax—and the beginnings of the conventionalization of grammar—is provided by different generations of users of Nicaraguan Sign Language. Nicaraguan Sign Language represents a situation in which deaf children, each of whom had developed on her own some skills with some form of home sign, were brought together in a school setting. They spontaneously developed ways of communicating with one another using a common set of signs, and new children coming to the school began learning this common set from them. The uniqueness of this situation is that it occurred just a few decades ago, and so the first generation of children is still alive, as adults, and two other generations of children and adults are available for study as well. The basic finding is that the younger signers seem to be more fluent with the signs, and they seem to have given them some added grammatical structure, as compared with the original creators represented by earlier generations.

Home signers, as noted above, are pretty much confined to whatever they and their parents can invent, with pressure to stay "natural" (iconic) arising from other persons not in on the inventing. But in the birth of a new language such as this, a new process enters the picture. As multiple users communicate with one another, new signs and constructions are created, and then as these are acquired by new learners via imitation (without always understanding the naturalness involved), we begin to get, again, "a drift to the arbitrary." We may call this process the conventionalization of grammar (or "grammaticalization," though this term has other connotations), and it will be treated at some length below. The important point for current purposes is simply that the addition of this creation and transmission process leads to the emergence of grammatical structure beyond that invented by individuals using their own idiosyncratic home sign.

In the case of Nicaraguan Sign Language, both analysis of spontaneous signing and experiments involving elicited production and comprehension have established that grammatical structure has been created in a very short time. First, later generations of Nicaraguan Sign Language users have learned to use space in a number of important ways to structure their utterances grammatically, in ways that resemble the devices of conventional sign languages (whereas first-generation signers have not). For example, they use space to identify nonpresent referents that might require multiple signs working together (constituency). Thus, they use a common spatial reference point to indicate items that go together in a constituent in some way—sometimes called agreement—so that, for example, an object and a modifying expression may be signed in the same location, indicating a modifying relationship—and the same for an agent and an action. In addition, spatial devices are also used to keep track of referents across time: once a signer has referred to an object with a sign, she may subsequently simply point to the location at which the object sign was originally produced to indicate that object a second time—in a manner very similar to the pronouns of spoken language. This is essentially using a spatial device to indicate things as a way that takes advantage of the already established joint attentional frame. Another interesting use of space by second-generation signers is the indication of perspectival reference point before gesturing, for example, signing onto a location in space associated with an already established object but from the point of view of someone other than the self (Senghas and Coppola 2001; Senghas 2003).

Second, with respect to sign order as a structuring device, in experiments in which subjects narrate what is happening in films, first-generation signers produce only one participant per action (as is mostly the case in home sign), so that the ordering of even fairly long narrations is an alternation of verb and participant signs. But second-generation signers prefer to produce verb-final utterances, no matter how many participants are involved, with actors/subjects/topics coming almost invariably before patients/objects/foci (Kegl, Senghas, and Coppola 1999). This verb-final ordering has also been found in another newly invented sign language, Bedouin Sign Language, with verb-final utterances outnumbering other types of orderings by about six to one (Sandler et al. 2005). Also, like some home signers, users of these newly created systems produce action signs toward objects to indicate that those objects are the patients or direct objects of the action.

Second-generation users of Nicaraguan Sign Language have thus begun employing—in a way that home signers and first-generation users have not—a number of grammatical structuring devices constituting serious syntax. Since sign languages have arisen spontaneously many times, and all of the mature ones have much grammatical structure, such conventionalization is presumably the normal process by which a community creates a full-blown sign language.

6.2.3 Speaking Children's Earliest Grammar

Not long after typically developing children begin producing multiword utterances—often in the pivot schemas, as described above—they begin structuring their utterances grammatically, as do deaf children acquiring a sign language. From fairly early their utterances show hierarchical structure in the sense that they have multi-item noun phrases and verb phrases that are identified by particular constructional patterns (see Tomasello 2003 for a review). They also use second-order syntactic devices for structuring the roles that participants play in events from fairly early as well, using ordering devices or other forms of syntactic marking such as case marking. Initially, these are typically tied locally to particular event types. For example, children may learn a particular ordering device to indicate agents and patients in particular kinds of events like giving or pushing, but not use those same devices for other types of events. These so-called verb island constructions (Tomasello 1992a, 2003) indicate that children's earliest syntactic marking is fairly local in scope and becomes general and abstract only gradually. The main lesson for current purposes is simply that syntactic devices—even conventional ones that change meaning in contrastive ways—may apply either more locally to specific word/signs or more broadly across whole categories of words/signs. In thinking about evolution, it is thus reasonable to suppose that at the early stages of serious syntax in the grammar of informing human beings may have structured their utterances with syntactic devices that did their work only locally with some particular words/signs, and not categorically across all known word/signs.

6.2.4 Summary

Again if we think evolutionarily, none of the situations we have examined here—Nicaraguan Sign Language or children acquiring a conventional signed or spoken language—fits any earlier stage in human evolution. The children creating and learning Nicaraguan Sign Language may be pretty close to some earlier stage, but they have more cognitive and social-cognitive skills than humans would have had at the point we are targeting (particularly with regard to issues of sharing and normativity), and they all begin their lives by learning home sign in interaction with mature, modern, speaking adults. What we are looking for here is something that is created *de novo* and that goes beyond the grammar of requesting to include more sophisticated grammatical structuring, but that still does not yet include all of the syntactic devices that will be required for sharing experience in narratives and also does not include the normative dimension of human cooperative communication.

The main innovation we are targeting in the grammar of informing is the communicator's use of conventional syntactic devices (i) to ground and so to identify the referents in the current joint attentional frame, including using multiunit constituents to do so; (ii) to structure the utterance as a whole for the recipient by indicating the different roles being played by the participants in the event; and (iii) to express motive and attitude conventionally (often still emotionally in face and voice). These innovations are motivated by a new communicative function—though obviously no particular devices are specifically determined by these functions, as different languages embody them in very different ways. In the grammar of requesting, tied to me and you in the here and now, none of these complexities is needed; in the grammar of informing, all of these complexities are needed. Presumably, the first conventional syntactic devices used evolutionarily were derived from "natural" principles—that is, ones that all human beings naturally employ based on their general cognitive, social, and motivation propensities, such as "actor first" or "topic first" or looking puzzled when asking for information—but the conventionalization process then transformed these into communicatively significant syntactic devices in human cooperative communication.

6.3   The Grammar of Sharing and Narrative

The sharing motive, as noted from the outset, is a species of informing. It concerns the basic human motivation to simply share information—and, most importantly, attitudes about that information—with others. We have speculated that sharing with others in this way serves to expand one's common ground with others—to be like others in the group and to, one hopes, be liked by them and be able to communicate with them more intimately— and so serves as a form of social identification and bonding. We also noted that this sharing/identification motive also led ultimately to the normativity of many social behaviors, the implicit social pressure to do it the way others do it. As language displays very strong normative structure—both in the way we refer to things with particular linguistic conventions and in the form of utterances as grammatical versus ungrammatical—it is possible that this motive is at least partially responsible for our judgment that "That's not the way it is said."

A major venue through which people of all the cultures of the world share information and attitudes with others in their group is in narratives. Basically all cultures have narratives that help define their group as a coherent entity through time—creation myths, folk tales, parables, and the like—and indeed these are passed on from generation to generation as a part of the cultural matrix. (Interestingly, even home signers without a truly conventional language appear to tell simple narratives via their iconic gestures—Goldin-Meadow 2003b—as do children acquiring Nicaraguan Sign Language—Senghas, Kita, and Özyürek 2004.) From a linguistic point of view, narratives that tell an extended story raise a host of problems of how to relate multiple events and their various participants to one another across time. These problems are solved with a number of different syntactic devices of what we might call fancy syntax, and indeed many of the seemingly inordinate complexities of modern grammars derive specifically from devices that, on the current hypothesis, were created to deal with the problems created by narratives and other forms of extended discourse. Indeed, even the grammar of individual utterance-level constructions has been affected, as the linguistic expression of event sequences in separate utterances, or even across conversational turns, may get compressed, grammaticalized, into a single construction involving multiple events produced more or less under one intonation contour. All of this can and does occur in both signed and spoken languages, and we will posit that it was characteristic of *Later Sapiens*.

6.3.1 Discourse and Narrative

To engage in narrative discourse we need ways for talking about multiple events and states of affairs related to one another in complex ways, and we need means for grounding our discourse not so much in the immediate nonlinguistic context as in the linguistic context formed by the previous discourse. Becoming a skillful narrator therefore requires mastery of a set of devices for providing coherence and cohesion across events in order to tell a good story.

The two major problems that narrative discourse sets are: relating events to one another in time, and keeping track of the participants in those events when they are sometimes the same and sometimes different across events (and playing different roles in different events when they are the same). First, keeping track of events in time leads to some incredibly complex grammatical structures. The simplest situation is of course when an event is located in time relative to now: I *slept* for an hour or I *will sleep* for an hour. But narratives require us also to situate events displaced in space and time relative to one another, so that I can say such things as:

While I *was sleeping,* a bomb exploded (one past event occurring inside of another past event).

After I *had slept* for an hour, mother came (one past event occurring after another past event).

By next month, I *will have finished* my book (a future time point relative to which another future event is past).

By the time I finish my book, I *will have been living* in Australia for ten years (a future event at which point another future extended event ends).

It is difficult to imagine any other communicative context, other than narrative discourse, that would require such arcane temporal bookkeeping in the form of different verb tenses and aspects.

Second, tracking referents across events is quite complicated as well. In some cases, the referent does not even need to be identified in the second event, as in "Bill drove to town and __ bought a shirt." In other cases the referent is identified with a pronoun, but this can be tricky if there are two previously mentioned participants who might be its referent, as in "Bill drove Sarah to town and __ bought a shirt," in which case the person who bought a shirt (Bill) is actually farther away from the word *bought* than is the other named referent (Sarah). But this can be overridden if a pronoun that is marked in some way is used, as in "Bill drove Sarah to town and she bought a shirt," in which the feminine pronoun *she* overrides the default case as in the previous example. Languages in which all nouns belong to different genders, or noun classes, are able to use this strategy much more productively than English. These simple examples only scratch the surface of the complexities of so-called reference tracking in discourse, but they at least illustrate in a very simple way some communicative pressures that might shape emerging grammars (e.g., the pressure to find ways to keep track of referents across events), which might be responsible for such things as a variety of different pronoun forms, different noun classes, some kinds of agreement marking, and so forth. As noted, this same function is often performed in sign languages by the signer making a sign for a person or object at a particular location in front of him or her, and then referring back to that person or object by pointing to that location subsequently.

The grounding of events in time in extended discourse and the tracking of referents across events are very much more complex than the simple discussion here would indicate—and there is great linguistic diversity in both of them. The main point is simply that communicative function drives the process, such that all linguistic communities who wish to tell narratives and engage in other forms of extended discourse must create grammatical conventions of the general type described here for getting these things done.

6.3.2   Complex Constructions

This kind of extended discourse leads to the most complex, utterance-level, syntactic constructions in a language, that is, those containing more than one event. In a process that will be described in more detail below, extended sequences of discourse indicating multiple events—loosely organized and expressed across different intonation units—"congeal" over historical time in the discourse community into more or less tightly organized grammatical constructions expressed within a single intonation contour. There are three basic types of such constructions that extend our identifying, structuring, and expressing functions in even more complex ways.

In terms of identifying, there are myriad different constructions that are used to identify referents using multiple elements, as in English noun phrases ("the big green car") and verbal complexes ("will have been sleeping"). The most complex of these—because they involve identifying a referent using an event—are relative clauses:

The man *who was wearing the green coat* left early.

There's that woman *who was at the shop yesterday.*

Other constructions change perspective and emphasis so as to identify a key participant for the recipient's benefit, such as:

It was the man who got robbed (not the woman, as you suppose).

It was the girl who robbed him (not the boy, as you suppose).

The details of how such constructions work should not divert us, as we only need to reiterate that they function to identify referents and derive from extended discourse in ways that will be spelled out in a bit more detail below.

In terms of structuring, all languages have complex constructions that relate events to one another and to participants in complex yet systematic ways. For example, in English we can say things involving two events like:

She finished$_1$ her homework, *and then* she went$_2$ to town.

She pulled$_1$ the door, *but* it wouldn't shut$_2$.

She rode$_1$ her bike *because* she needed to find$_2$ him quickly.

Such juxtaposed events, with a key word connecting them and specifying their relation, are mundane in discourse and narrative, and these are only a very few examples. There are many other types and there is great cross-linguistic diversity in these kinds of loosely organized complex constructions as well.

In terms of expressing, there are special constructions designed to indicate different speech act functions (motives) such as questions and commands:

Close the door! (Imperative)

Did you close the door? (Question)

He closed the door. (Informative)

In other constructions expressing speaker attitude, an event is reported within the framework of someone's psychological state or attitude. Some constructions of this type concern desire and volition, many of which—and those that are first in children's acquisition—express the communicator's attitude in the here and now toward the event. Most simply:

I *want* to *play* Batman.

I *must do* my homework.

I'm *trying* to *win*.

These may ultimately be generalized to reports about other people's psychological states or attitudes toward events. Other constructions in this category concern epistemic states. Some simple examples are:

I *know* I can *do* it.

I *think* he *went* home.

I *believe* she'll *come* to the party.

These may also be displaced to reports about other people's psychological states or attitudes toward events, of course.

Importantly, modern children's earliest complex constructions do not need to be grammaticalized out of discourse sequences, because children hear the constructions in their current complex form from adults (Diessel and Tomasello 2000, 2001; Diessel 2005). This is another manifestation of the more general cultural dialectic by which invented cultural products become ever more complex over historical time in social interaction and collaboration, but new generations simply acquire the new product by imitation or some other form of cultural learning (the ratchet effect; Tomasello, Kruger, and Ratner 1993). The critical point here is simply that many, if not most, of the very most complicated grammatical constructions of a language are conventionalized historically from larger discourse sequences in order to manage the many complexities of engaging in extended discourse and narrative with multiple-event structure—as we will outline in more detail below.

6.3.3 Grammaticality as Normativity

Why do all people in all cultures tell stories in the first place? In chapter 5 we laid out an evolutionary rationale for people sharing information, emotions, and attitudes with others. Basically, such sharing is a way of expanding our common ground with others and so expanding our communicative opportunities, and, in the end, making us more like them and enhancing our chances of social acceptance (with conformity to the group playing a critical role in processes of cultural group selection). Telling narratives contributes to this process as only members of our group know our stories, and our shared evaluations of the characters and their actions as we tell these stories are an important bonding mechanism as well (see Bruner

1986, who distinguishes within narratives "the landscape of action" and the "landscape of evaluation").

In chapter 5 we also argued that this process leads to social norms. Humans have a strong need to belong to some social group, and group-level norms for behavior—that you must be cooperative, that you must dress and eat and act like us—can emerge only because individuals are sensitive to social evaluation and sanctions (and actually preempt them by feeling on their own embarrassment, guilt, and shame). Importantly, normativity also extends to many of the everyday practices of the people in a social group, as a result of general pressure to conform and be a member of the group: this is the way we, the members of this group, harvest honey (as our forebears have done since the beginning of time); this is the way we use chopsticks to eat; and so forth.

The phenomenon of grammaticality—that certain utterances sound ungrammatical ("That's not English")—would seem to be very far removed from following social norms in order to avoid shame and guilt. But, we would argue, it is actually just another instantiation of social norms for everyday behaviors, like harvesting honey in our group-specific way and using chopsticks to eat—but reinforced by the fact that commonplace grammatical utterances are heard dozens or even hundreds of times every day so that their pattern is quite entrenched in our communicative activities (note that grammatical patterns heard less often do not sound as bad when violated as do more frequently heard patterns; Brooks et al. 1999).

Interestingly, the second-generation children acquiring Nicaraguan Sign Language seem to have a sense of grammaticality that home signers do not (i.e., they notice that the first generation does not always do it "right"; Senghas, Kita, and Özyürek 2004), suggesting that when the conventionalization process occurs with individuals possessing modern human cognitive and social skills and participating in a linguistic community, it creates the impression that things *must* be done this way—and that some others are not doing it correctly.

Many linguists and philosophers have puzzled over grammaticality: if it is not explicit rules as taught in school (that is, conscious, prescriptive grammar intended to signal to others one's education and social status) but something more basic, then what is it? In the current view, it is just another case of the normativity of group behavior, but with the added force of especially frequent habitual behavior so that violations sound strange. This is an unexpected, but extremely important, additional effect of the motive for sharing/conformity/group identification in the evolution of human communication.

6.3.4 *Summary*

I can see the linguists cringing now at the terrible oversimplifications of discourse and complex constructions (and indeed of serious syntax as well) that this brief account represents. But my goals here have been very concrete and simple. I have simply tried to show that:

• engaging in extended discourse and narrative creates certain functional demands such as relating events to one another, tracking participants, and taking perspectives;

• all known languages have grammatical devices for meeting these demands, but there are many different ways of doing this and so these devices vary greatly from one language to another;

• recurrent discourse sequences involving multiple events are the ultimate source of complex syntactic constructions (elaborated below).

Individuals engaged simply in requesting things from one another in the here and now, or even informing one another of things removed a bit from the here and now, would simply have no need for many of the fancy syntactic devices we see in modern languages whose function seems to be related in fairly straightforward ways to the functional demands of narrative discourse about structured series of events displaced in space and time.

In any case, we may summarize our evolutionary steps in terms of the grammar of requesting, the grammar of informing, and the grammar of sharing in narrative, as in figure 6.1. This figure is merely intended to depict, in a very general way, the grammatical properties characteristic of human communication as the different communicative motives emerged across evolutionary time. (In this figure, as in figure 5.1, we use the terms *Homo, Earlier Sapiens,* and *Later Sapiens* as handy and suggestive labels concerning evolutionary sequences, nothing more.)

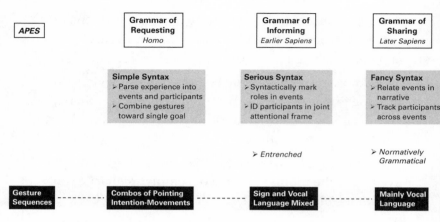

Figure 6.1
Evolutionary foundations of grammar in three steps.

The conventionalization process, taking place in cultural-historical time, is not depicted here, but it is to that (after a brief resummary in different terms) that we now turn.

As another way of summarizing our total, three-step evolutionary account, consider the modern-day creation of linguistic pidgins and creoles under special social circumstances by individuals who are native speakers of different vocal languages. The hypothesis would be that—even though they are cognitively very different from early humans—if these individuals only interacted in something like a work situation in which basically all of the communication was requesting that others do things in the context of the collaborative work activity, the resulting grammatical structure would lack most of the structuring devices of modern languages. To request that someone dig in this place now does not require the pluperfect tense or relative clauses, and indeed we know that in the very earliest stages many pidgins have very limited grammatical structure (so-called jargon; McWhorter 2005). But then, at Step 2, if these people needed to inform one another of things helpfully—especially third parties and other things removed in time and space—then this functional pressure would lead to the conventionalization of some serious syntactic devices (e.g., contrastive word order, syntactic marking, complex noun phrases, etc.) and more complex grammatical constructions, creating a "pidgin." As for Step 3, a pidgin typically begins to be called a creole, or even a normal natural language, when the speakers begin to identify themselves as a coherent cultural group, at least partly on the basis of their common language and perhaps the narrative stories they tell in sharing with one another in this common language.

6.4 The Conventionalization of Linguistic Constructions

The way that modern languages work is thus a complex mix of "natural" principles of communication and grammar—processes that derive directly from the way humans are built to cognize the world and interact socially—and conventionalized communicative devices created and passed along within specific cultural groups. Obviously, the processes by which communicative devices are conventionalized are not processes of biological evolution, but rather of cultural-historical evolution. The key to understanding these processes is the phenomenon of language change. To understand language change more clearly in the case of grammar, we must first understand what it is exactly that is created and passed along (answer: constructions). We then must understand why grammatical constructions change over historical time. The puzzle is that for efficient communication among all members of a group across generations, it would seem reasonable that communicative conventions, including grammatical conventions, stay always the same. And so the question is who is changing them and why (answer: no one is doing this on purpose), and in which modality (answer: both gestural and vocal languages).

6.4.1 Constructions

Communicators do not need to figure out totally creative ways of cobbling together multiunit utterances in every speech event—and they do not have "rules" out of grammar books (whatever those might be) for doing this. That is, they do not just have words and isolated grammatical devices; rather, they have already available in the speech community prepackaged, internally complex communicative conventions known as linguistic constructions. Linguistic constructions are essentially prefabricated, meaning-bearing structures for use in certain recurrent communicative situations. These constructions may involve particular words and phrases, such as "How ya doin'?," "See ya later," and "I dunno," or they may involve an abstract pattern not of particular words but of word types, for example, as in the English passive construction (X *was* VERB*ed by* Y) or past tense construction (VERB + *ed*).

One of the great theoretical advances in twentieth-century linguistics is the recognition that conventional-ized grammatical constructions may take on Gestalt properties of their own independent of the meanings of the individual words, and this creates a kind of auton-omy at the grammatical level of analysis (Langacker 1987; Fillmore 1989; Goldberg 1995, 2006; Croft 2001). Thus, if I say to you "The dax got mibbed by the gazzer," you know—without knowing the meaning of a single content word—that the gazzer did something (called mibbing) to the dax (and we have entered that event from the perspective of the dax, as patient). Indeed, the Gestalt properties of constructions can even "override" indi-vidual word meanings in many cases. For example, the grammar books will say that the verb *sneeze* is an intran-sitive verb, used with a single actor, the one who sneezes. But I can say something like "He sneezed her the tennis ball" and you will concoct a scene in which his sneezing causes a ball to go from him to her. That movement is not communicated by the verb *sneeze*, but rather by the construction as a whole (the ditransitive construction). It is thus not an exaggeration to say that the construction itself—the abstract pattern—is a linguistic symbol, albeit a complex one with internal structure (Goldberg 1995). This means that just as linguistic communities create and pass along particular words in their vocabulary, they also create and pass along grammatical constructions. Constructions comprising specific words and phrases may be passed along in the normal cultural way by imitation. But since abstract constructions are essentially patterns of use, they cannot be imitated directly, but rather children must (re-)construct them across individual learning experiences with different exemplars of the construction.

But neither words nor grammatical constructions get passed along totally faithfully. All one has to do is pick up some work of Chaucer and, as a modern speaker of English, attempt to read it. Much of it is incomprehensible, and that is only from a few hundred years ago. Modern linguistics actually began with the discovery that almost all of the European languages, and some that stretch as far away as India, have a common origin in a common ancestor language (proto-Indo-European), and that most of the different languages we see in Europe today have all arisen and differentiated almost completely from one another in just a few thousand years. And this change is not just in the words; the grammatical constructions of these languages have diverged radically from one another as well. Over a period of just a few hundred years, for example, English changed from using primarily case marking to indicate who did what to whom to using primarily word order (with remnants of the case system still visible in the pronouns: I-me, he-him, she-her, etc.). If we want to understand how linguistic constructions are created and transmitted across generations, we must begin by attempting to understand processes of language change.

6.4.2 Language Creation and Change

All individuals of all social species, with one exception, can communicate effectively using their evolved communicative displays and possibly signals with all other individuals of their species (even birds with different dialects still recognize and respond appropriately to songs in other dialects), and these displays and signals do not change appreciably across generations. The one exception is, of course, humans. Humans have over 6,000 different languages whose speakers cannot comprehend one another, and indeed even the speakers of the same language at different points in historical time would have great difficulties comprehending one another (e.g., Chaucer and us). The explanation for this is simply that human linguistic communities are constantly reinventing their languages—although not intentionally.

Language creation and change is what has been called a phenomenon of the "third kind" (also called, following Adam Smith, an invisible hand phenomenon; Keller 1994). Like such other societal-level phenomenon as inflation and resource depletion, it is something that results from intentional human actions, even though no single individual or even group of individuals intended for it to happen. Language creation and change result from the fact that human communication is open and dynamic, with interlocutors constantly adjusting to one another in order to communicate effectively and accomplish other social goals—relying to different degrees in different circumstances on different degrees and kinds of common ground. Although there is not much research on the cognitive dimensions of the process, one account of how it works that is generally consistent with the phenomena as observed in language histories is as follows (see Croft 2000; Dahl 2004; Deutscher 2005).

When people communicate with one another linguistically, the communicator is attempting to be efficient by saying as little as possible to get the message across. The recipient, of course, is interested in getting enough information to comprehend the message, relying both on the message and on the common ground she has with the communicator. And so if I ask a question "Where is Jeff?," appropriate answers are such curt things as "New York," "Sleeping," and other locutions that specify only the needed information, leaving the already shared information out of the utterance itself (i.e., I do not need to say "Jeff is in New York" or "Jeff is sleeping"). If you ask me a question to which I do not know the answer, my response in everyday English is typically something barely intelligible to a nonnative speaker, "I dunno," which I assume you will recognize since my possible responses are few and so this compressed utterance is probably sufficient to indicate the one intended. In specialized settings where people share much common ground—such as a dentist and her assistant who have worked together for years—a kind of abbreviated code arises in which participants communicate quickly and efficiently by taking advantage of their mutual experience to leave much unsaid. Low-information words in highly predictable places are typically barely articulated in everyday speech; for example, the actual articulation of a refusal might be something like "m-busy" ("I am busy"). The general principle is that the more common ground and predictability there is among interlocutors, the more reduced in form are the actual utterances produced. Speakers thus automatize and reduce certain utterances, and phrases within utterances, for purposes of efficiency—within the constraints of the recipient's ability to comprehend.

The utterances produced in particular situations of linguistic communication are thus basically compromises between the communicator's desire to say only what is needed to get across the message, and the recipient's desire to have all the information that is needed to comprehend the message. This happens at two levels. First, longer discourse sequences across intonation contours are reduced to utterance-level constructions produced mostly within a single intonation contour. Here are some examples, based on Givón (1979—although in many cases the historical record is not sufficiently detailed for confidence in the specifics):

• Loose discourse sequences such as *He pulled the door and it opened* may become telescoped into *He pulled the door open* (a resultative construction).

• Loose discourse sequences such as *My boyfriend . . . He plays piano . . . He plays in a band* may become *My boyfriend plays piano in a band.* Or, similarly, *My boyfriend . . . He rides horses . . . He bets on them* may become *My boyfriend, who rides horses, bets on them* (a relative clause construction).

• If someone expresses the belief that Mary will wed John, another person might respond with an assent *I believe that,* followed by a repetition of the expressed belief that *Mary will wed John*—which become telescoped into the single statement *I believe that Mary will wed John* (a sentential complement construction).

• Complex constructions may also derive from discourse sequences of initially separate utterances, as in *I want this . . . I buy it* evolving into *I want to buy it* (an infinitival complement construction).

The second level is one in which strings of words with many syllables are reduced to a smaller number of words with fewer syllables. A simple English example concerns the future marker *gonna,* a fusion of *going* and *to.* The original use of *going* was as a verb for movement, often in combination with the preposition *to* to indicate the destination (*I'm going to the store*), but sometimes also to indicate an intended action that the "going to" enabled (*Why are you going to London? I'm going to see my bride*).

This later became *I'm gonna VERB*, with *gonna* indicating not just the intention to do something in the future, but futurity only (with no movement or intention necessary; see Bybee 2002). This additional element—the notion of intention that was only a possible implication in the original—can only come from the common ground between interlocutors when such things are normally said. Other well-known examples include:

· The main future tense marker in English comes from the full lexical verb *will*, as in *I will it to happen*. This expression then at some point became something like *It'll happen* (with the volitional component of *will* "bleached" out).

· English phrases such as *on the top of* and *in the side of* evolved into *on top of* and *inside of* and eventually into *atop* and *inside*. In some languages relator words such as these spatial prepositions may also become attached to nouns as case markers)—in this instance as possible locative case markers.

· In French, the main negative is the expression *ne . . . pas*, as in *Je ne sais pas*. Currently in spoken French, the *ne* is becoming less often used and *pas* is becoming the main negative marker. But the word *pas* was at one point the word for "step," with the expression being something like the English "not one bit" or "not one step further."

A critical part of this process is the propagation and transmission of such changes in the linguistic community (e.g., spread of an innovation due to social prestige, etc.; Croft 2000), but of special importance for our account is transmission across generations. Recall that in accounting for the emergence of linguistic conventions in human evolution, we postulated a kind of "drift to the arbitrary" based on the fact that outsiders, who are missing some common ground as a basis for "naturalness," may have a difficult time comprehending and parsing the communicative signs of the others. What seems to happen in the case of grammar is something similar. Children hear utterances and just want to learn to do things like adults— they do not know or care anything for any "natural" roots of these. Thus, when they hear utterances whose constituent parts are hard to hear or absent (or they do not yet know them), they may understand how that utterance works in a different manner from the adult producing it (i.e., which parts of the utterance are serving which communicative functions). This is called functional reanalysis, and it results from the fact that comprehenders typically do two things simultaneously. On the one hand, they attempt to understand the overall meaning of the utterance: what does the speaker want me to do, know, or feel? But in addition they also engage in a kind of "blame assignment": in the overall meaning, what role is being played by each of the internal constituents of the utterance? Thus, if a child hears an adult say "I'd better go," she might not hear the -'d so well and just assume that *better* is a simple modal auxiliary like *must*, as in "I *must* go" or "I *should* go" or "I *can* go." That is then a blame assignment that differs from that of the adult, and so, if there are many similar children, at some historical point *better* will indeed become a modal auxiliary like *must* in the English language at large. This kind of reanalysis happens constantly, and it often spreads to related constructions by analogy (see Croft 2000 for a thorough discussion of these processes).

The cycle as we have characterized it is thus something like what is shown in figure 6.2. When predictability is high owing to strong common ground, speakers automatize and reduce constructions, which sometimes makes it difficult for new learners (who may then engage in a reanalysis), and these reduced, reanalyzed forms are then combined in discourse, and the whole process then starts over. Relatedly, if abstract constructions must be (re-)constructed by children from patterns of adult use, then "slippage" in the transmission may also occur if patterns of adult use change substantially—so that children end up with slightly different constructions from those of adults. For example, when English adults begin using an

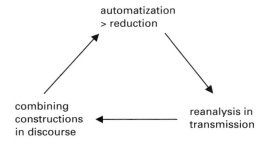

Figure 6.2

irregular past tense of a verb less frequently (e.g., *sneak-snuck* and *dive-dove*), children tend to regularize it (e.g., *sneaked* and *dived*) because many and frequent exemplars are needed to entrench irregular forms that differ from the predominant pattern—leading to change over time (Bybee 1995).

As with almost every aspect of my account of linguistic communication as presented here, I have oversimplified vastly and deleted important details. But that is because for current purposes we only need to understand enough of the process to make two key points of special relevance to the current account based on processes of shared intentionality. First, the conventionalization of grammar, as we have described it, can only take place if communicator and recipient have the common goal of successful communication. That is, we have characterized the outcome of grammaticalization processes as a kind of compromise between the needs of the communicator and those of the recipient. This compromise is possible only if the two participants are working together toward the common goal of the communicator's message being successfully comprehended by the recipient, and each of the participants is monitoring what the other is doing as they work toward that joint goal—so that, for example, the recipient may signal comprehension or noncomprehension as appropriate and the communicator may adjust the formulation of the message in response. This process is utterly different from the kind of compromise between communicator and recipient characteristic of great ape communication, described in chapter 2, in which each individual has its own individualistic end, and those signals survive which serve both of those individualistic ends adequately. As suggestive evidence, we may note again the fact that no nonhuman species, to our knowledge, ever asks for clarification of a communicative message or repairs one for the recipient.

Second, the creation and change of grammatical constructions—especially the process of reanalysis over time—depends crucially on the way common ground and joint attention work. Specifically, aspects of linguistic communication that are predictable owing to strong common ground (and which might be transparently iconic or compositional) become reduced in form as interlocutors are able to use this common ground, even with a weak linguistic signal, to make the appropriate inferences about the intended message. This is fine for the *cognoscenti*, but for outsiders, such as children, this makes the linguistic formulations less transparent, and so they must simply learn form-function parings arbitrarily (and imperfectly). In doing this, they engage in a blame assignment process—that is, they identify which parts of the construction are effecting which subfunctions—that may differ from that of mature speakers. Our specific proposal is thus that the conventionalization of grammatical constructions—grammaticalization and similar processes— can occur only in species who have cognitive skills for constructing common ground in joint attention, and in communities that have enough sociological complexity such that different individuals have different common ground with one another (see Croft 2000). This suggests that if we were to put various "linguistic" apes together, even if they did use some of their "linguistic" signs to communicate with one another, those signs and their combinations would not show any historical development because apes do not construct with one another the kind of common conceptual ground within which this process takes place.

Overall, it may be said without fear of contradiction that human skills of linguistic communication are multifarious and derive from multiple sources. The foundational aspects concerned with cooperative communication are due mainly to evolutionary processes, but the actual creation of the linguistic conventions and constructions that people use to structure their linguistic interactions with one another in particular languages are due both to cultural-historical processes that transcend individuals and to psychological processes during ontogeny of social learning, joint attention, analogy, and so forth. The shared intentionality inherent in communicating with a common goal within the context of common conceptual ground—in combination with various human tendencies of information processing and automatization—generates the possibility for language creation and change over cultural-historical time in particular linguistic communities.

6.4.3   Language Universals and Diversity

The empirical fact is that different cultural groups of the
world have conventionalized very different sets of linguistic conventions and constructions, in some cases
based on very different grammatical principles. It is possible to shoehorn all of these different linguistic conventions and constructions into some categories from classical
and modern formal linguistics, but it is not at all clear
that it is appropriate to do this. That is, just as all linguists
agree that it is no longer appropriate to shoehorn all
European languages into Latin grammar, as we once did,
it is also no longer appropriate to shoehorn all of our
recently discovered "exotic" languages into the categories of classical European grammars such as subject and
direct object, relative clauses, and so forth.

Linguistic typologists study linguistic diversity, and
those who are not bent on squeezing all languages into a
European Procrustean bed report an incredible panoply
of strange devices that different linguistic communities
use for structuring their utterances grammatically (Croft
2003). On just the most general level, some languages
have many small morphological endings on words,
whereas others have none. Some languages break complex
events and ideas down into many small units each
designated by a separate word, whereas others express
complex events and ideas in a single complex word.
Some languages work with the categories of subject and
direct object, whereas others do not. Some languages

have very clear classes of nouns and verbs, whereas others have mostly a single class whose items may play both roles (like the English words *brush* and *kiss*). Some languages have lots of embedding structures such as relative clauses, and others have very few. Some languages have noun phrases whose items come together (as in "the big green fish"), whereas in others the items in such phrases are "exploded" all over the sentence. Some languages have one or the other of prepositions, auxiliary verbs, modal verbs, conjunctions, articles, adverbs, interjections, complementizers, pronouns, whereas others are missing one or more of these. Some languages allow speakers to simply leave out referential terms freely when the referent is implicit in the context (ellipsis), whereas others do not. And this only scratches the scratches on the surface of all the wonders that abound in the different languages of the world.

But there are linguistic universals. These are perhaps not as straightforward as once believed, however, as they concern not specific syntactic devices or constructions, but rather general constraints or functions served. For example, one of the reasons for many language universals is that people speaking in any language conceptualize the world in similar ways in terms of such things as agents acting on objects, objects moving from and to locations, events causing other events, people possessing things, people perceiving and thinking and feeling things, people interacting and communicating with one another—all involving a basic event-participant distinction. Another reason is that people speaking in any language have a large set of communicative functions in common as well, because they have similar social intentions and motives: to request things of others, to inform others of things helpfully, and to share things with others, to name just the most general classes of motives. Another reason is that people speaking in any language manipulate the attention of others in similar ways, for example by treating things already in attention (topics) as different from things new to attention (foci). People all over the world also learn and process information in similar ways based on such things as visual perception, categorization, analogy, automatization, working memory, and cultural learning, within whose constraints all linguistic communication, conventionalization, and acquisition must operate. People all over the world also have the same vocal-auditory apparatus and process vocal-auditory information in similar ways. And, in terms of the dimension of things we have focused on here—skills and motives of individual and shared intentionality—people all over the world are similar as well, including a common evolutionary history of pointing and pantomiming in acts of cooperative communication.

In this context, the question arises whether specifically linguistic and grammatical principles—not based on general processes of human cognition and communication—have also evolved in the human species. The most well-known proposal of this type is, of course,

Chomskian universal grammar. Originally the hypothesis was fairly straightforward, as universal grammar contained such purely linguistic things as nouns, verbs, and basic rules of European grammar. But as it became clear that these things did not fit many non-European languages, the hypothesis changed to include very abstract linguistic things, supposedly representing the universal computational structure of language—such things as this subjacency constraint, the empty category principle, the theta-criterion, the projection principle, and so on. But as it has become clear that these things are totally theory-dependent and the theory has been abandoned, the proposal is now that there is simply one specifically linguistic computational principle, and that is recursion—and that may not even be specifically linguistic (Hauser, Chomsky, and Fitch 2002). The Chomskian hypothesis of an innate universal grammar thus currently has no coherent formulation (Tomasello 2004).

There is no question that there are general computational constraints on how languages may be created, acquired, and changed, and there are even implicational universals such that if a language accomplishes function X in this way, then it almost always accomplishes function Y in that way (Greenberg 1963). But the question is whether we need an innate universal grammar to account for these kinds of things. In recent research, many of these constraints and implicational relations have been accounted for in terms of the general way that people process information (Hawkins 2004) or the way that they focus on things informationally in different constructions (Goldberg 2006). In this view, then, universal computational constraints on all languages reflect general cognitive, social, and vocal-auditory principles and constraints inherent in human psychological functioning. Languages have been created within the constraints of preexisting human cognition and sociality, and if these are understood well enough, on the current hypothesis, these constraints will supply what is needed. It is not that the evolution of some kind of innate syntactic template such as universal grammar is impossible, it is just that currently there is no evidence for it empirically, no precise formulation of it theoretically, and no need for it at all—if the nature of language is properly understood.

Our conclusion is thus that although many aspects of human linguistic competence have indeed evolved biologically, specific grammatical principles and constructions have not. And universals in the grammatical structure of different languages have come from more general processes and constraints of human cognition, communication, and vocal-auditory processing, operating during the conventionalization and transmission of the particular grammatical constructions of particular linguistic communities. The question of why human groups each create their own linguistic conventions, including grammatical conventions, that change so incredibly rapidly over time is not so easy to answer. But presumably it is a reflection of more general processes of culture—humans are born to imitate and become like those around them—and language is just one manifestation of this. The most plausible explanation for this general pattern is the need for groups of humans to differentiate themselves from other groups, and indeed language is a major barrier for outsiders becoming full members of a cultural group later in life (a kind of cultural isolating mechanism). And conversely, as argued above, the use of language—including for sharing experiences and attitudes about common experiences in narratives—is a major way that cultural groups create their own internal group identities. Many of the changes of grammatical structure result from the inherent messiness of children reconstructing abstract constructions from individual instances of language use, given that every child has a slightly different linguistic experience from every other (Croft 2000).

6.4.4 Summary

There is a fundamental ambiguity in modern discourse in the cognitive sciences about what we mean when we use the terms grammar or syntax. Indeed, there is a whole line of recent research in which human infants or nonhuman primates detect recurrent patterns in streams of synthesized sounds and this is most often called "grammar learning" (more cautious researchers use "statistical learning"), even though the sounds have no meaning or communicative significance whatsoever. That is not what I mean here by grammar. Grammar presupposes intentional communication, at the very least, and then grammatical devices and constructions structure multiunit utterances in functionally meaningful ways. Conventional grammatical devices and constructions, just like simple conventions such as words, are cultural-historical products created by specific cultural groups for meeting their communicative needs. Universals of language are produced by commonalities in the social, cognitive, and vocal-auditory raw materials that both enable and constrain the conventionalization process. In the spirit of Bates (1979), there are universals of language because people all over the world have similar communicative jobs to get done and similar cognitive and social tools with which to do them.

Therefore, the challenge in attempting to reconstruct the evolution of human linguistic communication, as built on top of human cooperative communication in general, is that across modern human groups there are both universals and diversity. This presumably reflects a situation in which there was some modern human group, somewhere in Africa, that went quite a long way toward modern vocal languages—how far we do not know—but then, as subgroups from this larger group began to spread out all over the world, they conventionalized their own linguistic conventions and constructions. All of these groups retained the same basic cognitive, social-cognitive, communicative, and vocal-auditory capacities, of course, and so the conventionalization process was constrained in similar ways for all of them as well.

6.5   Conclusion

The answer to the question of where grammar comes from is: many places. Apes already string together gestures in sequences to communicate with others. "Linguistic" apes even produce true combinations in which they parse their intended message into multiple elements, often event and participants. The cognitive machinery for doing this, what we called simple syntax, thus has very deep evolutionary roots. And as long as the communicative motive involved is one of simple requesting—I want you to do something here and now—there will be no need for any more complex grammatical structuring of utterances.

Once cooperative communication and the motive to inform emerged—structured by common ground and communicative intentions—the way humans communicated became much more complex. The grammar of informing requires additional devices for specifying which particular events and participants are being talked about (perhaps in complex yet coherent constituents grounding them in the current joint attentional frame) and marking the roles they are playing in the talked-about event or situation. And when I need to narrate a whole sequence of events—for example, to relate what happened to me during yesterday's hunt—a grammar of sharing and narrative, involving even more grammatical devices, is required for relating events to one another and tracking the participants across those events. The evolutionary roots for the grammars of informing and sharing in narrative derive from basic competencies of cooperative communication and its complex shared intentionality infrastructure. But the actual grammatical conventions are, of course, not created by evolutionary processes at all; they are created by cultural-historical ("invisible hand") processes that we have called the conventionalization of grammatical constructions.

The grammatical constructions of modern human languages are thus products of a long and complex series of events in human history, involving both evolutionary and cultural processes—taking place within the constraints of a panoply of general cognitive and social-cognitive processes. Much of this happened in the gestural modality, which explains why it is that sign languages seem to spring into existence so easily today. The creation and modification of grammatical constructions is possible, in the current account, only because humans engage with one another communicatively as a joint activity with a common goal, and the communicator leaves much unsaid if it can be assumed to be in common ground and so pragmatically inferred by the recipient—so that individuals outside this joint attentional cocoon quite often analyze which parts of the utterance are serving which functions in novel ways. Even at the very latest stages of the process of language evolution, the fundamental skills and motives of shared intentionality with which humans began down the road of cooperative communication are still at the heart of the process.

7   From Ape Gestures to Human Language

Our talk gets its meaning from the rest of our activities.
—Wittgenstein, *On Certainty*

I promised it would be a complicated story, and so it is. But highly distinctive and complex phenotypic outcomes, such as human cooperative communication, almost always have complicated and circuitous evolutionary histories. And highly distinctive and complex cultural outcomes, such as conventional human languages, almost always have complicated and circuitous cultural histories laid on top of this. I thus choose to blame all of this complexity on reality—though it is of course possible that we just do not understand everything well enough to find the hidden simplicity. In any case, I make here a final attempt at simplicity by first summarizing the overall argument in a few pages, and by then revisiting our three hypotheses from chapter 1 to see how they have fared. I end with some thoughts on language as shared intentionality.

7.1   Summary of the Argument

A summary of the overall argument of these lectures (organized, approximately, by chapter) might go something as follows.

The road to human cooperative communication begins with great ape intentional communication, especially as manifest in gestures.

• Apes learn many of their gestures (by ontogenetic ritualization), and so they use them very flexibly, indeed intentionally, including with attention to the attention of specific others—which contrasts totally with their unlearned, inflexible, emotional vocalizations indiscriminately broadcast to the world.

• Apes always use their learned, intentional gestures to request/demand actions from others, including humans. They use their intention-movements to demand action directly. They use their attention-getters to demand action indirectly, that is, they use them to direct the other's attention so that she will see something and then do something as a result. Apes' learned attention-getters may be the only intentional communicative acts in the nonhuman world that operate with this split-level intentionality: that the other see something and so do something as a result.

• The comprehension and production of these gestures are underlain by skills for understanding individual intentionality—understanding that others have goals and perceptions—and result in a kind of practical reasoning (including inferences) about what others are doing and, perhaps, why they are doing it. Communicators and recipients each have their own distinct goals in the communicative process, with no jointly shared goals.

Human cooperative communication is more complex than ape intentional communication because its underlying social-cognitive infrastructure comprises not only skills for understanding individual intentionality but also skills and motivations for shared intentionality.

· The basic cognitive skill of shared intentionality is recursive mindreading. When employed in certain social interactions, it generates joint goals and joint attention, which provide the common conceptual ground within which human communication most naturally occurs.

· The basic motives for shared intentionality are helping and sharing. When employed in communicative interactions, these generate the three basic motives of human cooperative communication: requesting (requesting help), informing (offering help in the form of useful information), and sharing emotions and attitudes (bonding socially by expanding common ground).

· Mutual assumptions (and even norms) of cooperation and the Gricean communicative intention are generated as recursive mindreading is applied to the cooperative motives: we both know together that we are (and should be, from the point of view of the social group) cooperative. This leads human interactants to work together toward the joint goal of successful communication, and to engage in not just practical but cooperative reasoning, and so make inferences of communicative relevance, in the process.

• To communicate nonlinguistically, humans use the pointing gesture to direct the visual attention of others, and they use iconic gestures (pantomiming) to direct the imagination of others. These two types of gesture may be considered "natural" communication as they exploit, respectively, the recipient's natural tendency to follow gaze direction, and the recipient's natural tendency to interpret the actions of others intentionally. These simple gestures communicate in complex ways because they are used in interpersonal situations in which the participants share conceptual common ground as interpretive nexus, as well as mutual assumptions of cooperation.

• "Arbitrary" communicative conventions, including linguistic conventions, rely on the same cooperative infrastructure as "natural" human gestures, and indeed they derive originally from these natural gestures through a "drift to the arbitrary" as neophytes acquire the instrumental use of iconic gestures whose iconicity they do not fully grasp.

The ontogeny of human infants' gestural communication, especially pointing, provides evidence for the various components of the hypothesized cooperative infrastructure and a connection to shared intentionality—and before language acquisition begins.

• Experiments on infants' pointing demonstrate the critical role of the shared intentionality infrastructure: the joint attentional frame and common ground; the three basic motives of requesting, informing, and sharing; and, less certainly, the communicative intention and cooperative norms.

• Infants' pointing emerges developmentally only with their emerging skills of shared intentionality in collaborative action—not before, even though many other prerequisites are ready earlier—and this emergence antedates any substantial skills with a conventional language.

• Infants' iconic gestures emerge on the heels of their first pointing, requiring a communicative intention to be effective (otherwise they are just empty actions); they are quickly replaced by conventional language (while pointing is not displaced by the emergence of language) because both iconic gestures and linguistic conventions represent symbolic ways of indicating referents.

• The ontogenetic transition from gestures to conventional forms of communication, including language, also relies crucially on the shared intentionality infrastructure—especially joint attention in collaborative activities—to create the common ground necessary for learning "arbitrary" communicative conventions.

• The ontogenetic transition from gestures to language demonstrates the common function of (i) pointing and demonstratives (e.g., *this* and *that*); and (ii) iconic gestures and content words (e.g., nouns and verbs).

Human cooperative communication emerged phylogentically as part of a broader adaptation for collaborative activity and cultural life in general.

• Humans' skills and motives for shared intentionality arose initially within the context of mutualistic collaborative activities—with skills of recursive mindreading leading to the formation of joint goals, which then generated joint attention to things relevant to those joint goals. Great apes do not participate in collaborative activities of this type, and so they do not have the human-like skills and motives for shared intentionality.

• First pointing and then pantomiming arose as ways of coordinating the collaborative activity more efficiently, initially by requesting that the other do something—with compliance assured because it helped both participants. Initially, such cooperative communicative acts were used only within the context of collaborative activities—and so their intentional structure was cooperative all the way down. The use of skills of cooperative communication outside of collaborative activities (e.g., for lying), came only later.

• Actually offering help by informing may have arisen by processes of indirect reciprocity in which people sought to gain reputations as good collaborators. This created a public space of mutual expectations about how cooperative communication should work.

• Sharing emotions and attitudes with others may have arisen as ways of social bonding and expanding common ground within the social group (tied to cultural group selection)—with the actual norms that govern cooperative communication originating from group sanctions for not cooperating.

• Human skills of imitation enabled humans to create and acquire from others iconic gestures used as holophrases (requiring the communicative intention to even get off the ground), which quite naturally experience a "drift to the arbitrary" in the transmission process when those sharing less common ground are involved—thus creating communicative conventions.

• The eventual switch to totally arbitrary vocal conventions was only possible because these conventions were first used in conjunction with—actually piggybacked on—more naturally meaningful action-based gestures.

The grammatical dimension of human linguistic communication consists in the conventionalization and cultural transmission of linguistic constructions—based on general cognitive skills, as well as skills of shared intentionality and imitation—in order to meet the functional demands of the three basic communicative motives, leading to a grammar of requesting, a grammar of informing, and a grammar of sharing and narrative.

• Apes use sequences of gestures, and "linguistic" apes actually combine gestures toward a single communicative end and parse experience into events and participants—and so these basic grammatical skills are "given" as a starting point for the evolution of human grammatical competence.

• When "linguistic" apes—and so perhaps very early humans—produce multiunit utterances, they use them almost always for requestive functions—which typically involve only "me and you in the here and now," and which means that there is no functional pressure for any serious syntactic marking. These apes and early humans thus have only a grammar of requesting.

• With the emergence of the informing function and referents displaced in time and space, there arises a need for grammatical devices to (i) identify absent referents by grounding them in the current joint attentional frame (perhaps using multiunit constituents), (ii) syntactically mark the roles of participants, and (iii) distinguish requestive from informative communicative motives.

These functional demands lead to a grammar of informing.

• With the emergence of the sharing motive and utterances intended to narrate complex series of events displaced in time and space, there arises a need for grammatical devices to (i) time stamp and relate events to one another, and (ii) track participants across events. These functional demands lead to a grammar of sharing and narrative.

• The particular grammatical constructions of particular languages are created by a conventionalization process (grammaticalization and other processes) in cultural-historical time, depending crucially on joint goals for communicating, common conceptual ground, and some basic processes of cognition and information processing. The group-level processes involved here also create the normativity of constructions as "grammatical."

7.2   Hypotheses and Problems

In chapter 1 I proposed three hypotheses about the origins of human communication: (1) human cooperative communication evolved initially in the gestural domain (pointing and pantomiming); (2) this evolution was potentiated by skills and motivations for shared intentionality, themselves originally evolved in the context of collaborative activities; and (3) it is only in the context of inherently meaningful collaborative activities, coordinated by "natural" forms of communication such as pointing and pantomiming, that totally arbitrary linguistic conventions could have come into existence. We are now in a position to see how these three hypotheses have fared.

With regard to gestures, a number of theorists over the centuries have proposed that humans' first step on the evolutionary road to language was gestures (e.g., Hewes 1973; Corballis 2002; Kendon 2004; Armstrong and Wilcox 2007). These authors have offered a number of evolutionary arguments for this thesis, having to do mostly with various advantages of the visual-manual modality. Also important are the facts that human infants communicate meaningfully with gestures before language and that deaf infants not exposed to sign language soon begin to communicate in complex ways using invented gestures. Also, human beings who share no communicative conventions—everyone from strangers in a strange land to the creators of Nicaraguan Sign Language—find it relatively easy to begin communicating using gestures. And given a few generations and the appropriate social conditions, these may even end up being conventionalized into something that is arguably a full-blown human language. If humans were adapted for a vocal language only, then these gestural inventions are incredible, almost inexplicable, extensions of the core capacity. If humans were adapted first for something like gestural communication, and then the vocal modality took over only later, then these gestural inventions are much more readily explained.

I added to this two other arguments, one empirical and one theoretical. The empirical argument is that all four great ape species learn and use gestures in very flexible ways—which contrasts markedly with their unlearned, inflexible vocalizations. They also use their gestures with sensitivity to the attentional state of specific recipients, and even use some attention-getting gestures which already differentiate two levels of intention—referential and social—clearly presaging all of the sophisticated attention-directing that goes on in human referential communication. One may then easily imagine how these flexible gestures could have evolved into human pointing and iconic gestures, which already embodied, before vocal language, the most fundamental characteristics of human cooperative communication. It should be noted, however, that the vocalizations of great apes have not been so well studied—the vast majority of primate vocalization research is with monkeys—and so this is clearly an area that needs more research attention in the future. The attention-getters of apes, perhaps especially those that involve external objects (and including pointing for humans), need further investigation as well.

The theoretical argument is that it is very difficult to see how humans could have gone directly from ape-like vocalizations—associated basically with the communicator's emotions—to created, learned, and mutually known communicative conventions, shared by all members of a group. To dramatize the point, I used a somewhat grotesque *Gedankenexperiment* of nonlinguistic children on a desert island who either could not vocalize or could not gesture. The children who could not vocalize would gesture up a storm and communicate quite nicely, but it is difficult to imagine that the children who could not gesture would create vocal conventions easily—since vocalizations tend to draw attention to the self and the self's emotional state and not to external referents at all. The proposal was thus that the path to human vocal conventions had to pass through an intermediary stage of more naturally meaningful, action-based gestures based on humans' natural tendencies to follow the gaze direction of others and to interpret their actions as intentional. Indeed, I even argued that vocal conventions came to possess communicative significance originally only by piggybacking on—being used redundantly with—naturally meaningful gestures.

In terms of the second hypothesis—shared intentionality as the basis for human cooperative communication—there are two lines of empirical evidence and a few theoretical arguments. The first line of empirical evidence comes from comparing great apes and humans. Experimental research, much of it reviewed in section 2.4, demonstrates that great apes understand individual intentionality. Some researchers believe that our assessment here is too generous, and that apes and other nonhuman animals have only simple behavioral rules for predicting what others will do in certain situations (Povinelli and Vonk 2006). Our response is that the studies speak for themselves—providing converging evidence using several different methods for all key points (see Tomasello and Call, in press, for a more systematic argument). And the analysis of apes' gestural communication here would seem to be consistent with an understanding of individual intentionality as well. However, in contrast to this strong evidence for understanding individual intentionality, there is no experimental evidence that great apes participate in shared intentionality, as their synchronized activities in experiments do not seem to have the structure of human collaboration, nor do they participate in joint attention in human-like ways. In this case there are researchers who believe that my assessment is too negative; for example, Boesch (2005) believes that naturalistic observations of chimpanzee hunting establish its collaborative nature. But to demonstrate underlying cognitive processes, naturalistic observations are not sufficient; we need experiments. And the experiments that have been done—in fairness, there are not so many—have demonstrated apes' ability to synchronize with others in problem-solving situations, but not to form joint goals, joint plans, and joint attention with them while doing so. Negative results from experiments are always difficult to interpret, of course, and so experimental research on great ape collaboration is another area in dire need of greater scientific attention.

Because they do not engage in truly collaborative activities in general, great apes' communication, in the current hypothesis, is basically individualistic as well—just as

that of other mammals. Their intentional communication
is aimed exclusively at making demands/requests. There
are some observations of great apes communicating in
ways that do not seem like prototypical requests; for
example, the researchers who have trained "linguistic"
apes typically report some utterances used when the
ape apparently does not want anything. Experimental
research is needed here, however, because a viable alternative hypothesis is that the apes are simply exercising
their skill by "naming" something as they see it—without
any prosocial desire to inform others of things helpfully
or to declaratively share emotions or attitudes with them.
Another example is the several experiments showing that
when apes want food, and a human needs to find a
hidden tool in order to fetch it for them, the apes will
point to that tool's hidden location (see section 2.3 for
references). One could say they are informing the human
here, but since apparently apes do not point in this way
when the human only wants something for herself
(research is ongoing)—and they certainly do not do anything like this with conspecifics—one could also view
this as something more like "social tool use": requesting
that the human fetch and use the tool for the ape. And
note that there is no evidence anywhere that apes employ
common ground or mutual expectations of helpfulness
or that they comprehend the Gricean communicative
intention, since they routinely fail to make simple relevance inferences in experiments testing their comprehen-

sion of the human pointing gesture (see section 2.3). In any case, our interpretation of these two sets of data, on ape collaboration and communication, suggests to us that great apes do not engage in either truly collaborative activities or truly cooperative communication. Since humans engage in both, and since from a theoretical point of view these both involve cooperative skills and motives, a reasonable hypothesis is that these two skills share a common psychological infrastructure of shared intentionality. This shared infrastructure suggests a common evolutionary origin of the two skills.

The second line of evidence for the central role of shared intentionality comes from human ontogeny. Human infants have the physical ability to point and gesture with their hands and bodies from fairly early in development, and they would seem to have at least some motives that cooperative communication could satisfy, for example, getting others to do things by requesting (and perhaps sharing emotions). But they do not engage in cooperative communication until they are close to one year of age, which just happens to be the same age that they begin displaying skills of shared intentionality in their collaborative activities with other persons. The temporal synchrony is not so straightforward here because a number of things all happen at around the first birthday, but this developmental coemergence is certainly very suggestive. And from the first birthday, infants' pointing and other gesturing already shows evidence of the use of common ground, cooperative motives, and, perhaps, mutual assumptions of cooperativeness and the Gricean communicative intention—though more research is needed here for sure.

Again, as in the case of apes, we have critics coming from both directions. Although not addressing these issues specifically, there are some infancy researchers who would very likely believe that infants actually engage in something like cooperative communication much earlier than is manifest in the pointing gesture at one year of age (e.g., Trevarthen 1979). In contrast, there are other theorists who think we are too generous in interpreting one-year-olds' pointing as manipulating the mental states of others altruistically (e.g., Carpendale and Lewis 2004). But as in the case of apes, these are mostly researchers who are more focused on natural observations than on experiments, and we believe that the current experimental research, as reviewed in chapter 4, supports our position on the mentalistic and altruistic structure of early communication. There are certainly no experimental studies that argue against this conclusion.

The major theoretical arguments for shared intentionality as the basis for human cooperative communication derive from the philosophical analyses of communication provided by classic scholars such as Wittgenstein (1953), Grice (1957, 1975), and Lewis (1969), and more contemporary scholars such as Sperber and Wilson (1986), Clark (1996), Levinson (1995, 2006), and Searle (1969, 1995). I certainly do not claim to have done anything theoretically that goes beyond their insights in significant ways, but I have tried to put together something new from their seminal ideas as applied to the communicative activities of great apes, human children, and perhaps our human forebears. What is clear in doing this is that the central unifying concept is something like recursive mindreading (as summarized in table 3.1, for example). Thus, we see apes' understanding of intentions and attention turn into human joint intentions, joint attention, and communicative intentions; we see humans' cooperative motives for communicating turn into mutual assumptions and even norms of cooperation; and we see humans' "natural" communicative gestures turn into human communicative conventions. These transformations all result from some kind of recursively structured mutual understanding between two or more human beings who each know that the other knows, and so forth, back and forth indefinitely—at least in one way of looking at it.

The notion of mutual knowledge was first employed in the context of communication by Lewis (1969) in his analysis of coordinating conventions. Sperber and Wilson (1986) do not like the connotations of mutual knowledge (as implying certainty), and so prefer to speak of mutual cognitive environments and mutual manifestness to capture some of the same insights. Clark (1996) opts for talk of common ground as a more neutral way of describing the phenomenon, and Searle (1995) simply speaks of collective or we-intentionality. There is much debate about whether the notion of recursivity is needed in all of this or whether it is more reasonable to simply characterize we-intentionality in all its various forms as a psychological primitive without all of the backing-and-forthing. My own view is that whether we treat we-intentionality theoretically as a primitive or as something derived from a back-and-forth between individuals depends on what we are trying to explain. In explaining how contemporary humans operate in real time, it is possible that no notion of recursivity is actually operative, but rather humans simply possess a primitive notion of we-intentionality. Indeed, I think that this is exactly what young infants do; they simply distinguish situations in which we are sharing attention to something from those in which we are not. But as development proceeds, the various individual perspectives embodied in sharing are articulated out (presumably on the basis of bumpy interactions in which things thought to be shared turn out not to be), perhaps as hypothesized by Barresi and Moore (1996). I earlier cited as evidence for recursivity the fact that breakdowns can occur at various levels in the back-and-forth—and humans diagnose these differently and repair them in different ways as a result—but the actual data for this hypothesis are not so numerous. And when we turn to evolution, I think it would be extremely implausible to posit that we-intentionality arose full-blown as a one-shot innovation. Rather, it is almost certainly the case that there was a point at which individuals simply began to understand something like "he sees me seeing it," and then only later did the full recursivity of this understanding become manifest.

Finally, with respect to the third hypothesis about the origin of communicative conventions specifically, I have suggested that totally arbitrary communicative conventions, such as those in spoken language, could only have arisen through the intermediary of more "natural," action-based gestures within collaborative interactions structured by joint attention—taking advantage of humans' natural tendencies to follow the gaze direction of others and to interpret actions intentionally. Perhaps the best evidence for this proposal comes from early child language. Even though young infants are perfectly capable of associating sounds and experiences from several months of age (and even imitating vocalizations), they do not begin acquiring linguistic conventions until they begin participating with others in collaborative activities structured by joint attention at around the first birthday. And indeed, infants' participation in such activities correlates quantitatively very strongly with how quickly they acquire their initial communicative conventions (see Tomasello 2003 for a review). Also required for conventional communication, of course, are strong skills of action imitation—perhaps even role reversal imitation—to ensure that the conventions are both passed along across generations and mutually known to be shared among all who participate in this cultural-historical process.

And in the child's transition to grammar, the use of pointing and other gestures seems to supply a critical bridge, even though of course modern children are keen to acquire both communicative and grammatical conventions straightaway, simply to be like others, and so they may acquire them without any support from natural gestures if the joint attentional frame is strong enough. Deaf children who create with their parents idiosyncratic communicative conventions in the form of home sign must perforce start with natural gestures in joint attentional interactions or else they would not be understood—with any move to the arbitrary in such signing systems requiring a community in which a mutually known shared learning history may develop (as in Nicaraguan Sign Language).

The origin of grammar in human evolution, in the current hypothesis, was part of a single process in which humans began to conventionalize means of communication. That is, it was a stepwise process in which emerging new communicative motives for informing and sharing/narrative placed new functional pressures on individuals already requesting things from one another with "natural" gestures, and then holophrastic conventions. In response, humans created conventional syntactic devices for structuring multiunit utterances grammatically—and so meeting the new communicative needs precipitated by informing and sharing—and these became conventionalized into Gestalt-like linguistic constructions: prepackaged patterns of linguistic conventions and syntactic devices for recurrent communicative functions. Importantly, the process by which linguistic constructions are conventionalized (grammaticalized) depends crucially on interactants who have a shared communicative goal and are able to "negotiate" with one another the form the utterance needs to take based ultimately on their common conceptual ground. Thus, the grammatical dimension of human cooperative communication very likely originated in combinations of pointing and pantomiming within collaborative activities, and it moved outside this restricted context by means of a "drift to the arbitrary" in the same manner as holophrastic linguistic conventions. The passing along of grammatical constructions across generations requires not just cultural learning and imitation, but also the ability to (re-)construct patterns of language use from experienced acts of linguistic communication.

Overall, then, the analysis presented here suggests that, following Bates (1979), human language is best seen as "a new machine made out of old parts." And indeed, though it is difficult to imagine this in the twenty-first century, it could have ended up a different machine if some of its parts had evolved differently initially—since the parts are many and each has its own contingent evolutionary history. Thus, in the current analysis, skills for understanding individual intentionality gave an adaptive advantage to primate individuals originally in the context of competition; skills of action imitation evolved originally in humans' tool use and making; joint intentions and joint attention evolved originally in the context of human collaborative activity; the Gricean communicative intention emerged in the context of mutual expectations of cooperation; human motives for informing others of things evolved originally in the context of concerns about reputation for helpfulness; human motives for sharing emotions and attitudes with others evolved originally in the context of group-level processes and norms; human norms arose to maximize within-group homogeneity in the context of cultural group selection; human gestures have a deep history in great apes, but new ones such as pointing and pantomiming arose in human evolution based on primates' natural tendency to follow gaze direction and to interpret action intentionally; human communicative conventions arose in situations with joint goals based on human skills of role reversal imitation and cooperative motives, and are transmitted based on human skills of social imitation; human vocal skills have a deep history in great apes, but also have evolved unique features fairly recently presumably to facilitate conventional communication (and so, perhaps, to distinguish natal members of our group); human skills of grammar have deep roots in the primate tendency to parse experience into events and participants and to combine acts toward a single goal; conventionalizing grammatical constructions takes place above the level of individuals and depends on human skills of shared intentionality, imitation, and vocal-auditory processing, among others. And on and on.

The point is simply that if any of these parts had been different in significant ways—for any of a zillion evolutionary reasons—human languages could have turned out very differently as well. Perhaps we could have evolved only to request things from others using natural gestures. Perhaps we could have evolved linguistic conventions, but still only to request things—so that we would have conventionalized only a simple syntax. Or perhaps we could have created linguistic conventions and constructions for informing others of things helpfully but not to narrate events displaced in time and space—so that we would have no fancy syntax involving complex verb tenses and aspects or devices for tracking referents across events. Even more arresting is to try to imagine what human "language"—if we would even want to call it that at all—would look like if it had evolved not in the context of cooperation but competition. In this case, there would be no joint attention and common ground and so acts of reference could not be made in the human-like way, certainly not for perspectives or absent referents. There would be no communicative intention based on mutual assumptions of cooperation, and so no reason to try hard to discover why someone is trying to communicate with me—and no norms of communication. There would be no conventions, which can only arise when individuals have common, cooperative understandings and interests. And without the motives of informing and sharing, this hypothetical competitive form of "language" could only be used for coercion and deception—and actually not even that, as the communicators could not collaborate to get the message across, owing to a lack of trust. So basically, there could in fact be no language as we know it based on competition. And if the cooperation had evolved differently—for example in the scenarios outlined above—the form of language would have been different as well. Simply put, if human social life had evolved in a different direction, our means of communication would have evolved in a different direction as well. To imagine a language is to imagine a form of life, says Wittgenstein.

7.3 Language as Shared Intentionality

If one were to ask a panel of scientists and laypersons what accounts for the remarkably complexity of human cognitive abilities, social institutions, and culture, the most common response would almost certainly be "Language." But what is language? At least partly because there is written language, which may be looked at and examined, and reexamined, and then put on a shelf, we intuitively think of language as some kind of object (Olson 1994). But it is not an object—at least not in any interesting sense—any more than a university or a government or a game of chess is an object in any interesting sense. In the formulation of Searle (1995, p. 36):

In the case of social objects . . . process is prior to product. Social objects are always . . . constituted by social acts; and, in a sense, the object is just the continuous possibility of the activity.

Linguistic acts are social acts that one person intentionally directs to another (and highlights that he is doing this) in order to direct her attention and imagination in particular ways so that she will do, know, or feel what he wants her to. These acts work only if the participants are both equipped with a psychological infrastructure of skills and motivations of shared intentionality evolved for facilitating interactions with others in collaborative activities. Language, or better linguistic communication, is thus not any kind of object, formal or otherwise; rather it is a form of social action constituted by social conventions for achieving social ends, premised on at least some shared understandings and shared purposes among users.

Like many cultural products, human languages may in their turn contribute to further developments in the originating skills. This is true in at least two fundamental ways. First, and most obviously, modern human collaboration and culture are as complex as they are mainly because they are typically organized and transmitted via linguistic conventions. Human collaboration for building skyscrapers and creating universities, for example, is unimaginable without conventional forms of communication for setting the shared goals and subgoals and formulating the coordinated plans to achieve them. Human collaboration is the original home of human cooperative communication, but then this new form of communication facilitates ever more complex forms of collaboration in a coevolutionary spiral.

Second, and less obviously, participating in conventional linguistic communication and other forms of shared intentionality takes basic human cognition in some surprising new directions. Although it is taken completely for granted by cognitive scientists, human beings are the only animal species that conceptualizes the world in terms of different potential perspectives on one and the same entity, thus creating so-called perspectival cognitive representations (Tomasello 1999). The key point here is that these unique forms of human conceptualization depend crucially on shared intentionality—in the sense that the whole notion of perspective presupposes some jointly focused entity that we know we share but are viewing from different angles (Perner, Brandl, and Garnham 2003; Moll and Tomasello 2007b). Importantly, perspectival cognitive representations are not a format of human conceptualization given at birth, but are actually constructed by children as they participate in the process of cooperative communication—in the to-and-fro of various kinds of discourse in which different perspectives are expressed toward shared topics in the participants' common conceptual ground (Tomasello and Rakoczy 2003). The cooperative infrastructure of human communication, including conventional linguistic communication, thus not only arises from but also contributes to humans' uniquely cooperative, cultural ways of living and thinking.

The origins of human cooperative communication are thus many, and their culmination in skills of linguistic communication represents one more instance—perhaps the fundamental instance—of the coevolutionary process by which basic cognitive skills evolve phylogenetically, enabling the creation of cultural products historically, which then provide developing children with the biological and cultural tools they need to develop ontogenetically.

References

Acredelo, L. P., and Goodwyn, S. W. (1988). Symbolic gesturing in normal infants. *Child Development, 59,* 450–466.

Akhtar, N., Carpenter, M., and Tomasello, M. (1996). The role of discourse novelty in early word learning. *Child Development, 67,* 635–645.

Akhtar, N., Jipson, J., and Callanan, M. (2001). Learning words through overhearing. *Child Development, 72,* 416–430.

Armstrong, D., Stokoe, W., and Wilcox, S. (1995). *Gesture and the Nature of Language.* Cambridge: Cambridge University Press.

Armstrong, D., and Wilcox, S. (2007). *The Gestural Origin of Language.* New York: Oxford University Press.

Bakeman, R., and Adamson, L. (1984). Coordinating attention to people and objects in mother-infant and peer-infant interactions. *Child Development, 55,* 1278–1289.

Baldwin, D. (1991). Infants' contributions to the achievement of joint reference. *Child Development, 62,* 875–890.

Bard, K., and Vauclair, J. (1984). The communicative context of object manipulation in ape and human adult-infant pairs. *Journal of Human Evolution, 13,* 181–190.

Barresi, J., and Moore, C. (1996). Intentional relations and social understanding. *Behavioral and Brain Sciences, 19*(1), 107–129.

Bates, E. (1979). *The Emergence of Symbols: Cognition and Communication in Infancy.* New York: Academic Press.

Bates, E., Camaioni, L., and Volterra, V. (1975). The acquisition of performatives prior to speech. *Merrill-Palmer Quarterly, 21,* 205–224.

Bateson, P. (1988). The biological evolution of cooperation and trust. In *Trust: Making and Breaking Cooperative Relations,* ed. D. Gambetta (pp. 14–30). Oxford: Blackwell.

Behne, T., Carpenter, M., Call, J., and Tomasello, M. (2005). Unwilling versus unable? Infants' understanding of intentional action. *Developmental Psychology, 41,* 328–337.

Behne, T., Carpenter, M., and Tomasello, M. (2005). One-year-olds comprehend the communicative intentions behind gestures in a hiding game. *Developmental Science, 8,* 492–499.

Bergstrom, C. T., and Lachmann, M. (2001). Alarm calls as costly signals of anti-predator vigilance: The watchful babbler game. *Animal Behavior 61*(3), 535–543.

Bloom, P. (2000). *How Children Learn the Meanings of Words.* Cambridge, Mass.: MIT Press.

Boesch, C. (2005). Joint cooperative hunting among wild chimpanzees: Taking natural observations seriously. *Behavioral and Brain Sciences, 28,* 692–693.

Boesch, C., and Boesch, H. (1989). Hunting behavior of wild chimpanzees in the Tai Forest National Park. *American Journal of Physical Anthropology, 78*(4), 547–573.

Boesch, C., and Boesch-Achermann, H. (2000). *The Chimpanzees of the Taï Forest: Behavioural Ecology and Evolution.* Oxford: Oxford University Press.

Boyd, R., and Richerson, P. (1985). *Culture and the Evolutionary Process.* Chicago: The University of Chicago Press.

Braine, M. (1963). The ontogeny of English phrase structure. *Language, 39,* 1–14.

Bratman, M. (1992). Shared co-operative activity. *Philosophical Review, 101*(2), 327–341.

Bräuer, J., Call, J., and Tomasello, M. (2005). All four great ape species follow gaze around barriers. *Journal of Comparative Psychology, 119*, 145–154.

Bräuer, J., Kaminski, J., Call, J., and Tomasello, M. (2006). Making inferences about the location of hidden food: Social dog—Causal ape. *Journal of Comparative Psychology, 120*, 38–47.

Bretherton, I., Bates, E., McNew, S., and Shore, C. (1981). Comprehension and production of symbols in infancy. *Developmental Psychology, 17*, 728–736.

Brinck, I. (2004). The pragmatics of imperative and declarative pointing. *Cognitive Science Quarterly, 3*(4), 1–18.

Brooks, P., Tomasello, M., Lewis, L., and Dodson, K. (1999). Children's overgeneralization of fixed transitivity verbs: The entrenchment hypothesis. *Child Development, 70, 1325–1337.*

Brown, P., and Levinson, S. (1978). Universals in language usage: Politeness phenomena. In *Questions and Politeness,* ed. E. Goody. Cambridge: Cambridge University Press.

Bruner, J. (1983). *Child's Talk.* New York: Norton.

Bruner, J. (1986). *Actual Minds, Possible Worlds.* Cambridge, Mass.: Harvard University Press.

Bühler, K. (1934/1990). *Theory of Language: The Representational Function of Language.* Trans. D. F. Goodwin. Amsterdam and Philadelphia: John Benjamins.

Burling, R. (2005). *The Talking Ape.* Oxford: Oxford University Press.

Buttelmann, D., Carpenter, M., Call, J., and Tomasello, M. (2007). Enculturated apes imitate rationally. *Developmental Science, 10,* F31–38.

Butterworth, G. (2003). Pointing is the royal road to language for babies. In *Pointing: Where Language, Culture, and Cognition Meet,* ed. S. Kita (pp. 9–33). Hillsdale, N.J.: Lawrence Erlbaum.

Bybee, J. (1995). Regular morphology and the lexicon. *Language and Cognitive Processes, 10*, 425–455.

Bybee, J. (2002). Sequentiality as the basis of constituent structure. In *From Pre-language to Language*, ed. T. Givón and B. Malle. Amsterdam: John Benjamins.

Call, J. (2004). Inferences about the location of food in the great apes *(Pan paniscus, Pan troglodytes, Gorilla gorilla, Pongo pygmaeus)*. *Journal of Comparative Psychology, 118*, 232–241.

Call, J., Hare, B., Carpenter, M., and Tomasello, M. (2004). Unwilling or unable? Chimpanzees' understanding of intentional action. *Developmental Science, 7*, 488–498.

Call, J., and Tomasello, M. (1994). The production and comprehension of referential pointing by orangutans. *Journal of Comparative Psychology, 108*, 307–317.

Call, J., and Tomasello, M. (1998). Distinguishing intentional from accidental actions in orangutans *(Pongo pygmaeus)*, chimpanzees *(Pan troglodytes)*, and human children *(Homo sapiens)*. *Journal of Comparative Psychology, 112*(2), 192–206.

Call, J., and Tomasello, M. (2005). What chimpanzees know about seeing, revisited: An explanation of the third kind. In *Joint Attention: Communication and Other Minds*, ed. N. Eilan, C. Hoerl, T. McCormack, and J. Roessler (pp. 45–64). Oxford: Oxford University Press.

Call, J., and Tomasello, M. (2007). *The Gestural Communication of Apes and Monkeys*. Mahwah, N.J.: Lawrence Erlbaum.

Camaioni, L. (1993). The development of intentional communication: A re-analysis. In, *New Perspectives in Early Communicative Development*, ed. J. Nadel and L. Camaioni (pp. 82–96). New York: Routledge.

Camaioni, L., Perucchini, P., Muratori, F., Parrini, B., and Cesari, A. (2003). The communicative use of pointing in autism: Developmental profiles and factors related to change. *European Psychiatry, 18*(1), 6–12.

Campbell, A. L., Brooks, P., and Tomasello, M. (2000). Factors affecting young children's use of pronouns as referring expressions. *Journal of Speech, Language, and Hearing Research, 43*, 1337–1349.

Capirci, O., Iverson, J. M., Pizzuto, E., and Volterra, V. (1996). Gestures and words during the transition to two-word speech. *Journal of Child Language*, *23*, 645–673.

Caron, A. J., Kiel, E. J., Dayton, M., and Butler, S. C. (2002). Comprehension of the referential intent of looking and pointing between 12 and 15 months. *Journal of Cognition and Development*, *3*(4), 445–464.

Carpendale, J. E. M., and Lewis, C. (2004). Constructing an understanding of mind: The development of children's understanding of mind within social interaction. *Behavioral and Brain Sciences*, *27*, 79–150.

Carpenter, M. (2006). Instrumental, social, and shared goals and intentions in imitation. In *Imitation and the Development of the Social Mind: Lessons from Typical Development and Autism*, ed. S. Rogers and J. Williams. New York: Guilford.

Carpenter, M., Akhtar, N., and Tomasello, M. (1998). Fourteen- through 18-month-old infants differentially imitate intentional and accidental actions. *Infant Behavior and Development*, *21*, 315–330.

Carpenter, M., Nagell, K., and Tomasello, M. (1998). Social cognition, joint attention, and communicative competence from 9 to 15 months of age. *Monographs of the Society of Research in Child Development*, *63*(4).

Carpenter, M., Pennington, B. F., and Rogers, S. J. (2001). Understanding of others' intentions in children with autism and children with developmental delays. *Journal of Autism and Developmental Disorders*, *31*, 589–599.

Carpenter, M., Tomasello, M., and Savage-Rumbaugh, S. (1995). Joint attention and imitative learning in children, chimpanzees, and enculturated chimpanzees. *Social Development*, *4*(3), 217–237.

Carpenter, M., Tomasello, M., and Striano, T. (2005). Role reversal imitation and language in typically-developing infants and children with autism. *Infancy*, *8*, 253–278.

Chafe, W. (1994). *Discourse, Consciousness, and Time: The Flow and Displacement of Conscious Experience in Speaking and Writing*. Chicago: The University of Chicago Press.

Chalmeau, R. (1994). Do chimpanzees cooperate in a learning task? *Primates, 35*(3), 385–392.

Chalmeau, R., and Gallo, A. (1996). What chimpanzees *(Pan troglodytes)* learn in a cooperative task. *Primates, 37,* 39–47.

Cheney, D. L., and Seyfarth, R. M. (1990a). *How Monkeys See the World: Inside the Mind of Another Species.* Chicago: The University of Chicago Press.

Cheney, D. L., and Seyfarth, R. M. (1990b). Attending to behaviour versus attending to knowledge: Examining monkeys' attribution of mental states. *Animal Behaviour, 40,* 742–753.

Chomsky, N. (1965). *Aspects of the Theory of Syntax.* Cambridge, Mass.: MIT Press.

Clark, A. P., and Wrangham, R. W. (1994). Chimpanzee arrival pant-hoots: Do they signify food or status? *International Journal of Primatology, 15,* 185–205.

Clark, H. (1996). *Uses of Language.* Cambridge: Cambridge University Press.

Clark, H., and Marshall, C. R. (1981). Definite reference and mutual knowledge. In *Elements of Discourse Understanding,* ed. A. K. Joshi, B. L. Webber, and I. A. Sag (pp. 10–63). Cambridge: Cambridge University Press.

Clark, H. H. (1992). *Arenas of Language Use.* Chicago: The University of Chicago Press.

Corballis, M. C. (2002). *From Hand to Mouth: The Origins of Language.* Princeton: Princeton University Press.

Crawford, M. P. (1937). The cooperative solving of problems by young chimpanzees. *Comparative Psychology Monographs, 14,* 1–88.

Crawford, M. P. (1941). The cooperative solving by chimpanzees of problems requiring serial responses to color cues. *Journal of Social Psychology, 13,* 259–280.

Crockford, C., and Boesch, C. (2003). Context-specific calls in wild chimpanzees, *Pan troglodytes verus*: Analysis of barks. *Animal Behaviour, 66,* 115–125.

Croft, W. (1991). *Syntactic Categories and Grammatical Relations: The Cognitive Organization of Information*. Chicago: The University of Chicago Press.

Croft, W. (1995). Intonation units and grammatical units. *Linguistics*, 33(5), 839–882.

Croft, W. (2000). *Explaining Language Change: An Evolutionary Approach*. London: Longmans.

Croft, W. (2001). *Radical Construction Grammar: Syntactic Theory in Typological Perspective*. Oxford: Oxford University Press.

Croft, W. (2003). *Typology and Universals*, second ed. Cambridge: Cambridge University Press.

Csibra, G. (2003). Teleological and referential understanding of action in infancy. *Philosophical Transactions of the Royal Society, London B, 358*, 447–458.

Csibra, G., Gergely, G., Bíró, S., Koós, O., and Brockbank, M. (1999). Goal attribution without agency cues: The perception of "pure reason" in infancy. *Cognition, 72*, 237–267.

Dahl, O. (2004). *The Growth and Maintenance of Linguistic Complexity*. Studies in Language Companion Series. Amsterdam/Philadelphia: John Benjamins.

Darwin, C. R. (1872). *The Expression of the Emotions in Man and Animals*. London: Murray.

Dawkins, R., and Krebs, J. (1978). Animal signals: Information or manipulation. In *Behavioral Ecology: An Evolutionary Approach*, ed. J. Krebs and N. Davies (pp. 282–309). Oxford: Blackwell.

DeLoache, J. S. (2004). Becoming symbol-minded. *Trends in Cognitive Sciences, 8*, 66–70.

de Saussure, F. (1916/1959). *Course in General Linguistics*. New York: Philosophical Library.

Dessalles, J.-L. (2006). *The Evolutionary Origins of Language*. Cambridge: Cambridge University Press.

Deutscher, G. (2005). *The Unfolding of Language*. London: William Heinemann.

de Waal, F. B. M. (1986). Deception in the natural communication of chimpanzees. In *Deception: Perspectives on Human and Nonhuman Deceit*, ed. R. W. Mitchell and N. S. Thompson (pp. 221–244). Albany: SUNY Press.

de Waal, F. B. M., and Lutrell, L. M. (1988). Mechanisms of social reciprocity in three primate species: Symmetrical relationship characteristics or cognition? *Ethology and Sociobiology, 9*, 101–118.

Diessel, H. (2005). *The Acquisition of Complex Sentences*. Cambridge: Cambridge University Press.

Diessel, H. (2006). Demonstratives, joint attention, and the emergence of grammar. *Cognitive Linguistics, 17*, 463–489.

Diessel, H., and Tomasello, M. (2000). The development of relative constructions in early child speech. *Cognitive Linguistics, 11*, 131–152.

Diessel, H., and Tomasello, M. (2001). The acquisition of finite complement clauses in English: A usage based approach to the development of grammatical constructions. *Cognitive Linguistics, 12*, 97–141.

Donald, M. (1991). *Origins of the Modern Mind*. Cambridge, Mass.: Harvard University Press.

Enard, W., Przeworski, W., Fisher, S., Lai, L., Wiebe, V., Kitano, T., Monaco, A., and Pääbo, S. (2002). Molecular evolution of FOXP2, a gene involved in speech and language. *Nature, 418*, 869–872.

Fehr, E., and Fischbacher, U. (2003). The nature of human altruism. *Nature, 425*, 785–791.

Fillmore, C. (1989). Grammatical construction theory and the familiar dichotomies. In *Language Processing in Social Context*, ed. R. Dietrich and C. F. Graumann. North Holland: Elsevier.

Folven, R., and Bonvillian, J. (1991). The transition from nonreferential to referential language in children acquiring American Sign Language. *Developmental Psychology, 27*, 806–816.

Gardner, R. A., and Gardner, B. T. (1969). Teaching sign language to a chimpanzee. *Science, 165,* 664–672.

Gergely, G., Bekkering, H., and Király, I. (2002). Rational imitation in preverbal infants. *Nature, 415,* 755.

Gergely, G., and Csibra, G. (2006). Sylvia's recipe: The role of imitation and pedagogy in the transmission of cultural knowledge. In *Roots of Human Sociality: Culture, Cognition, and Interaction,* ed. N. J. Enfield and S. C. Levinson (pp. 229–255). Oxford: Berg Press.

Gilbert, M. (1989). *On Social Facts.* International Library of Philosophy series. Princeton: Princeton University Press.

Gilby, I. C. 2006. Meat sharing among the Gombe chimpanzees: Harassment and reciprocal exchange. *Animal Behaviour, 71*(4), 953–963.

Gilby, I. C., Eberly, L. E., Pintea, L., and Pusey, A. E. (2006). Ecological and social influences on the hunting behaviour of wild chimpanzees, *Pan troglodytes schweinfurthii. Animal Behaviour, 72*(1), 169–180.

Givón, T. (1979). *On Understanding Grammar.* New York: Academic Press.

Givón, T. (2001). *Syntax,* volume 2. Amsterdam : John Benjamins.

Goldberg, A. (1995). *Constructions: A Construction Grammar Approach to Argument Structure.* Chicago: The University of Chicago Press.

Goldberg, A. (2006). *Constructions at Work.* Oxford: Oxford University Press.

Goldin-Meadow, S. (2003a). *Hearing Gesture: How Our Hands Help Us Think.* Cambridge, Mass.: Harvard University Press.

Goldin-Meadow, S. (2003b). *The Resilience of Language: What Gesture Creation in Deaf Children Can Tell Us about How All Children Learn Language.* New York: Psychology Press.

Goldin-Meadow, S., and Mylander, C. (1984). Gestural communication in deaf children: The effects and non-effects of parental input on early language development. *Monographs of the Society for Research in Child Development, 49,* 1–151.

Golinkoff, R. M. (1986). "I beg your pardon?": The preverbal negotiation of failed messages. *Journal of Child Language, 13*, 455–476.

Gómez, J. C. (1990). The emergence of intentional communication as a problem-solving strategy in the gorilla. In *"Language" and Intelligence in Monkeys and Apes*, ed. S. T. Parker and K. R. Gibson (pp. 333–355). Cambridge: Cambridge University Press.

Gómez, J. C. (2004). *Apes, Monkeys, Children, and the Growth of Mind.* Cambridge, Mass.: Harvard University Press.

Goodall, J. (1986). *The Chimpanzees of Gombe. Patterns of Behavior.* Cambridge, Mass.: Harvard University Press.

Gouzoules, H., Gouzoules, S., and Ashley, J. (1995). Representational signalling in nonhuman primate vocal communication. In *Current topics in primate vocal communication*, ed. E. Zimmermann, J. Newman, and U. Jürgens (pp. 235–252). New York: Plenum Press.

Greenberg, J. (1963). Some universals of grammar with particular reference to the order of meaningful elements. In *Universals of Language*, ed. J. Greenberg (pp. 73–113). Cambridge, Mass.: MIT Press.

Greenfield, P. M., and Savage-Rumbaugh, E. S. (1990). Grammatical combination in *Pan paniscus*: Processes of learning and invention in the evolution and development of language. In *"Language" and Intelligence in Monkeys and Apes*, ed. S. T. Parker and K. R. Gibson (pp. 540–578). Cambridge: Cambridge University Press.

Greenfield, P. M., and Savage-Rumbaugh, E. S. (1991). Imitation, grammatical development, and the invention of protogrammar by an ape. In *Biological and Behavioral Determinants of Language Development*, ed. N. A. Krasnegor, D. M. Rumbaugh, R. L. Schiefelbusch, and M. Studdert-Kennedy (pp. 235–258). Hillsdale, N.J.: Lawrence Erlbaum.

Greenfield, P. M., and Smith, I. H. (1976). *The Structure of Communication in Early Language Development.* New York: Academic Press.

Grice, H. P. (1957). Meaning. *Philosophical Review, 64*, 377–388.

Grice, P. (1975). Logic and conversation. In *Syntax and Semantics*, volume 3: *Speech Acts*, ed. P. Cole and J. Morgan (pp. 43–58). New York: Academic Press.

Gundel, J., Hedberg, N., and Zacharski, R. (1993). Cognitive status and the form of referring expressions in discourse. *Language, 69,* 274–307.

Habermas, J. (1987). *The Theory of Communicative Action.* New York: Beacon Press.

Haith, M., and Benson, J. (1997). Infant cognition. In *Handbook of Child Psychology,* volume 2, ed. D. Kuhn and R. Siegler. New York: Wiley.

Hannan, T., and Fogel, A. (1987). A case study assessment of "pointing" in the first three months of life. *Perceptual and Motor Skills, 65,* 187–194.

Hare, B., Brown, M., Williamson, C., and Tomasello, M. (2002). The domestication of social cognition in dogs. *Science, 298,* 1634–1636.

Hare, B., Call, J., Agnetta, B., and Tomasello, M. (2000). Chimpanzees know what conspecifics do and do not see. *Animal Behaviour, 59,* 771–785.

Hare, B., Call, J., and Tomasello, M. (1998). Communication of food location between human and dog *(Canis familiaris). Evolution of Communication, 2,* 137–159.

Hare, B., Call, J., and Tomasello, M. (2001). Do chimpanzees know what conspecifics know? *Animal Behaviour, 61*(1), 139–151.

Hare, B., Call, J., and Tomasello, M. (2006). Chimpanzees deceive a human by hiding. *Cognition, 101,* 495–514.

Hare, B., and Tomasello, M. (2004). Chimpanzees are more skillful in competitive than in co-operative cognitive tasks. *Animal Behaviour, 68,* 571–581.

Hare, B., and Tomasello, M. (2005). Human-like social skills in dogs? *Trends in Cognitive Science, 9,* 439–444.

Hauser, M. D., Chomsky, N., and Fitch, W. T. (2002). The faculty of language: What is it, who has it, and how did it evolve? *Science, 298,* 1569–1579.

Hauser, M. D., and Wrangham, R. W. (1987). Manipulation of food calls in captive chimpanzees: A preliminary report. *Folia Primatologica, 48,* 207–210.

Hawkins, J. (2004). *Efficiency and Complexity in Grammars*. Oxford: Oxford University Press.

Heine, B., and Kuteva, T. (2002). On the evolution of grammatical forms. In *The Transition to Language*, ed. A. Wray. Oxford: Oxford University Press.

Henrich, J., Boyd, R., Bowles, S., Gintis, H., Fehr, E., Camerer, C., McElreath, R., Gurven, M., Hill, K., Barr, A., Ensminger, J., Tracer, D., Marlow, F., Patton, J., Alvard, M., Gil-White, F., and Henrich, N. (2005). "Economic Man" in cross-cultural perspective: Ethnography and experiments from 15 small-scale societies. *Behavioral and Brain Sciences, 28*, 795–855.

Herman, L. (2005). Intelligence and rational behavior in the bottlenosed dolphin. In *Rational Animals?*, ed. S. Hurley and M. Nudds. Oxford: Oxford University Press.

Herrmann, E., and Tomasello, M. (2006). Apes' and children's understanding of cooperative and competitive motives in a communicative situation. *Developmental Science, 9*(5), 518–529.

Hewes, G. W. (1973). Primate communication and the gestural origins of language. *Current Anthropology, 14*, 9–10.

Hill, K., and Hurtado, A. M. (1996). *Ache Life History: The Ecology and Demography of a Foraging People*. Glenside, Penn.: Aldine Press.

Hirata, S., and Fuwa, K. (2006). Chimpanzees *(Pan troglodytes)* learn to act with other individuals in a cooperative task. *Primates, 48*(1), 13–21.

Iverson, J., Capirci, O., and Caselli, M. C. (1994). From communication to language in two modalities. *Cognitive Development, 9*, 23–43.

Iverson, J., and Goldin-Meadow, S. (2005). Gesture paves the way for language development. *Psychological Science, 16*, 367–373.

Jensen, K., Hare, B., Call, J., and Tomasello, M. (2006). Chimpanzees are self-regarding maximizers in a food acquisition task. *Proceedings of the Royal Society, 273*, 1013–1021.

Kagan, J. (1981). *The Second Year: The Emergence of Self-Awareness*. Cambridge, Mass.: Harvard University Press.

Kaminski, J., Call, J., and Tomasello, M. (2004). Body orientation and face orientation: Two factors controlling apes' begging behavior from humans. *Animal Cognition, 7,* 216–223.

Kegl, J., Senghas, A., and Coppola, M. (1999). Creation through contact: Sign language emergence and sign language change in Nicaragua. In *Language Creation and Language Change: Creolization, Diachrony, and Development,* ed. M. DeGraff (pp. 179–237). Cambridge, Mass.: MIT Press.

Keller, R. (1994). *On Language Change: The Invisible Hand in Language.* New York: Routledge.

Kendon, A. (2004). *Gesture: Visible Action as Utterance.* Cambridge: Cambridge University Press.

Kita, S. (ed.) (2003). *Pointing: Where Language, Culture, and Cognition Meet.* Mahwah, N.J.: Lawrence Erlbaum.

Kobayashi, H., and Kohshima, S. (2001). Unique morphology of the human eye and its adaptive meaning: Comparative studies on external morphology of the primate eye. *Journal of Human Evolution, 40,* 419–435.

Kuhlmeier, V., Wynn, K., and Bloom, P. (2003). Attribution of dispositional states by 12-month-olds. *Psychological Science, 14*(5), 402–408.

Lambrecht, K. (1994). *Information Structure and Sentence Form.* Cambridge: Cambridge University Press.

Langacker, R. (1987). *Foundations of Cognitive Grammar,* volume 1. Stanford, Calif.: Stanford University Press.

Langacker, R. (1991). *Foundations of Cognitive Grammar,* volume 2. Stanford, Calif.: Stanford University Press.

Leavens, D. A., and Hopkins, W. D. (1998). Intentional communication by chimpanzees: A cross-sectional study of the use of referential gestures. *Developmental Psychology, 34,* 813–822.

Leavens, D. A., Hopkins, W. D., and Bard, K. A. (2005). Understanding the point of chimpanzee pointing: Epigenesis and ecological validity. *Current Directions in Psychological Science, 14,* 185–189.

Lederberg, A., and Everhart, V. (1998). Communication between deaf children and their hearing mothers: The role of language, gesture, and vocalization. *Journal of Speech, Language, and Hearing Research, 41*, 887–899.

Leslie, A. (1987) Pretense and representation: The origins of "theory of mind." *Psychological Review, 94*, 412–426.

Levinson, S. (2006). On the human interactional engine. In *Roots of Human Sociality,* ed. N. Enfield and S. Levinson (pp. 39–69). New York: Berg Publishers.

Levinson, S. C. (1995). Interactional biases in human thinking. In *Social Intelligence and Interaction,* ed. E. Goody (pp. 221–260). Cambridge: Cambridge University Press.

Lewis, D. (1969). *Convention.* Cambridge, Mass.: Harvard University Press.

Liddell, S. K. (2003). *Grammar, Gesture, and Meaning in American Sign Language.* Cambridge: Cambridge University Press.

Liebal, K., Behne, T., Carpenter, M., and Tomasello, M. (in press). Infants use shared experience to interpret a pointing gesture. *Developmental Science.*

Liebal, K., Call, J., and Tomasello, M. (2004). The use of gesture sequences by chimpanzees. *American Journal of Primatology, 64*, 377–396.

Liebal, K., Columbi, C., Rogers, S., Warneken, F., and Tomasello, M. (2008). Cooperative activities in children with autism. *Journal of Autism and Developmental Disorders, 38*, 224–238.

Liebal, K., Pika, S., Call, J., and Tomasello, M. (2004). To move or not to move: How apes adjust to the attentional state of others. *Interaction Studies, 5*, 199–219.

Liebal, K., Pika, S., and Tomasello, M. (2006). Gestural communication in orangutans. *Gesture, 6*, 1–38.

Liszkowski, U. (2005). Human twelve-month-olds point co-operatively to share interest with and provide information for a communicative partner. *Gesture, 5*, 135–154.

Lizskowski, U., Albrecht, K., Carpenter, M., and Tomasello, M. (in press). Infants' visual and auditory communication when a partner is or is not visually attending. *Infant Behavior and Development*.

Liszkowski, U., Carpenter, M., Henning, A., Striano, T., and Tomasello, M. (2004). 12-month-olds point to share attention and interest. *Developmental Science, 7*, 297–307.

Liszkowski, U., Carpenter, M., Striano, T., and Tomasello, M. (2006). 12- and 18-month-olds point to provide information for others. *Journal of Cognition and Development, 7*, 173–187.

Liszkowski, U., Carpenter, M., and Tomasello, M. (2007a). Reference and attitude in infant pointing. *Journal of Child Language, 34*, 1–20.

Liszkowski, U., Carpenter, M., and Tomasello, M. (2007b). Pointing out new news, old news, and absent referents at 12 months of age. *Developmental Science, 10*, F1–F7.

Maestripieri, D. (1998). Primate social organization, vocabulary size, and communication dynamics: A comparative study of macaques. In *The Evolution of Language: Assessing the Evidence from Nonhuman Primates*, ed. B. King. Santa Fe: School of American Research.

Matthews, D., Lieven, E. V., Theakston, A. L., and Tomasello, M. (2006). The effect of perceptual availability and prior discourse on young children's use or referring expressions. *Applied Psycholinguistics, 27*, 403–422.

Matthews, D., Lieven, E., and Tomasello, M. (2007). How toddlers and preschoolers learn to uniquely identify referents for others: A training study. *Child Development, 34*, 381–409.

Maynard Smith, J., and Harper, D. (2003). *Animal Signals*. Oxford: Oxford University Press.

McNeill, D. (1992). *Hand and Mind: What Gestures Reveal about Thought*. Chicago: The University of Chicago Press.

McNeill, D. (2005). *Gesture and Thought*. Chicago: The University of Chicago Press.

McWhorter, J. (2005). *Defining Creole*. Oxford: Oxford University Press.

Melis, A., Call, J., and Tomasello, M. (2006). Chimpanzees conceal visual and auditory information from others. *Journal of Comparative Psychology, 120*, 154–162.

Melis, A., Hare, B., and Tomasello, M. (2006a). Engineering cooperation in chimpanzees: Tolerance constraints on cooperation. *Animal Behaviour, 72*, 275–286.

Melis, A., Hare, B., and Tomasello, M. (2006b). Chimpanzees recruit the best collaborators. *Science, 31*, 1297–1300.

Meltzoff, A. (1995). Understanding the intentions of others: Re-enactment of intended acts by 18-month-old children. *Developmental Psychology, 31*, 1–16.

Menzel, C. (1999). Unprompted recall and reporting of hidden objects by a chimpanzee after extended delays. *Journal of Comparative Psychology, 113*, 426–434.

Millikan, R. G. (2005). *Language: A Biological Model*. Oxford: Oxford University Press.

Mitani, J. C., and Nishida, T. (1993). Contexts and social correlates of long-distance calling by male chimpanzees. *Animal Behaviour, 45*, 735–746.

Moll, H., Koring, C., Carpenter, M., and Tomasello, M. (2006). Infants determine others' focus of attention by pragmatics and exclusion. *Journal of Cognition and Development, 7*, 411–430.

Moll, H., Richter, N., Carpenter, M., and Tomasello, M. (2008). 14-month-olds know what "we" have shared in a special way. *Infancy, 13*, 90–101.

Moll, H., and Tomasello, M. (2004). 12- and 18-month-olds follow gaze to hidden locations. *Developmental Science, 7*, F1–F9.

Moll, H., and Tomasello, M. (2007a). How 14- and 18- month-olds know what others have experienced. *Developmental Psychology, 43*, 309–317.

Moll, H., and Tomasello, M. (2007b). Co-operation and human cognition: The Vygotskian intelligence hypothesis. *Philosophical Transactions of the Royal Society, 362,* 639–648.

Moore, C. (1996). Theories of mind in infancy. *British Journal of Developmental Psychology, 14,* 19–40.

Moore, C., and Corkum, V. (1994). Social understanding at the end of the first year of life. *Developmental Review, 14,* 349–372.

Moore, C., and D'Entremont, B. (2001). Developmental changes in pointing as a function of parent's attentional focus. *Journal of Cognition and Development, 2,* 109–129.

Mundy, P., and Burnette, C. (2005). Joint attention and neurodevelopment. In *Handbook of Autism and Pervasive Developmental Disorders,* volume 3, ed. F. Volkmar, A. Klin, and R. Paul (pp. 650–681). Hoboken, N.J.: John Wiley.

Mundy, P., and Sigman, M. (2006). Joint attention, social competence, and developmental psychopathology. In *Developmental Psychopathology,* volume 1: *Theory and Methods,* second ed., ed. D. Cicchetti and D. Cohen. Hoboken, N.J.: John Wiley.

Namy, L. L., Acredolo, L., and Goodwyn, S. (2000). Verbal labels and gestural routines in parental communication with young children. *Journal of Nonverbal Behavior, 24,* 63–79.

Namy, L. L., Campbell, A., and Tomasello, M. (2004). Developmental change in the role of iconicity in symbol learning. *Journal of Cognition and Development, 5,* 37–56.

Namy, L. L., and Waxman, S. R. (1998). Words and gestures: Infants' interpretations of different forms of symbolic reference. *Child Development, 69,* 295–308.

Namy, L. L., and Waxman, S. R. (2000). Naming and exclaiming: Infants' sensitivity to naming contexts. *Journal of Cognition and Development, 1,* 405–428.

Nelson, K. (1985). *Making Sense: The Acquisition of Shared Meaning.* New York: Academic Press.

Nelson, K. (1996). *Language in Cognitive Development.* New York: Cambridge University Press.

Nowak, M. A., and Sigmund, K. (1998) Evolution of indirect reciprocity by image scoring. *Nature, 393,* 573–577.

Okamoto-Barth, S., Call, J., and Tomasello, M. (2007). Great apes' understanding of others' line of sight. *Psychological Science, 18,* 462–468.

Olson, D. (1994). *The World on Paper: The Conceptual and Cognitive Implications of Writing and Reading.* New York: Cambridge University Press.

O'Neill, D. K. (1996). Two-year-old children's sensitivity to a parent's knowledge state when making requests. *Child Development, 67,* 659–677.

Onishi, K. H., and Baillargeon, R. (2005). Do 15-month-old infants understand false beliefs? *Science, 308,* 255–258.

Orlansky, M., and Bonvillian, J. D. (1984). The role of iconicity in early sign language acquisition. *Journal of Speech and Hearing Disorders, 49,* 287–292.

Owings, D. H., and Morton, E. S. (1998). *Animal Vocal Communication: A New Approach.* Cambridge: Cambridge University Press.

Owren, M. J., and Rendell, D. (2001). Sound on the rebound: Bringing form and function back to the forefront in understanding nonhuman primate vocal signaling. *Evolutionary Anthropology, 10,* 58–71.

Ozcaliskan, S., and Goldin-Meadow, S. (2005). Gesture is at the cutting edge of language development. *Cognition, 96,* B101–113.

Padden, C. A. (1983). Interaction of morphology and syntax in American Sign Language. Doctoral dissertation. University of California, San Diego.

Panchanathan, S., and Boyd, R. (2003). A tale of two defectors: The importance of standing for the evolution of indirect reciprocity. *Journal of Theoretical Biology, 224,* 115–126.

Pepperberg, I. M. (2000). *The Alex Studies: Cognitive and Communicative Abilities of Grey Parrots.* Cambridge, Mass.: Harvard University Press.

Perner, J., Brandl, J., and Garnham, A. (2003). What is a perspective problem? Developmental issues in understanding belief and dual identity. *Facta Philosophica, 5*, 355–378.

Pinker, S. (1999). *Words and Rules.* New York: Morrow Press.

Pollick, A., and de Waal, F. (2007). Ape gestures and language evolution. *Proceedings of the National Academy of Sciences, 104*, 8184–9189.

Povinelli, D. J., and Davis, D. R. (1994). Differences between chimpanzees *(Pan troglodytes)* and humans *(Homo sapiens)* in the resting state of the index finger: Implications for pointing. *Journal of Comparative Psychology, 108*, 134–139.

Povinelli, D. J., and Eddy, T. J. (1996). What young chimpanzees know about seeing. *Monographs of the Society for Research in Child Development, 61*(3).

Povinelli, D. J., and O'Neill, D. (2000). Do chimpanzees use their gestures to instruct each other? In *Understanding Other Minds: Perspectives from Developmental Cognitive Neuroscience,* second ed., ed. S. Baron-Cohen, H. Tager-Flusberg, and D. Cohen. Oxford: Oxford University Press.

Povinelli, D. J., and Vonk, J. (2006). We don't need a microscope to explore the chimpanzee's mind. In *Rational Animals,* ed. S. Hurley (pp. 385–412). Oxford: Oxford University Press.

Quine, W. V. (1960). *Word and oObject.* Cambridge, Mass.: MIT Press.

Ratner, N., and Bruner, J. (1978). Games, social exchange, and the acquisition of language. *Journal of Child Language, 5*, 391–401.

Richerson, P., and Boyd, R. (2005). *Not by Genes Alone.* Chicago: The University of Chicago Press.

Rivas, E. (2005). Recent use of signs by chimpanzees *(Pan Troglodytes)* in interactions with humans. *Journal of Comparative Psychology, 119*(4), 404–417.

Rochat, P. (2001). *The Infant's World.* The Developing Child series. Cambridge, Mass.: Harvard University Press.

Ross, H. S., and Lollis, S. P. (1987). Communication within infant social games. *Developmental Psychology, 23*(2), 241–248.

Sandler, W., Meir, I., Padden, C., and Aronoff, M. (2005). The emergence of grammar: Systematic structure in a new language. *Proceedings of the National Academy of Science, 102*(7), 2661–2665.

Savage-Rumbaugh, S., McDonald, K., Sevcik, R., Hopkins, W., and Rupert, E. (1986). Spontaneous symbol acquisition and communicative use by pygmy chimpanzee *(Pan paniscus). Journal of Experimental Psychology, 115*, 211–235.

Savage-Rumbaugh, S., Murphy, J., Sevcik, R., Brakke, K., Williams, S., and Rumbaugh, D. (1993). Language comprehension in ape and child. *Monographs of the Society for Research in Child Development, 58*(3–4).

Savage-Rumbaugh, E. S., Rumbaugh, D. M., and Boysen, S. (1978). Linguistically mediated tool use and exchange by chimpanzees *(Pan troglodytes). Behavioral and Brain Sciences, 4*, 539–554.

Saylor, M. (2004). 12- and 16-month-old infants recognize properties of mentioned absent things. *Developmental Science, 7*, 599–611.

Schachter, S. (1959). *The Psychology of Affiliation*. Stanford, Calif.: Stanford University Press.

Schelling, T. C. (1960). *The Strategy of Conflict*. Cambridge, Mass.: Harvard University Press.

Schick, B. (2005). *Advances in the Sign Language Development of Deaf Children*. Oxford: Oxford University Press.

Schwier, C., van Maanen, C., Carpenter, M., and Tomasello, M. (2006). Rational imitation in 12-month-old infants. *Infancy, 10*, 303–311.

Searle, J. R. (1969). *Speech Acts: An Essay in the Philosophy of Language*. Cambridge: Cambridge University Press.

Searle, J. R. (1983). *Intentionality*. Cambridge: Cambridge University Press.

Searle, J. R. (1990). Collective intentions and actions. In *Intentions in Communication*, ed. P. Cohen, J. Morgan, and M. Pollack. Cambridge, Mass.: MIT Press.

Searle, J. R. (1995). *The Construction of Social Reality*. New York: Free Press.

Searle, J. R. (1999). *Mind, Language, and Society: Philosophy in the Real World*. New York: Basic Books.

Senghas, A. (2003). Intergenerational influence and ontogenetic development in the emergence of spatial grammar in Nicaraguan Sign Language. *Cognitive Development, 18*, 511–531.

Senghas, A., and Coppola, M. (2001). Children creating language: How Nicaraguan Sign Language acquired a spatial grammar. *Psychological Science, 12*(4), 323–328.

Senghas, A., Kita, S., and Özyürek, A. (2004). Children creating core properties of language: Evidence from an emerging sign language in Nicaragua. *Science, 305*, 5691, 1779–1782.

Seyfarth, R. M., and Cheney, D. L. (2003). Signalers and receivers in animal communication. *Annual Review of Psychology 54*, 145–173.

Shatz, M., and O'Reilly, A. (1990). Conversation or communicative skill? A re-assessment of two-year-olds' behavior in miscommunication episodes. *Journal of Child Language, 17*, 131–146.

Shwe, H. I., and Markman, E. M. (1997). Young children's appreciation of the mental impact of their communicative signals. *Developmental Psychology, 33*(4), 630–636.

Silk, J. B., Brosnan, S. F., Vonk, J., Henrich, J., Povinelli, D. J., Richardson, A. S., Lambeth, S. P., Mascaro, J. and Schapiro, S. J. (2005). Chimpanzees are indifferent to the welfare of unrelated group members. *Nature 437*, 1357–1359.

Spencer, P. (1993). Communication behaviors of infants with hearing loss and their hearing mothers. *Journal of Speech and Hearing Research, 36*, 311–321.

Sperber, D. (1994). Understanding verbal understanding. In *What Is Intelligence?*, ed. J. Khalfa (pp. 179–198). Cambridge: Cambridge University Press.

Sperber, D., and Wilson, D. (1986). *Relevance: Communication and Cognition*. Cambridge, Mass.: Harvard University Press.

Stanford, C. B. (1998). *Chimpanzee and Red Colobus: The Ecology of Predator and Prey*. Cambridge, Mass.: Harvard University Press.

Stern, D. N. (1985). *The Interpersonal World of the Infant: A View from Psychoanalysis and Developmental Psychology*. New York: Basic Books.

Sugiyama, Y. (1981). Observations on the population dynamics and behavior of wild chimpanzees at Bossou, Guinea, 1979–1980. *Primates, 22*, 432–444.

Tanner, J. E., and Byrne, R. W. (1993). Concealing facial evidence of mood: Perspective-taking in a captive gorilla? *Primates, 34*, 451–457.

Tanner, J. E., and Byrne, R. W. (1996). Representation of action through iconic gesture in a captive lowland gorilla. *Current Anthropology, 37*, 162–173.

Tinbergen, N. (1951). *The Study of Instinct*. New York: Oxford University Press.

Tomasello, M. (1988). The role of joint attentional process in early language development. *Language Sciences, 10*, 69–88.

Tomasello, M. (1992a). *First Verbs: A Case Study of Early Grammatical Development*. Cambridge: Cambridge University Press.

Tomasello, M. (1992b). The social bases of language acquisition. *Social Development, 1*(1), 67–87.

Tomasello, M. (1995). Joint attention as social cognition. In *Joint Attention: Its Origin and Role in Development*, ed. C. Moore and P. J. Dunham (pp. 103–130). Hillsdale, N.J.: Lawrence Erlbaum.

Tomasello, M. (1996). Do apes ape? In *Social Learning in Animals: The Roots of Culture*, ed. C. M. Heyes and B. G. Galef (pp. 319–346). San Diego: Academic Press.

Tomasello, M. (1998). Reference: Intending that others jointly attend. *Pragmatics and Cognition, 6*, 229–244.

Tomasello, M. (1999). *The Cultural Origins of Human Cognition*. Cambridge, Mass.: Harvard University Press.

Tomasello, M. (2001). Perceiving intentions and learning words in the second year of life. In *Language Acquisition and Conceptual Development*, ed. M. Bowerman and S. Levinson (pp. 132–158). Cambridge: Cambridge University Press.

Tomasello, M. (2003). *Constructing a Language: A Usage-Based Theory of Language Acquisition*. Cambridge, Mass.: Harvard University Press.

Tomasello, M. (2004). What kind of evidence could refute the UG hypothesis? *Studies in Language, 28*, 642–644.

Tomasello, M., and Call, J. (1997). *Primate Cognition*. Oxford: Oxford University Press.

Tomasello, M., and Call, J. (2006). Do chimpanzees know what others see—or only what they are looking at? In *Rational Animals?*, ed. M. Nudds and S. Huley. Oxford: Oxford University Press.

Tomasello, M., and Call, J. (in press). Chimpanzee social cognition. In *Chimpanzee Minds*, ed. E. Londsdorf and S. Ross. Chicago: The University of Chicago Press.

Tomasello, M., Call, J., and Gluckman, A. (1997). The comprehension of novel communicative signs by apes and human children. *Child Development, 68*, 1067–1081.

Tomasello, M., Call, J., Nagell, K., Olguin, R., and Carpenter, M. (1994). The learning and use of gestural signals by young chimpanzees: A trans-generational study. *Primates, 37*, 137–154.

Tomasello, M., Call, J., Warren, J., Frost, T., Carpenter, M., and Nagell, K. (1997). The ontogeny of chimpanzee gestural signals: A comparision across groups and generations. *Evolution of Communication, 1*, 223–253.

Tomasello, M., and Carpenter, M. (2005). The emergence of social cognition in three young chimpanzees. *Monographs of the Society for Research in Child Development, 70*(279).

Tomasello, M., Carpenter, M., Call, J., Behne, T., and Moll, H. (2005). Understanding and sharing intentions: The origins of cultural cognition. *Behavioral and Brain Sciences, 28*, 675–735.

Tomasello, M., Carpenter, M., and Lizskowski, U. (2007). A new look at infant pointing. *Child Development, 78*, 705–722.

Tomasello, M., and Farrar, J. (1986). Object permanence and relational words: A lexical training study. *Journal of Child Language, 13*, 495–506.

Tomasello, M., George, B., Kruger, A., Farrar, J., and Evans, A. (1985). The development of gestural communication in young chimpanzees. *Journal of Human Evolution, 14,* 175–186.

Tomasello, M., Gust, D., and Frost, T. (1989). A longitudinal investigation of gestural communication in young chimpanzees. *Primates, 30,* 35–50.

Tomasello, M., and Haberl, K. (2003). Understanding attention: 12- and 18-month-olds know what is new for other persons. *Developmental Psychology, 39*(5), 906–912.

Tomasello, M., Hare, B., and Agnetta, B. (1999). Chimpanzees, *Pan troglodytes,* follow gaze direction geometrically. *Animal Behaviour, 58*(4), 769–777.

Tomasello, M., Hare, B., Lehmann, H., and Call, J. (2007). Reliance on head versus eyes in the gaze following of great apes and human infants: The cooperative eye hypothesis. *Journal of Human Evolution, 52,* 314–320.

Tomasello, M., Kruger, A., and Ratner, H. (1993). Cultural learning. *Behavioral and Brain Sciences, 16,* 495–552.

Tomasello, M., and Rakoczy, H. (2003). What makes human cognition unique? From individual to shared to collective intentionality. *Mind and Language, 18*(2), 121–147.

Tomasello, M., Striano, T., and Rochat, P. (1999). Do young children use objects as symbols? *British Journal of Developmental Psychology, 17,* 563–584.

Tomasello, M., Strosberg, R., and Akhtar, N. (1996). Eighteen-month-old children learn words in non-ostensive contexts. *Journal of Child Language, 23,* 157–176.

Tomasello, M., and Zuberbüler, K. (2002). Primate vocal and gestural communication. In *The Cognitive Animal: Empirical and Theoretical Perspectives on Animal Cognition,* ed. M. Bekoff, C. Allen, and G. Burghardt. Cambridge, Mass.: MIT Press.

Tomonaga, M., Myowa-Yamakoshi, M., Mizuno, Y., Yamaguchi, M., Kosugi, D., Bard, K., Tanaka, M., and Matsuzawa, T. (2004) Development of social cognition in infant chimpanzees *(Pan troglodytes)*: Face recognition, smiling, gaze and the lack of triadic interactions. *Japanese Psychological Research, 46,* 227–235.

Trevarthen, C. (1979). Instincts for human understanding and for cultural cooperation: Their development in infancy. In *Human Ethology: Claims and Limits of a New Discipline,* ed. M. von Cranach, K. Foppa, W. Lepenies, and D. Ploog (pp. 530–571). Cambridge: Cambridge University Press.

Uzgiris, I. C. (1981). Two functions of imitation during infancy. *International Journal of Behavioral Developmental, 4,* 1–12.

Vygotsky, L. (1978). *Mind in Society: The Development of Higher Psychological Processes.* Ed. M. Cole. Cambridge, Mass.: Harvard University Press.

Warneken, F., Chen, F., and Tomasello, M. (2006). Cooperative activities in young children and chimpanzees. *Child Development, 77,* 640–663.

Warneken, F., Hare, B., Melis, A., Hanus, D., and Tomasello, M. (2007). Roots of human altruism in chimpanzees. *PLOS: Biology,* 5(7): e184.

Warneken, F., and Tomasello, M. (2006). Altruistic helping in human infants and young chimpanzees. *Science, 31,* 1301–1303.

Warneken, F., and Tomasello, M. (2007). Helping and co-operation at 14 months of age. *Infancy, 11,* 271–294.

Watts, D., and Mitani, J. C. 2002. Hunting behavior of chimpanzees at Ngogo, Kibale National Park, Uganda. *International Journal of Primatology, 23,* 1–28.

Whiten, A., Horner, V., Litchfield, C., and Marshall-Pescini, S. (2004). How do apes ape? *Learning and Behaviour, 32,* 36–52.

Wittek, A., and Tomasello, M. (2005). German-speaking children's productivity with syntactic constructions and case morphology: Local cues help locally. *First Language, 25,* 103–125.

Wittgenstein, L. (1953). *Philosophical Investigations.* Oxford: Basil Blackwell.

Wittgenstein, L. (1969). *On Certainty*. Oxford: Basil Blackwell.

Wittgenstein, L. (2005). *The Big Typescript: TS 213*. Oxford: Basil Blackwell.

Woodward, A. (1998). Infants selectively encode the goal object of an actor's reach. *Cognition, 69*, 1–34.

Woodward, A. (1999). Infants' ability to distinguish between purposeful and non-purposeful behaviors. *Infant Behavior and Development, 22*(2), 145–160.

Woodward, A. L., and Hoyne, K. L. (1999). Infants' learning about words and sounds in relation to objects. *Child Development, 70*, 65–77.

Wrangham, R. W. (1975). The behavioural ecology of chimpanzees in Gombe National Park, Tanzania. Doctoral dissertation, University of Cambridge.

Wray, A. (1998). Protolanguage as a holistic system for social interaction. *Language and Communication, 18*, 47–67.

Zahavi, A., and Zahavi, A. (1997). *The Handicap Principle: A Missing Piece in Darwin's Puzzle*. New York and Oxford: Oxford University Press.

Zuberbühler, K. (2000). Causal cognition in a non-human primate: Field playback experiments with Diana monkeys. *Cognition, 76*, 195–207.

Zuberbühler, K. (2005). The phylogenetic roots of language: Evidence from primate communication and cognition. *Current Directions in Psychological Science, 14*(3), 126–130.

Author Index

Subject Index

Note: Page numbers followed by *f* or *t* indicate figures and tables, respectively.